Public Native America

Public Native America

Tribal Self-Representations in Casinos, Museums, and Powwows

M ARY L AWLOR

R UTGERS U NIVERSITY P RESS
OCM 61748368
New Brunswick, New Jersey, and London

Library of Congress Cataloging-in-Publication Data

Lawlor, Mary
    Public Native America : tribal self-representations in casinos, museums, and powwows / Mary Lawlor.
        p. cm.
    Includes bibliographical references and index.
    ISBN-13: 978-0-8135-3864-8 (hardcover : alk. paper)
    ISBN-13: 978-0-8135-3865-5 (pbk. : alk. paper)
    1. Indians of North America—Public opinion.   2. Indians of North America—Psychology.   3. Indians of North America—Ethnic identity.   4. Ethnopsychology—North America.   5. Self-perception—North America.   6. Indians in popular culture—North America.   7. Powwows—North America.   8. Museum exhibits—North America.   9. Gambling on Indian reservations—North America.   10. Public opinion—North America.   I. Title.
    E98. P99L39   2006
    305.897—dc22   2005028059

A British Cataloging-in-Publication record for this book is available
from the British Library.

All photos by Mary Lawlor.

Copyright © 2006 by Mary Lawlor

Manufactured in the United States of America

To John and to Abbey and to the memory of Fred Pfeil, Pat (Ajowa) Poole, and Luis Kemnitzer

Contents

ACKNOWLEDGMENTS

I WANT TO THANK *American Quarterly* for permission to use material from my essay "Identity in Mashantucket" (57, no. 1, March 2005) in chapter 1; *Ariel: A Review of International English Literature* for permission to quote from my "Keeping History at Wind River and Acoma" (26, no. 3, July 1995) in sections of chapters 3 and 4; and *Comparative American Studies* for permission to use portions of my essay "Indigenous Internationalism: Native Rights and the UN" (1, no. 3, 2003) in chapter 5.

I want to express my gratitude to the people at the reservations I visited who shared information or guided me through the public institutions I describe in this book. In doing so, I don't want to convey the impression that they agreed with what has ended up in print here, but that they were all generous and obviously very learned hosts. At the Mashantucket Pequot Public Relations Office, Suzanne Viafora kindly let me interview her and answered many questions about the recent history of the Mashantucket Pequots and helped me get my facts straight. Although I only had the opportunity to meet him once briefly, Richard Hayward, the former tribal council chairman at Mashantucket who did so much to get his tribe back on its legs again, has been a source of inspiration from a distance for a long time. I am grateful to Ferlin Clark, then development officer and now president of Diné College, for welcoming me to Navajoland the first time I went there. The Dajo'baii Days Seminar he invited me to attend at Diné College provided an amazing introduction to Navajo history, religion, and geography. Char Tullie, who was registrar in the Historic Preservation Department at the Navajo Nation Museum during my second visit there, showed me around the museum and not only offered valuable historical data but shared personal responses to the exhibits as well. Christopher Morris at the Navajo Tribal Council Speaker's Office provided important facts about attitudes toward gaming on the Navajo Reservation, judiciously explaining all sides of the issue. Reba Jo Teran and others at the Eastern Shoshone Cultural Center patiently explained to me how Sacagawea is remembered at Wind River and pointed out many useful research sources among their holdings. Ernie Over of the Riverton (WY) *Ranger* and the Wind River Heritage Center introduced me to Riverton's annual "Powwow Primer" and provided lively demonstrations of the town's commitment to its multicultural heritage. I especially want to thank Fred S. Vallo Sr. for spending a generous hour of his time talking to me when he was governor of Acoma Pueblo. His clarity and directness were immensely helpful, particularly his emphasis on the gravity of the issue of sovereignty for American Indian people. I also want to say thank you to Emerson Vallo for facilitating communications between his brother and me and to two guides at Sky City (the mesa village, not the casino) whose masterful performances as tour leaders introduced me to the complications and intricacies that can pertain in tribal public self-representations.

Elsa Stamatopoulou, the director of the Secretariat for the Permanent Forum on Indigenous Issues at the United Nations, spent precious time with me explaining the history and bureaucratic systems that produced the Permanent Forum and reading an early draft of what appears here as chapter 5, "Indigenous Internationalism: Native Rights and the United Nations." I have benefited not only from her acute understanding of the political actualities of indigenous rights but also from what she has shown me and others about what it means to make ideas walk and talk and do things in the public square. I'm thankful, too, to Patricia Jimenez and Pierrette Biraux-Ziegler of DoCip (Indigenous Peoples' Center for Documentation, Research, and Information) for opening their doors to Muhlenberg College interns at the Permanent Forum's annual conference in New York, for showing them what it all means, and for helping me understand how much crucial and yet unrecognized logistical work goes into making the forum function as well as it does for such a young organization.

Marc Manganaro gave me the opportunity to talk about the material that went into the chapters on the Eastern Shoshones and Acoma Pueblo with his graduate class at Rutgers University. His comments and those of his students gave me much to think about and inspired many revisions. Fred Pfeil and Grant Scott both read an early version of the Mashantucket chapter and helped me steer away from potentially problematic statements and positions. Lucy Maddox gave me much relished support for the Mashantucket chapter as well as good advice as I prepared it for submission to *American Quarterly*. Louise Barnett was kind enough to listen to the argument and, not surprisingly, gave me very knowledgeable responses to it as well as support. Dorothy Hodgson shared her intelligence and experience with indigenous issues in East Africa during our conversations at the Permanent Forum over the last couple of years.

I also want to thank Marita Sturken at *American Quarterly* for her sound advice on the revisions of "Identity in Mashantucket," Pamela McCallum at *Ariel* for her guidance and support in the earlier work on Acoma Pueblo and the Eastern Shoshones of Wind River, and Winfred Flück for his encouragement of my work and that of other participants in a panel on human rights at the meeting of the European Association of American Studies in Bordeaux in 2002. My essay for that panel became the basis for chapter 5.

Much gratitude goes as well to Leslie Mitchner at Rutgers University Press for her energetic interest in the project and for being such a great editor in all ways. Two anonymous readers for Rutgers University Press gave me expert, meticulous advice for revisions, for which I am deeply grateful.

The Class of 1932 of Muhlenberg College provided a generous grant for the academic year 2002–2003, during which I was able to do research for this book. Thanks too, once again, to my friends in the English Department at Muhlenberg who helped throughout the life of this project by their interest, their encouragement, questions, challenges, comments, and readings: Jim Bloom, Tom Cartelli, Francesca Coppa, Barri Gold, Alec Marsh, Linda Miller, David Rosenwasser, Grant Scott, and Jill Stephen. The Humanities Seminar in Performance Studies over the past two years inspired many new ways of looking at public self-representation. I'm grateful to Francesca, Chris Kovats-Bernat, Karen Dearborn, Larry Hass, Jim Peck, Beth Schachter, and Susan Schwartz for many good discussions and stimulating arguments.

My friends Pat Badt, Scott Sherk, and Virginia Wiles have been the best of companions during the years I've worked on this book. Their immense talents, intellects, hearts, and humor have given me great joy and seen me through many trying moments. My sisters Nancy Pennington, Sarah Pearce, and Elizabeth Davis (in spirit) have been great supporters and intimate confidants. Thanks as well to Luis Kemnitzer for much wisdom on visiting and writing about Native America and to my cousin Moher Downing for her great friendship and many good conversations about our work.

Most of all my gratitude goes to Abbey and John McClure. Abbey's work with Madre has impressed me immensely and inspired fuel for finishing up work on *Public Native America*. John, as always, has been my most important resource. He engendered many of the ideas in this book by his observations, not only about the museums, casinos, and powwows I studied, but also about other situations elsewhere in the Third and Fourth Worlds, where struggles for recognition of cultural identity and political sovereignty are so clearly and immediately related to material well-being. A learned student of empire, he has helped me understand the strange and tragic legacies of colonialism more than I ever would have been able to without him. For this influence, for finding a way to be with me in Gaucin, and for countless graces of mind and heart, *gracias.*

Public Native America

Introduction

OVER THE COURSE of the past thirty years, roughly since the 1973 standoff at Wounded Knee on the Pine Ridge Reservation in South Dakota, attention to American Indian tribes in the U.S. media has been noticeably on the rise. The increase marks a significant shift from the relative disinterest in Native affairs that characterized much of U.S. public culture during the first half of the twentieth century. At Wounded Knee, Oglala Lakota elders, political activists of the American Indian Movement (AIM), and three hundred residents of Pine Ridge along with their supporters took control of the community in a gesture of protest against a long list of offenses by the federal government. The list included generations of disregard for the legally binding terms of the 1868 Fort Laramie Treaty and neglect of responsibility for the prosecution of major crimes against Indians on and off the reservation. Faced by a cadre of FBI agents, U.S. marshals, tribal police, and other paramilitaries enlisted by the pro-Washington tribal council president, the occupiers of Wounded Knee made their demands, held their ground, and captured the attention of the nation.

National newspapers, which had focused on AIM during the previous year when the group had taken control of the Bureau of Indian Affairs headquarters in Washington, joined with the local South Dakota press in reporting on events at Wounded Knee regularly from February 28 through April 30, 1973.[1] Much of the reporting dragged out exoticizing iconographies of the nineteenth century, including portraits of Indians as unassimilated losers in the progressive and competitive social environment of modern North America and as romantic resistance heroes. The coverage at first concentrated on the hostility of officials and off-reservation neighbors toward the occupiers, but shortly into the seventy-one-day affair, journalists began emphasizing a growing sympathy for the

I

besieged rebels on the part of many local as well as distant observers. In general, the commentary invoked its own range of stereotypes, but it also called attention to the civil rights at stake in the standoff and to the moral as well as civil upper hand the Oglala traditionals and their AIM allies were enjoying. The very fact that the Native political position was so much in the limelight spoke to another fact, in many ways more resonant: the Oglalas were managing to control the way they were represented in the public sphere.

In the end, the conflict won only promises from the state and the federal government to the Oglalas. Many of those involved in the occupation were arrested. Nevertheless, the episode made for a dramatic story that heralded a revised and more complex discourse concerning Native America than had existed in the past. Since Wounded Knee, public images of indigenous peoples in the United States have emphasized, far more so than they had in the past, Native political organization and the legally articulate claims of tribal political sovereignty, in addition to the distinctiveness of tribal cultural identities within the social landscape of North America.[2] In the process of emerging more prominently in U.S. public life, Native Americans have not only broadcast these claims of political and cultural autonomy, but they have taken substantial control over the production of images and narratives of tribal pasts and contemporary experience in complex styles of public tribal self-representations.

The venues where this work of tribal self-representation gets done are the focus of this book. The tribal institutional sites I describe here, museums, powwows, and casinos, are oriented toward tourism, since tourism is the medium by which most non-Natives find opportunity to face Native America and to witness or experience what tribal collectives, insofar as institutions of tourism speak for them, offer the public to know about their histories and public identities.

Rather than seeking to comprehend tribal daily life or esoteric knowledges, the questions animating *Public Native America* speak to the public interfaces where non-tribal audiences are addressed: How do indigenous North American tribes represent themselves *as* particular tribal collectives to non-tribal visitors? What are the ideational and material terms of tribal experience and knowledge that get foregrounded in public encounters? What ideological, aesthetic, and social factors are most commonly featured? What vocabularies and visual repertoires get deployed? What are some of the more implied, less overt, but nonetheless easily readable representations? What links or breaks are generated between these particular tribal identifications and the category of Native America in general? How and how much do they acknowledge and account for cultural hybridization and similarities to the general culture in the process of publicly establishing their differences? What strategies do tribal groups use in public self-representations to seal off what is private, what is not to be represented? Finally, to what extent are non–Native audiences notified, quietly or overtly, that such displays and performances present circumscribed accounts of the people producing them, that things are being withheld?[3]

AT PRESENT, more than five hundred tribal entities and hundreds more unacknowledged groups consider themselves and ask to be considered in the eyes of the general public as American Indian, Native American, or indigenous peoples. The U.S. Census Bureau statistics for November 2003 show an estimated total of self-identified American Indians and Alaska Natives of 4.3 million, 3.1 million of whom claim membership in specific tribes.[4] In spite of these growing numbers and the increased public attention to Native matters, the very concept of an Indian tribe is still held in contempt in much U.S. public discourse, in great part due to the idea, common as well in the late nineteenth century, that tribal identity is "dying out" if not already lost. A common assumption holds that the differences which once characterized distinct tribal cultures have sifted down into the hybrid cultures of the United States such that "Native" styles of being appear at best as nostalgic re-enactments of long-gone practices and world views. The Pawnee and Otoe writer Anna Lee Walters notes, "Indian people today . . . have often been told that all the 'real Indians' are gone, and that those who remain are somehow less than their predecessors." She then rehearses some of the questions that such comments insinuate: "Where is it that the real Indian has gone? And who are *we,* the grandchildren of those who are gone?"[5]

The many academic books and articles published since the early 1970s that address the cultural and political complexities of a revitalized Native America, particularly in the fields of anthropology, history, and ethnohistory, seem to have had little effect on the impressions held by many Americans, particularly those of European decent whose families have historically had little contact with non-European people. In spite of the countless newspaper articles appearing since Wounded Knee devoted to issues of reservation life—the growth of Indian casinos, land use, tribal campaign contributions, and jurisdictional disputes between tribes and the states, to cite the most prominent examples—Native American tribes are poorly understood by many, if not most, of the non-Native populations of North America.

In the wake of Wounded Knee, tribal projects of self-representation have been aimed at correcting these misinterpretations and at instructing non-Native audiences about tribal histories, aesthetics, and the cultural properties that distinguish contemporary tribal life: languages, religions, kinship systems, and ethics. Expositions of traditionalism commonly include descriptions and performances emphasizing the vitality of these systems at the present time; and they often demonstrate as well the efforts under way to reinvigorate or to restore older practices and concepts in tribal communities where they have not flourished in recent generations.

The answers to the questions posed at the end of the first section, above, suggest a central conflict in these self-representations that the book attempts to map and analyze. In the processes of displaying tribal experiences and identities in terms of distinct, unassimilated cultures, tribal public institutions often resort to modes of thought and expression that would be somewhat disparagingly termed "essentialist" in Western academic discourse; while, by contrast, representations of tribal identity that thematize connections with the larger public sphere are often characterized by the mixtures, contradictions, and playful significations that characterize the postmodern. I will claim that the two modes of essentialism and postmodernism are not simply contradictory: they are most often articulated to each other in ways that can promote cultural effectiveness, economic advantage, and broader social recognition. Essentialism lends cultural stability where instability threatens and demarcates a place for the community at issue to stand, so to speak, in the process of negotiating with more powerful others. The presence of essentialist cultural claims in tourist venues where non-Native audiences meet the tribe can also function, somewhat paradoxically perhaps, to attract consumerist desire to the exotic and to the distinctly "other." Such attraction can work to the economic advantage of the tribe and, together with the expressions of distinct cultural heritage, can also have the effect of furthering social recognition and respect in the broader public sphere beyond the reservation.

Most of the questions suggested here are in some sense appended to the last one, and I will argue that, however rich and interesting a tribe's self-display may be, it can often be understood as precisely a public skin, a public face, for non-Indian audiences; and an important, though subtle, component of the representation is what, for want of a better term, I will call "displayed withholding": a practice of showing that something is not being shown and that this something marks the crucial difference which furnishes distinctly Navajo, Acoma, Mashantucket, or Eastern Shoshone styles of being and knowing. Indeed, the term "public" in the title to this book implies its opposite term, "private," the broad category of experience that flourishes off of the high road of public exchange. "Public" also implies its opposite, "secret." Much is secret in Native communal systems, and public displays often make this clear. Displayed withholding is not only an issue of optics but of audibility. Debates exist within tribes about what is to be made visible to the non-Native public; and while these debates are not made known to us in detail, we hear and read about what we will not be permitted to hear or read. The presentation of a dance at a powwow, of a pot or fabric in a museum, might call attention not only to the object's or event's aesthetic appeal and historical valence, but also to the fact that the seemingly resonant iconography of its design is not being explained to non-tribal audiences. In some cases, the use of Native language in the description of an object or dance movement can serve this purpose, insofar as the words will only speak to select witnesses. Anna Lee Walters describes—and, it could be said, simultaneously performs—this method in noting that the "use of even a single word in extant tribal vocabularies . . . is often enough to spring . . . core ideas and experiences forward into light, where they will have particular significance for another of the same language background, and less meaning for others who do not share that background."[6] This presence of the visibly invisible and the audibly inaudible, as Walters describes it, has a great deal to do with the effective evocation of a specific tribal difference, of a discourse that is not shared and which provides gravity to the lived idea of identity in difference.

In a sense, the spaces and mechanisms of self-representation that emerge operate as obverse versions of what Mary Louise Pratt has famously designated "contact zones." Pratt's term refers to those zones of interaction between, on the one hand, European American explorers, conquistadors, and government agents and, on the other hand, indigenous, colonized subjects in the Western Hemisphere. The terms of exchange that Pratt describes are played out in situations of "coercion, radical inequality and intractable conflict."[7] While it goes without saying that the political and material advantage to which Pratt refers is on the side of the Europeans, she takes into consideration the agency of indigenous actors in resisting and collaborating in the development of imperial scenarios. In the scenes I describe in this book, the "contact zones" in an immediate sense favor the indigenous hosts, whose self-designed situations of display allow them to assert authority in the encounter, in terms of what gets displayed and how the exhibition is shaped. Whether aimed at political or at cultural self-representation, these projects do the work of correcting narratives that have gained ascendancy through historiographies and images orchestrated from Euro-American perspectives.

Each chapter looks at one of four tribal museums and compares its representation of tribal history and cultural legacy with those implicitly or overtly featured in either casinos or powwows. Chapter 1, "Identity at Mashantucket," examines the conflicting but in key ways overlapping constructions of Mashantucket styles of collective identity at the Mashantucket Pequot Museum and Research Center and at Foxwoods Resort Casino. Drawing on Stuart Hall's theories of articulation and of cultural identity formation among colonized and formerly colonized peoples, the chapter argues that the casino and the museum compete with and complement each other in their projects to demonstrate a distinct Pequot collective cultural reality embedded in the circuits of global capitalism that have made much of the tribe's recent successes possible. Chapter 2, "Displaying Loss at Navajoland," charts the apparently seamless conjunctions of contrasting cultural methods and materials at the Navajo Nation Museum with those at the Northern Navajo Fair powwow and open-to-the-public Nightway ceremony. The chapter focuses on representations of cultural loss and continuation as expressions of mourning and resistance, citing David Eng and David Kazanjian's theory of melancholy, where melancholy is understood as an unresolved, chronic state of mourning, a form of politicized sadness that sustains memory as a practice of cultural difference and a method of resistance.[8] Chapter 3, "Wind River Lessons," explores the ways that the Shoshone Cultural Center honors the memory of Sacagawea and Chief Washakie and instructs visitors on the relationships of these icons of tribal history to the present-day tribe. The chapter contrasts and connects the museum's focus on historical biographies of Sacagawea and Washakie and their functions as representative figures of an inherited Shoshone cultural character with the complex, postmodern self-representations at the Eastern Shoshone Indian Days Powwow and at the Powwow Primer, a program of instruction for non-Natives held in the Anglo city of Riverton, located within the reservation. The chapter then turns to an analysis of contemporary claims of tribal sovereignty at Acoma as well as elsewhere in Native America in order to show how the visual and verbal rhetoric of melancholic loss has political efficacy and fuels political and legal action as well as self-representation by tribal peoples in the public sphere. Chapter 4, "Keeping History at Acoma Pueblo," looks at the Acoma Pueblo Museum and tours of old Acoma Village, where recitals of Acoma history sustain a somber, reserved tone and texture in comparison with the flashy gregariousness of the tribe's Sky City Casino, located fifteen miles away. Here, too, I use Eng and Kazanjian's interpretations of colonial melancholia as a mechanism for preserving both a lively sense of the past in the present and a stance of resistance to normalization, to status quo expectations of assimilation that seek to resolve the pain of mourning and depathologize the wounds of history.

The final chapter, "Indigenous Internationalism: Native Rights and the United Nations," takes up the matter of pan-indigenous "articulated" (in Hall's sense), political formations in the late twentieth and early twenty-first centuries. The differences between self-representations described in the separate chapters speak to one of the central points of the book, that there is no singular Native America, nor a limitable category of ethnic subjectivity, "Native American." On the other hand, since the late 1960s, activist Native movements have prompted the linking or articulation of tribal interests toward a transcontinental political sense of Nativism. The occupation of Alcatraz in 1969; the emergence of the American Indian Movement, Indians of All Tribes, and other political groups that crossed tribal boundary lines; and landmark events such as the Trail of Broken Treaties march to Washington and the occupation of the Bureau of Indian Affairs in 1972, followed by the standoff at Wounded Knee in 1973, shaped a pan-tribal political force. To some extent, this movement had been connected with civil rights and black power groups that had been at the center of activist movements throughout U.S. society in the late 1960s. Native interests, however, took institutional form with the creation of American Indian Studies programs in universities across the country and the establishment of what are still the central organs of trans-tribal Native legal and political life, the Native American Rights Fund, the Indian Law Resource Center, and the National Congress of American Indians.

One of the most interesting and perhaps promising developments in the past twenty years has been the linking up of pan–Native American activist organizations with representatives of indigenous populations around the globe in human rights forums hosted by the United Nations. These movements make up the central topic of the final chapter. Non-governmental organizations and tribal governments speaking for the indigenous populations of the Americas, Africa, Asia, and Europe have drawn on common experiences and aspirations to lobby the United Nations for recognition of their status as nations and "peoples" whose cultures and histories are distinct from those of the states that have colonized them.[9] In 2002, a Permanent Forum on Indigenous Issues was initiated at the United Nations, providing a landmark entry of tribal peoples into the strata of global state diplomacy, solidified by the creation of a secretariat—a fixed bureaucratic structure within the UN system.

The chapter is an attempt to weigh the promises of political efficacy gained by this world-scale process of tribal self-representation. The focus here thus shifts from particular tribal self-representations in the United States to the struggle for world indigenous recognition at the United Nations. Indeed, indigenous efforts at the United Nations are of a different order from those I address in earlier chapters, where tribal displays are aimed at less powerful audiences: tourists, scholars, and neighbors. The audiences for the Permanent Forum are states and international agencies. The self-representations have distinctly political aims. In the end, however, the stakes are very similar: recognition in the general public sphere of cultural and historical distinctiveness; honoring of political sovereignty; and economic stimulation to compensate for the marginalization and material losses that are the legacies of colonialism. Prefaced by a brief history of international law in the West regarding indigenous peoples from the time of the Columbian conquests, the chapter seeks to answer the question of whether self-representations before the United Nations work to continue or contest the colonial legacy.

I HAVE DELIBERATELY chosen to write about generically different tribal institutions at each reservation, enterprises that tend at first sight to contrast with if not openly contradict each other in their representations of the particular tribe. My purpose in focusing on these conflicting displays and performances is not to point out intra-tribal conflicts in methods of self-representation to non-Native publics but to emphasize the complexity and the multiple positions taken in plans for tribal self-displays for such audiences. A common misunderstanding among reservation tourists, as often enough among academics, is to assume that tribal communities operate more or less in unison on most decisions and plans for collective, public life. This, of course, is manifestly not the case; nevertheless, it seems to me that the point needs to be made clearly, extensively, and somewhat repeatedly in order to shake the presumption loose. Thus, while my arguments often show that the great differences between a single tribe's institutional representations are on closer inspection not so hugely conflicting, they nevertheless attempt to keep in view the extensive dialogues and debates that go into these productions. When I use the term "tribe" through the course of the book, therefore, I do not assume a singular voice, with all members lining up consistently in support of the particular practices or designs of the institutions under discussion. "Tribe," as I use it, refers to the tribal leadership and its agents that, officially at least, act on behalf of the tribal citizenry in general, by virtue of election and appointment, even when, as is often the case, disputes exist. Where disputes become significant in the productions and meanings of institutional tribal self-representations, I will address them; but in the main, I have not taken on the task of analyzing intra-tribal differences of opinion on these productions.

THE RELENTLESS MOMENTUM of colonialism as a factor in the social, political, and cultural dimensions of indigenous life everywhere challenges processes of traditional tribal identity formations. Since colonial histories have had such impact on what tribes understand as their proper cultural legacies, self-representations in public arenas are often complicated by efforts to sort out specifically tribal signification from the layers of Western influence. As many scholars have argued over the past twenty years, the practices and beliefs coined as "tradition" and felt as the signatures of culture in Native communities get revised with each generation, given the political, geographical, economic, and even religious differences that attend each historical moment.[10] This concept of revisionary genealogy, which features centrally in contemporary cultural studies, has gained such wide acceptance in the academy as to have become virtually self-evident by the present time. The argument that traditions and the cultures they mark necessarily change with generational descent, however, can be an anxious matter to many Indian people, particularly those who subscribe to precisely what poststructuralist critics object to: a notion of tradition and culture as constant, stable essences which transcend the material and ideational dynamics of history. This kind of thinking has been looked at askance in the academy for decades now, and with good reason. Since the publication in 1961 of Frantz Fanon's *Les Damnés de la Terre*, published in English in 1968 as *The Wretched of the Earth*, students of colonial and postcolonial discourse have kept a wary eye on claims of transcendent nativist identity. In his penultimate chapter, Fanon wrote, "It has been remarked several times that this passionate search for a national culture which existed before the colonial era finds its legitimate reason in the anxiety shared by native intellectuals to shrink away from that Western culture in which they all risk being swamped. . . . [They] relentlessly determine to renew contact once more with the oldest and most pre-colonial springs of life of their people."[11]

But, he adds, "colonialism is not satisfied merely with holding a people in its grip. . . . By a kind of perverted logic, it turns to the past of the oppressed people, and distorts, disfigures, and destroys it."[12] Because colonialism smothers native pasts as extensively as it does, Fanon argues, its own influences develop a nearly irresistible momentum among subjugated populations. Thus, "at the very moment when the native intellectual is anxiously trying to create a cultural work he fails to realize that he is utilizing techniques and language which are borrowed from the stranger in his country. He contents himself with stamping these instruments with a hallmark which he wishes to be national, but which is strangely reminiscent of exoticism. . . . In the sphere of plastic arts, for example, the native artist who wishes at whatever cost to create a national work of art shuts himself up in a stereotyped reproduction of details."[13]

In Fanon's view, the simplifications that emerge as "culture" are the products of a grasping for traditional identity by once-colonized peoples who have at best a hazy view of the customs of daily life, the cosmologies, or rituals of community before colonization. From this perspective, the very idea of a discrete Native American knowledge, surviving the horrors and accommodations of the past intact, furnishing a discrete influence for identity formation in late colonial time, would certainly appear an anxious construction.

Achille Mbembe's more recent critique of native identity politics—which he also refers to as "the burden of the metaphysics of difference"—is part of an effort to get at the "heart of the matter" of the violence and the social and political chaos of contemporary Africa. Nativism, he argues, as one of the prevailing themes of contemporary Africanist scholarly discourse, is too dependent on concepts of victimhood and loss to have much beneficial effect.[14] In the spirit of Fanon, Mbembe charges nativism with offering a "faked philosophy" that insists on the possibility of "a return to an ontological and mythical 'Africanness' in which the African subject might once again say 'I' and express him- or herself in his or her own name."[15] As "discourses of inversion," nativism and African nationalism are both based on the "myths they claim to oppose and reproduce their dichotomies: racial difference . . . cultural confrontation . . . [and] religious opposition." In addition, Mbembe argues, race, as a key term in the nativist lexicon of autochthony, however violent its influence in postcolonial as well as colonial thought and action, is simply embraced in Afro-nativism without being challenged at all.[16]

There is no denying the memorable power and persuasion of Fanon's and Mbembe's arguments. Each in his way points directly at the problems of fundamentalist approaches to identity, particularly the dangers of reproducing exclusivist binaries. I will argue, however, that the radical vision of the death of native cultures in Fanon's and Mbembe's writings and their projection that effective cultural difference is impossible to sustain in the face of global Western cultural and economic influence are too drastic in their modernist understandings of the efficaciousness of cultural performance and reinvention. One of the most challenging tasks of this book is, indeed, to make this argument; this is, to read tribal self-representations in such a way as to honor notions of cultural essentialism evident in American Indian communities and at the same time to deploy constructivist notions of cultural inheritance in framing the postmodern styles of many Native American public venues.

To do this I will turn to analysts of colonial and postcolonial situations who have addressed the problem as it arises in comparable situations in other zones of the developing world. In doing so, these writers have recognized the presence, for good or ill, of rooted notions of cultural identity and treated them effectively within a discursive climate that almost exclusively privileges arguments from social and historical construction. I refer to Diana Fuss's studiously cautious project to demonstrate the afterlife of essentialism in the age of deconstruction and to Gayatry Spivak's influential legitimization of circumscribed forms of essentialism. The theoretical work that Fuss and Spivak have spawned opens the possibility for seeing essentialism as a viable mode, not in and of itself but as one of several strands of thought, including constructivism, instability, and hybridization, that overlap and challenge each other in the rhetoric of contemporary tribal public self-representation.

I also make use of Stuart Hall's commentaries on the pragmatics of essentialism in colonized and decolonized situations, and his theories of articulation as a way of mapping claims to transcendent cultural identity within the complex terrain of tribal self-representations. Hall reminds us that for Fanon the problem of cultural identity formation among colonized peoples lies not only in colonialism's production of stereotypes to replace native self-knowledges; but in the fact that these reductions become internalized: "The epistemic violence is both outside and inside . . . in here as well as out there. That is why it is a question of . . . the internalization of the self-as-other." To address this difficult dynamic, cultural essentialism in communal self-representations can function as "a still point in a turning world," in Hall's terms, a grounded reference that might be remembered and deployed to renegotiate identity in the midst of any of the dramatically altering effects of colonialism.[17] Hall recognizes that the fact of marginal peoples "coming into representation" constitutes a virtual cultural revolution and a key feature of global, postmodern society.[18] The enormous weight, force, and speed of contemporary Western circuits of capital and political power make it all the more important for colonized peoples to resuscitate their own "hidden histories." This is the moment of decolonization, according to Hall, when history begins not only to include accounts of marginalized peoples, but to be produced by them in various forms of self-representation. The process involves the rediscovery of origins in order to "return to some kind of roots . . . to snatch from the hidden histories another place to stand in, another place to speak from."[19] These places are both "imaginary" and "knowable," in the sense that they must be reconstructed from memories, stories, bits of material evidence that suggests rather than represents in a relation of part-for-whole an integrated field of cultural practice, ideology, and belief. The pasts recalled are not simple or literal but narrativized out of great need and desire. "I do not think the margins could speak up without first grounding themselves somewhere," Hall writes; and he quotes bell hooks to ask the question, "Where would we be . . . without a touch of essentialism?"[20]

The problem arises with the binary relations on which essentialism rests: a view of the world as constituted by us and them and "a rediscovery of identity which constitutes a form of fundamentalism."[21] This method of self-identification that centers on positioning oneself in opposition to others is, of course, the seed of much that is most dangerous in the present global scene. Hall cites Paul Gilroy's invocation, in relation to black diasporic society in Britain, that one must refuse the binary and instead position oneself as both black and British.[22] The coupling of such identities does not, according to Gilroy, obviate either of them; and the moment of self-representation that stakes out the boundaries of a specific identity formation makes possible the "imaginary political re-identification [and] reterritorialization" of marginalized groups, like, I would argue, the tribal communities of the postmodern United States.

This territory and the tribe's relation to it not only help to materialize the "still point" to which Hall refers, but allow as well for what Frederic Jameson calls "disalienation" in the "reconquest of a sense of place and the construction or reconstruction of an articulated ensemble which can be retained in memory and which the individual subject can map and remap along the moments of mobile, alternative trajectories."[23]

Jameson's term "articulation" is key to his and to Hall's understanding of the relations between such a group and such a place, or between the other components, including language, religion, politics, and daily life practices that make up a cultural formation. Hall's elaboration of an articulation theory over the course of several essays and interviews is especially useful at this juncture. In "On Postmodernism and Articulation," he stresses the linked but contingent relations between elements that make up a social or cultural formation. While Hall resists any notion that

these fittings are necessary or natural, emphasizing instead their historical and social constitution, he insists, as in his example of religion and
ideology, "When I say the connections are 'not necessary,' I don't mean
religion is free-floating. It exists historically in a particular formation,
anchored very directly in relation to a number of different forces. . . . Its
meaning . . . comes precisely from its position within a formation. It
comes with what else it is articulated to."[24]

The value of this model for my study is in the possibilities it opens
for making sense of the cultural essentialisms in tribal self-representations.
Religion, language, daily life practices, and land can be understood as
linked to each other in centuries-old relations that would be difficult
indeed to sever and that have the look and feel of nature but are as historically influenced as the contemporary situations in the midst of which
they are reproduced. The simultaneity of essentialist and historicist accounts of tribal identities so familiar in tribal museums would suggest
that the former is at some level qualified, attenuated, limited precisely by
the historical shapings that explain present circumstances; and yet the stability, the rootedness, of tradition as the bedrock of lived reality is nevertheless asserted.

Articulation theory also helps to explain how Euro-American motifs
and the ideas they reference in American Indian self-representations are
not inevitable features of present-day tribal identities. The "techniques and
language which are borrowed from the stranger in his country," to quote
Fanon, have not, it appears to me, become naturalized dimensions of tribal
consciousness but linked components of the social and cultural formation
that could potentially be unlinked, albeit their fastenings are sure and
durable. In spite of this firm grasp, the links of Western cultural materials
and ideas are not necessarily the inevitably or unconsciously imposed effects of U.S. colonial history but are just as likely consciously deployed signifiers. By the same token, tribal use of images and other tokens of Native
America that appear to be drawn from Western archives need not be
viewed simply as evidence of the internalization of Western reductions.

Native American self-representations to non-Native audiences that
include openly displayed images of tribal culture certainly in the process
deploy Western rhetorical methods, institutional frameworks, even, at
times, reductive stereotypes. In many cases, however, these discourses and
the practices they inform have been submitted to what Arjun Appadurai

has called "indigenization" and what Mbembe himself refers to as "creative assimilation": the deployment of the developed world's systems, methods, and objects for local uses that differ from those for which they were originally intended.[25] In addition, the productions at issue are not necessarily devoid of expressed consciousness of their Western derivations, and this self-consciousness itself could be said to imply a certain distance from what is referred to in the representations themselves. Why should this distance necessarily be defined as Western?

In his widely cited essay of 1988, "Identity in Mashpee," James Clifford read the difficulties of influence that Fanon described in 1961 in the context of the Mashpee Wampanoag 1976 court case in which the Cape Cod tribe attempted to gain federal recognition.[26] Focusing on the problem of establishing evidence for cultural identity, Clifford argued that the Mashpee claimed to perform ceremonies and retain beliefs that made them a distinct, historical tribe; but that these claims were also aimed at satisfying certain reductive assumptions about Indianness held by the judge and jury. Because their demonstrations did not go far enough in this direction, and because their clothing, speech, professions, and social affiliations were so patently "Western," Clifford argued, that the Mashpee lost their case.

Clifford's point is that neither the Mashpees' position (that the tribe had continued to thrive since the seventeenth century) nor the defense argument (that the Mashpee had not existed as a coherent tribe for many generations) was elastic enough to accommodate the ruptures, discontinuities, and reinventions that characterize cultural inheritance, particularly for people who have been subject to colonization. If we think about Clifford's argument in comparison with Fanon's, we might consider that, left with this compromised cultural inheritance, Native American groups seeking recognition in a legal or more broadly social sense might with good reason deploy constructions of their cultures "borrowed from the stranger in [their] country"—not only because their imaginations are inevitably saturated with the borrowed tropes, as Fanon implies, but because they find these tropes strategically useful. If the Mashpee had made recourse to such self-representations, Clifford suggests, they might have won their case; and they would now be free, if they so chose, to discard such devices and to show their various audiences and interlocutors who they are by other means.

Unlike Fanon, Clifford finds it advantageous for tribal groups to accept what he sees as the inevitably constructed texture of identity and to embrace the disjunctures that attend them as part of the modern (or postmodern) condition. But while Clifford's arguments in the 1988 essay take into account the eclecticism common in Native self-representations in the public sphere, they neglect the extent to which such rhetorics do indeed often include, however implicitly or openly, reference to a fund of stable cultural material lying "behind" or apart from the iconic devices that appear in proffered images and accounts. These gestures strongly imply that something different remains which might furnish the means for a strand, if not much more, of discrete Native identity.

In a sense, Clifford reproduced his own "either-or" binary by disallowing that such boundary making and essentialism might very well emerge from consciously chosen positions. For many generations now, tribes have been facing a powerful if changeful field of non-Native cultural influences which they have had to negotiate, willingly or not. Such negotiations might take the form of resistance, affiliation, or anything in between; and native people have surely been aware for a long time of the fact that these encounters have left their marks on cultural forms, practices, and even ideas. The decision to represent culture as a bounded entity, then, becomes a rhetorically strategic one which tribes have deployed, not just for the sake of assuring their own people—if that indeed is one of the reasons for such choices—but as a form of resistance that marks off the space of Native cultural phenomena as distinct, as constituting an experiential as well as conceptual difference.

Perhaps precisely because of the long history of exposure to powerful Western influences, and to contain the effects, Indian communities often represent their cultural identities as existing in stable, transcendent essences. To expect tribal self-definition to systematically operate without it would, at the least, be to expect Native Americans to bracket one of the most deeply held notions of subjectivity and cultural identity in the West and one to which tribes have been exposed since first contact (if they didn't already subscribe to it before): the notion of identity as fixed and continuous, whether it refers to an individual or a nation. To assume that tribal identity would or should be systematically represented without recourse to this concept would be tantamount to suggesting that Native Americans be more consistently non-Western—and perhaps more effectively postmodern as well—than anyone else, a suggestion that I doubt very much Clifford would want to embrace.

In a more recent argument, Clifford takes a different approach and more openly recognizes the endurance of essentialism, in this case in Native Pacific identity claims, particularly in connection with land, citing "the indigenous *longue durée,* the precolonial space and time that tends to be lost in postcolonial projections." These indigenous identities virtually cry out what Clifford does not now deny: "we were here before all that; we are still here; we will make a future here."[27] Drawing on Stuart Hall's model of articulation, Clifford continues to object, as in "Identity in Mashpee," to the imaging of a cultural formation as an organic entity and still asserts that, whatever any Native speaker may claim, "there is no eternal or natural shape to their configuration." But in this later work, Clifford takes up Hall's method of giving place to commentary and self-description of local populations in his argument. While articulation theory assumes linking and delinking rather than enduring fixity, what is linked in the collective voice of cultural identity includes, for Clifford, the rooted. Contemporary Native movements to restore and refurbish "old cultural dispositions" work to locate themselves as particular, discreet formations within the global circuit of influences and exchanges, "to exist in a multiplex modernity . . . with a difference, a difference derived from cultural tradition, from landedness, and from ongoing histories of displacement, travel, and circulation."[28]

The models of cultural articulation that Hall, Jameson, and the later Clifford propose seem to me the most promising methods for taking account of Native American essentialism in tribal self-representations in the U.S. public sphere at the present time.[29] Rather than dismissing expressions of a transcendental tribal core existing in material as well as ideational and spiritual terms, I treat them as linked to openly historicist accounts of tribal change and reformation in the context of the long colonial history. At moments this linkage, or articulation, of differing accounts of current tribal identities will present conflicts, even contradictions with which American Indian communities have long since been familiar. Rather than crowding each other out of the picture, these competing narratives, performances, and other displays of contemporary tribal identity exist, I will argue, in linked relationships. Just as visions of cultural essentialism can be delinked from the composition, so too can the seemingly ineluctable pressures of Western thought and image. What emerges in the rhetorics of display at the tribal tourist venues I study here invites non-Native audiences to witness the aspirations, anxieties, the promises, confusions, and, indeed, the complexity of contemporary Native American public life.

AT EACH of the four reservations I address in this book, the museum functions as the most formal vehicle of tribal self-display. Although Native American tribal museums began appearing as early as the mid-nineteenth century, modern institutional structures did not emerge until almost the middle of the twentieth century. Steve Maxwell writes in the journal of the National Museum of the American Indian that the oldest tribal museum on record "goes back to the mid-1800s." Maxwell's research shows that Caroline Parker Mount Pleasant, wife of a Tuscarora chief, set up a collection of tribal artifacts for public viewing on the Tuscarora Indian Reservation in upstate New York.[30] The Osage intellectual historian Robert Allen Warrior writes that the Osage Tribal Museum appeared in 1938 under the tutelage of the fiction writer and memoirist John Joseph Matthews.[31] Since the late 1960s, tribal museums have become virtually commonplace in Native communities. Maxwell notes that in the past ten years more than a dozen have "opened their doors to the public, and the pace shows no sign of slowing." Currently, over two hundred of these institutions are operating in the United States and in Canada.[32] They offer visitors opportunities to contemplate and learn about the histories and the revered objects of tribal pasts. The historical narratives evoked by the displays reach back to precolonial daily life and extend forward through more recent pasts to the present, exposing in the process not only cultural information that tribal curatorial staffs want visitors to know, but the sources of material deprivation and cultural marginalization common to reservation society as well. Objects on display serve as material links to these various pasts and as precious evidence of the connections between then and now. As Laurie Webster notes in an essay on a Navajo weaving exhibit discussed in chapter 2, since the 1970s a significant shift has occurred in exhibitions of indigenous histories and material cultures, with many more Native people acting as curators, rather than strictly informants, than was the case in the past. Webster writes that "with this has come a fundamental change in the type of cultural information conveyed, based on what Native people think outsiders need to know and what they deem appropriate for sharing."[33]

Similar comments about the cultural politics of contemporary American Indian self-exhibition have emerged in connection with the most publicized Native museum project in recent times, the National Museum of the American Indian in Washington, D.C. Richard West, the NMAI's founding director, has written that the museum's effort has been to "bring the essential voices of native people themselves to the interpretation of our cultures and the things we have made."[34] As a branch of the Smithsonian Institution, the NMAI has distinct functions and intended audiences from what we find in specific tribal museums. First, the National Museum of the American Indian is a federally sponsored organization, and its staff, even though it is largely Native, answers to the non-Native bureaucratic hierarchy of the Smithsonian. Tribal museums by their very nature seek to operate with autonomy and without agendas set by off-reservation or non-Native agents. The top-down organizational structure of NMAI mimics its emergence out of the governmental system; while tribally generated museums on reservations tend to arise from more locally organized interests and histories. Secondly, while tribal museums tend to emphasize differences, and perhaps dialogue drawn from difference, NMAI seems so far at least to evoke an ethos of relationship and connection of shared experiences of oppression. It is this last issue in particular that distinguishes NMAI from most tribal museums. My arguments in each of the first four chapters emphasize the importance of difference as a feature of identity and the central roles that tribal museums play in publicly representing the historical and cultural experiences that demarcate difference. Thus, apart from references to West's and other curators' commentaries that help clarify my arguments, the NMAI does not have much of a place in this book—even though it may be the one Native museum with which readers are most likely familiar. The concluding chapter, which looks at indigenous internationalism as it is taking shape at the United Nations Permanent Forum on Indigenous Issues, begins by showing how tribal communities from around the globe are indeed engaging in relationship and attempting to articulate connections based on common histories of colonization and of continued political and cultural marginalization. But here, too, my efforts are to show how the participation in deliberations at the United Nations are aimed, finally, at securing the cultural and political rights that will allow the indigenous nations involved to confirm and reproduce their differences, even as they have the capacity to engage on the world stage.

The changes in tribal museum practices that Laurie Webster and Richard West refer to include greater emphasis on survival and on the continuation of Native life and cultural knowledges and practices in the present. The Indian museums I study here, like many of those located on reservations elsewhere, do not neglect, in the process of staging continuity, to demonstrate the profound reconfigurations which tribes have undergone, given the powerful pressures of a host of Western influences. While some Native curators lay claim to what in the academy might be called essentialist accounts of cultural survival, such accounts are nevertheless accompanied by narratives of historical change and adaptation mandated in particular by the experiences of colonialism. What emerge are displays of contemporary tribal identities that simultaneously elaborate and perform traditionalism and at the same time reveal how contemporary Native America is shaped by the deprivations of colonial history and the tension-provoking effects of colonialism on Native social and cultural inheritances. Each chapter addresses the particular ways in which the tribal museum at issue stages the relations between these different effects and their bearing on current reservation collective self-representation.

Powwows feature tribal self-images and performances that are not so overtly didactic as what we find in museums. Outsiders are usually welcome; indeed, as they are at Navajo Nation, powwows are often folded into the agendas of annual tribal fairs. The dances, songs, and procedures of powwows are not, generally speaking, however, accompanied by narration or commented on in any overt sense; rather, the familiarity of Native participants with powwow processes is assumed. Outsiders in the bleachers observe the intricate spectacle without any instruction about their origins, meanings, or effects. If non-Natives take part in activities on the dance grounds, they must act on their own, exhibiting the same knowledge of dance movements and other practices or attempting to imitate them on the spot. Dances, songs, and regalia deploy designs and ideas understood as traditional, but while particular tribal histories are referenced in the very locations of powwows, in the narratives and commentaries of the master of ceremonies, and in titles of powwow "royalty," powwows tend to draw on more pan-tribal genealogies for their representational styles than do museums. As the principle form of ostensibly secular, inter-tribal ceremonial gathering which non-Natives are invited to observe and even participate in, powwows have become an important means for tribal self-representation to off-reservation audiences. Robert DesJarlait describes the powwow as a "community-based, inter-cultural event."[35] At most powwows, the hosting community invites members of other tribes and bands as well as non-Native dancers and observers to participate, whether the event at issue is a traditional or "contest" powwow where material prizes are awarded for what judges deem the best dancing. David Whitehorse writes, however, that for many non-Indians, "it is an event to be curiously viewed, but always from a safe distance."[36]

Casinos have drawn more crowds and more media attention in recent years than any other form of Native American tourism. Obviously, their primary concerns are not to educate off-reservation audiences or to entertain them with performances of tribal culture. Nevertheless, the themes and designs of Indian casinos make the most of tribal motifs and images in the process of pursuing profit. In the halls and corridors of Native gambling institutions, we are confronted with a plethora of tribal self-representations that might appropriately be described as postmodern for their dramatically mixed designs that run a gamut from the historically accurate to the reductive and stereotypical. Given their functions as advertising logos and even incitements to consumption, we would not expect these devices to have the seriousness or the steady focus of museum displays, or the more casual traditionalism of powwows. They do, however, project ideas about Native America that prompt more than simply buying or playing. They tell stories and promote images of the identities of the tribal communities that produce them.

Some further words about casinos. With the passage of the Indian Gaming Regulatory Act in 1988, the ongoing Native gaming practices that had been slowly building on reservations across the United States were codified, regulated, and taken into control by the federal government. The ruling stipulates that the form of casino gaming a tribe wishes to operate must have precedent in the state where the tribe is located and that the state must negotiate a compact with the tribe in good faith. As the National Indian Gaming Commission's overview of the law emphasizes, "although Congress clearly intended regulatory issues to be addressed in tribal-state compacts, it left a number of key functions in federal hands."[37] Thus some Native leaders argue that these measures are seen to challenge Native sovereignty since state and federal governments have determining roles in the establishment of Native casinos. For others, however, the regulations are understood to have helped American Indian tribes gain economic advantages for the first time in the history of their colonization. The National Indian Gaming Commission reports that revenues to tribes from gaming operations in 2002 reached nearly 15 billion dollars and that the 330 Indian gaming facilities across the United States provided work for over three hundred thousand people.[38]

Gambling has its opponents among Indians, however. Rather than focusing on addiction or crime, opposition to casino gaming on reservations is generally centered around perceptions that gambling cultivates a materialist orientation at the expense of a spiritual or cultural one and that this tendency threatens the coherency, the difference, the vibrancy of Native traditions and societies. In addition, while the Indian Gaming Regulatory Act confirms and secures certain opportunities for Native American tribes to enter the economic circuits to which they have been denied entry for the past hundred years, the legislation also compromises tribal sovereignty, insofar as it requires tribes to negotiate with state governments and to deal with them in the establishment of gaming compacts. Passionate, complex disputes have happened in the past and continue to rage over the propriety of gaming and casinos operating on ancient homelands, an issue I take up in more detail in chapter 1 in discussing the recent history of the Mashantucket Pequots. My own position in support of casinos is based on the simple fact that gaming has indisputably provided substantial material benefits for tribes. I share the position that, by and large, casinos have made possible not only the improvement of social health in any number of fields but the cultural reinvigoration that fuels as well as complicates public displays of tribal collective identity.[39]

No matter how well gaming is regarded within reservation borders, tribal casinos have been criticized almost continuously in the non-Native media. Particularly in non-Native communities that border reservations, charges that unfair advantages are preserved for Native casinos have become virtually commonplace, and legislation has been attempted on several occasions to stop Indian gaming on these grounds. Stories having to do with Indian casinos and the legislation that has enabled them have appeared often in the mainstream U.S. press during the past decade, making the most of the dramatic tensions in casino legal negotiations and public relations, in addition to imbuing Indian casinos with a certain moral ambiguity.[40] My position is that these Native American gaming enterprises are beneficial if for no other reason than that they have made it possible for several indigenous communities that have been mired in deep poverty for generations to find a foothold out of that hell. Global corporate capitalism and its cultural machinery by definition find their way into nearly every corner of human society, including Native America, and the fewer material resources a tribe has to meet these trends, the less chance it will have to shape, much less determine, the methods, quantities, or effects these influences will continue to have on their society. Even if casino profits derive from the community's participation in global circuits of exchange, and to that extent evidence global modernity's part in the community's cultural makeup, these earnings allow for more control over the pressures and flows of powerful economic and political forces in daily life than would exist without them.

But I also want to say before going further with this necessary introductory discussion of casinos—and I hope to convince readers to take this point seriously—that casinos make up a very small part of the socioeconomic profile of contemporary Native America. They can be powerful media attractors, nevertheless, because of their many shimmering effects: the glamour of wealth, the potential for underworld involvement, the passion of land disputes, indeed, the *frisson* of scandal that commonly attends the very idea of gambling. But casinos are not so common, nor so categorically successful, as the abundant attention they have gotten would imply. The singular focus on the disputes, risks, and ironies of Indian casinos, it seems to me, often serves to distract attention from the continuing poverty on reservations, the continuing marginalization of American Indians from the structures of power in the United States, and the heinous history of colonization that rarely gets looked at in the face in this country—by academics any more than by the neighbors of Native American communities who are in competition with them over land and sovereignty.

Indeed, gambling has long been associated with corruption and decadence in Western societies. John Findlay shows in his history of gambling in colonial America and the United States that the practice has continuously been denigrated when communities perceive themselves as having reached certain levels of civic development and want to confirm their identities as morally as well as socially sophisticated places. Gambling, according to Findlay's well-documented argument, has typically enjoyed support in "frontier" regions throughout the United States at different moments in the history of the nation, but gambling's association with risk and players' traditional lack of concern for class and race difference when involved in gaming have made the practice vulnerable in locations aspiring to respectability. More than particular, material reasons for condemning gaming—as, for instance, that players consistently lose too much or that gaming inevitably opens doors to criminal practices—communities have reacted to gaming's unsuitability to a conventional profile of successful social life.[41] In other recent studies, the venerable antipathy to gambling in the West and has been revisited, with the assumptions on which it is built called into question. In their comprehensive 1990 study of the sociology of gambling, Reuven and Gabrielle Brenner concluded that "behind the condemnation has lurked, at times, a resistance to the idea that chance, rather than divine will or talent, can have a significant effect on the allocation and reallocation of property. In other words, the condemnation was linked with the idea that people can get rich because of sheer luck and the fact that people's hopes could be ritualized around the idea of chance, embodied in some market institutions, rather than that of providence, embodied in some religious institutions."[42] The Brenners find that criticism of gambling based on the argument that it is immoral also emerges as a disguise for self-interest on the part of "groups"—the authors appear to mean marketers and managers of other forms of entertainment—"whose responses to gambling are based on fears of losing their fortunes when people suddenly preferred to devote their time and money to gambling. . . . In societies committed to the idea of competition, such groups, who thus feared falling behind, could not be expected to state bluntly that this threat shaped their opposition to gambling. Thus, words were used as a curtain to cover these groups' selfish motivations. Unfortunately, later generations frequently seemed to take words at their face value, leading both to the invention of some theories and to prejudice."[43] Statistics provided by the National Indian Gaming Association, a Native organization, would seem to in some degree confirm the Brenners' argument. The NIGA shows that the national prevalence rate for lifetime pathological gambling is 0.8 percent, compared with 13.8 percent for alcoholism and 6.2 percent for drug dependence.[44]

IT NEEDS TO BE KEPT IN MIND that several of the venues I study here are, of course, connected in some fashion to global tourist markets. Visitors are drawn to tribal museums, casinos, fairs, and powwows through advertising, news, and other media that circulate across national boundaries; and tribes must regularly do business with U.S. and world-scale corporations that function as suppliers as well as clients. The chapters demonstrate how tribal self-representations on the reservations I study here contribute to a growing understanding among Native Americans that, beyond the familiar and more immediately visible "flows" between reservation and metropolitan cultures, tribal collectives and their projects are inscribed within circuits of global exchange.[45] In Achille Mbembe's words, such tourism, hosted by colonized and formerly colonized nations, becomes "another vehicle for re-enchanting tradition and recycling local identities" and not only helps shape tribal identities but exoticizes indigenous environments for visitors' consumption.[46] My readings of tribal projects of self-representation to non-Native audiences suggest that they are not, however, simply caught up in the net of market forces, recycling and reconfirming dominant motifs of "Indianness." Rather, my effort is to emphasize Native agents' tactical deployment of these processes and devices in order to secure specific tribal benefits having to do with recognition as well as material profit.

AS A STUDENT of contemporary Native literature, I have spent the past decade attempting to understand what is at stake for individual authors in their fictional interpretations of tribal processes in postmodern time. The complex rhetoric of showing and withholding information about these processes in narratives centering on the problematics of Native identity in the contemporary United States restage, time and again, two mutually troubling dynamics of contemporary Native self-representation: a need to honor and in many cases re-enliven a damaged tribal cultural imaginary as a primary ontology and a demand, given the impositions of history, to respond to the needs and interests of the non-Native politically and socially dominant. Conflicts between these two in most ways opposing dynamics are central to much late twentieth-century and millennial Native fiction, and the relentlessness of the problem, of course, speaks to the degree of difficulty in these same matters as they develop off the literary page.

The central historical fact that keeps these two modes positioned parallel to each other, without intersecting and without either of them utterly overtaking the other, is colonialism. The long colonial history that Native tribes have endured at the hands of the United States has meant not only the loss of homelands and the compromising of political sovereignty but lengthy exposure to cultural modernity. It is easy enough to see how European American popular culture, bureaucratic methods, and institutional structures saturate Native collectives as much as they do other non-American regional societies around the globe in the early twenty-first century. The structures of modernity, in place among Indian tribes in the United States since the late nineteenth century, however, were never imposed by means of slow or cautious persuasion. They were forced into place through domination and coercion: boarding schools, missionary programs, a host of Bureau of Indian Affairs programs aimed at imposing the English language, Christianity, and Western administrative logic. The economic means necessary to a plausible assimilation of Native America into the fabric of a democratic nation were never fostered sufficiently for these hallmarks of modernity to take hold in an integrated way.

These means were superimposed in the manner that Ranajit Guha has described, in the case of colonial India, as "dominance without hegemony."[47] In this formulation, Guha refers to Antonio Gramsci's "hegemony" as a form of power secured through persuasion and coercion such that those who are dominated become convinced, to one degree or another, of the plausibility of the social arrangements and ideologies of the powerful. Left out of the economic and political mainstream of American modernity over the course of the nineteenth and early twentieth centuries and having been dominated by means of violent oppression instead of persuasion, the indigenous population of North America has not represented itself as "convinced" in any substantial, comprehensive degree of the rectitude of U.S. ideology or its military, political, and social practices. Of course there have been many exceptions, particularly where individuals have come to prominence within the hierarchies of

U.S. government and religious life; and in the present time, television and advertising, which saturate reservations with images and ideas of the dominant society, do much of the work of extending hegemony. But the experience of dominance without hegemony is evident particularly in the way that Native America has come to live beside mainstream American modernity, feeling its effects, framed by its institutional and political structures, but rarely imbued with means by which to reproduce its wealth. Without this deeper inscription in the modern European American state, tribes continue to exist apart, sustaining a familiarity with the modern as well as certain means of addressing it; but the lack of hegemony has meant that difference itself has been ineluctably sustained. Thus, tribal ways of being and knowing have been contested from nearly every direction by modern American cultural and political processes; and yet tribal people have not had sufficient access to the economic engines of their contemporaries in the dominant society for comprehensive assimilation or hegemony to occur, for the differences to be forgotten or left aside. Older styles of collective life change with the powerful pressures of colonialism, but they are themselves the means of dealing with those pressures and the substance of what survives them. The need to move in both worlds is unavoidable, as is the pressure of living with the contradictions. As the Standing Rock Sioux writer Susan Power has her narrator conclude in the remarkable story "First Fruits," "to remain Indian in this world, one must learn to accommodate contradiction."[48]

The fictional representation of the anguish of such experiences draws, of course, on the particular intellectual, emotional, and visionary powers of individual native writers as well as on their social and cultural experiences as Native Americans. Tribal collectives, on the other hand, deal with these conflicts via political, economic, and cultural means. The tensions get expressed in reservation public institutions where tribes face non-Native audiences, offering representations of collective experiences and histories that enact the complicated negotiations of display and withholding thematized in Native literary production.

I have chosen to dwell on the rhetoric of institutional representations of Native America in this book as a way of honoring the intricate, often difficult positions in which tribal collectives as well as individual Native speakers find themselves, and to contribute, insofar as it is possible to do so, to Native efforts at correcting public misconceptions that

American Indians are a "vanishing race" or that the reappearance of Native America on the public stage in the past thirty years constitutes a form of romantic nostalgia.

My effort is to demonstrate that the tribal public self-representations studied here define tribal cultural identity as distinct styles of being and knowing thriving in the present time. These public projects reiterate in so many ways the point that American Indians, having been left out of the economic development of bourgeois America, have not substantially assimilated to the dominant cultural paradigms. But Native tribes have not been out of the sight or sound of modernity, and they have certainly not been beyond its touch.

THE PRINCIPLE I have born in mind in planning and drafting these chapters is that we are all, Natives and non-Natives alike, inheritors of a colonial history that both joins and divides us, a history that supplements cultural difference in making our mutual recognition and respect difficult, when they exist at all. My hope is thus to contribute to the dialogues, such as they are, between American Indians and the larger public, dialogues, I will argue, of which these representations are themselves components.

In preparing this project, I have benefited from the research provided by many excellent books and essays in Native American Studies, particularly those devoted to tribal museums, powwows, and other institutions intimately connected to cultural recuperation and identity. Many fine studies have recently emerged that pursue the more theoretical question about just what academic studies can hope to know about Indians.[49] None of these, however, focus on the rhetoric—verbal, visual, or performative—of Native self-representations directed toward non-Native audiences. Neither have studies appeared that attempt to gauge the ways in which those audiences' responses have affected the methods or the terms of subsequent representations. Several recent books offer brief interpretations of tribal rhetoric to the non-Native public, but their interests lie primarily in analyses of histories and current issues of identity within the tribes, among their own members, in the tradition of ethnographic study.[50] *Public Native America* offers a different kind of study, devoted to precisely those neglected interfaces where tribes address non-Indian audiences, demonstrating what they deem appropriate among beliefs, histories, and identities.

As a European American academic writer, I take the risk of positioning myself among the many non-Native analysts who have taken it upon themselves to interpret Native American life from the outside, so to speak. I must acknowledge, therefore, that this work gives rise to questions long since framed by students of colonial and postcolonial culture concerning the voicing of tribal interests and the interpretation of their efforts in public engagements that extend beyond the walls and doors of tribal daily life. These questions, pushed to the foreground of postcolonial studies in particular by the Subaltern Studies group, continue to haunt such projects as this one. The title to Gayatry Spivak's "Can the Subaltern Speak?" has acquired a spirit-life of its own, airborne, ubiquitous, whispering itself into our ears.[51] I hope this book will draw less fire, however, when readers take two issues into account. First, the Native American tribal collectives whose self-representations I address here are not in an exclusive sense subaltern subjects since, in addition to inhabiting different "worldings," to use Spivak's term, they are surrounded by a postmodern United States and operate in part within its economic, social, political, and cultural circuits. Native American tribal representatives, therefore, not only know how to speak of—and display, perform, narrate—themselves to audiences that emerge from these environments but can do so quite eloquently. The differences from and similarities to off-reservation visitors' experiences that one finds in tribal representations of Native American cultural reality make possible the shaping of these representations such that they "make sense" for Western ears and eyes. In addition, as Dipesh Chakrabarty has written, in the contemporary universe marked by secularism and rationalism, " 'disenchantment' is not the only principle by which we 'world' the earth. The supernatural can inhabit the world in these other modes of worlding, and not always as a problem or a result of conscious belief or ideas."[52] In pointing out the continuity of the magical and the religious in the midst of rational, secularist regimes of knowledge, Chakrabarty reminds us that non-tribal viewers of tribal public displays are also divided, hybridized, in our selves and in our lived experiences. We can register the plausibility of the existence of tribal belief even when we cannot know its contents.

Secondly, in the chapters that follow, I attempt to interpret many different levels of signification in tribal displays for off-reservation audiences. As public statements, these self-representations are open to commentary and debate, to investigation of implied as well as overt levels of meaning. My arguments often challenge or call attention to contradictions in the apparently intended effects of specific performances, images, and narratives even as I attempt, as far as possible, to honor the apparent intentions in the spirit of constructive dialogue. All of this means, of course, that I do not assume to grasp a specific, stable meaning to any particular element of the institutions I analyze. My own experiences and preoccupations, of course, have a good deal to do with what I see. Nevertheless, I have proceeded for the most part without calling a great deal of attention to my own psychological and cultural lenses, since such information would make the text rather tortuously self-conscious. In any case, I trust that readers will see my angles of perception, and the limits those angles bring to my readings, without my needing to thematize them. The important thing is to take notice of Native America as it shows itself to the public and to recognize the continuing presence of this colonized, properly sovereign world within the United States.

CHAPTER 1

Identity in Mashantucket

LOCATED NEAR THE VILLAGE of Ledyard in southeastern Connecticut, the Mashantucket Pequot Reservation extends over 1,250 acres of thickly wooded terrain and is home to some 650 people. The Pequots are the owners of Foxwoods Resort Casino, an enterprise that has made business history and remained a remarkable success since opening day in 1992. Building on the tribe's highly profitable bingo operation that began in 1986, Foxwoods has made the Pequots wealthy beyond anyone's expectations.[1] As a Native American institution, however, it has been the site of much controversy and a favorite case in point for debates about the propriety and ethics of commercial gambling on Indian reservations across the United States.

By examining the effects of Foxwoods and of the more recently opened Mashantucket Pequot Museum and Research Center as vehicles of intentional as well as inadvertent public rhetoric, this chapter shows how Pequot public identity is being renegotiated in the context of overtly capitalist enterprises and the accumulation of wealth. By "public identity," I mean here articulations of collective world views, experiences, and practices that the Mashantucket Pequots, like other tribes, project for largely non-Native audiences visiting their reservations. This public identity, in my reading of it, is produced from competing self-representations that emerge in the interfaces where the Pequots meet their off-reservation visitors and interlocutors. Simultaneously emphasizing the distinctiveness of contemporary Pequot cultural foundations and the connectedness of the tribe to the economic and social flows of larger national and global circuits, Pequot self-displays elaborate recognizably postmodern modalities. Tribal identities emerging at these interfaces include an essentialist portrait approaching autochthony that is overlaid with and contested by the marks and postures of not-quite-other, popular styles of being.

Both the casino and the museum manifest the tribe's tendency to accept such stark contrasts in its public self-representations. For reasons I trust will become clear, the obvious discordances work as effective strategies for solidifying productive relations with the Pequots' neighbors; and, however paradoxical it may appear at this point, for simultaneously increasing the viability of cultural identity within the tribal collective. I should state my position at the outset that the Mashantucket Pequots have a culturally as well as legally legitimate claim to the term "tribe," defined as a group of people who share descent from indigenous residents of a particular homeland. I am also convinced that Foxwoods is a constructive, worthwhile enterprise, since its financial sponsorship has helped significantly to revitalize the Pequot tribe.[2]

Since the passage of the Indian Gaming Regulatory Act in 1988, more than four hundred tribal gaming operations have been established through contracts between tribes and state governments.[3] The IGRA was intended to promote tribal economic development and to protect tribes from the hands of organized crime. It evolved in the wake of the 1979 federal case that reconfirmed the sovereignty of the Seminole Tribe of Florida over its own bingo operations and of the 1987 Supreme Court ruling in *California v. Cabazon Band of Mission Indians,* which secured tribes' rights to operate games that were already legal in a given state without external regulation.[4] In some cases, by no means all, the gambling operations that have opened under the auspices of IGRA have been quite successful: in 2004, they earned $18.5 billion.[5] A few Native casinos have had the singular effect of drawing their tribal communities out of the deep poverty that has characterized reservation life from the beginning.[6] The IGRA stipulates that federally recognized Native American tribes, as sovereign entities, can decide for themselves if they wish to pursue gaming ventures. Casino gaming, however, can only be conducted if a precedent exists within the legal framework of the state at issue. If this is so, and a tribe wishes to build a casino, the state government is required to negotiate a compact with the tribe and to do so in good faith.[7]

Responses to these negotiations as well as to the casinos that emerged from them have been passionate and passionately divided, on as well as off reservations.[8] Indian casinos can, in theory, emerge anywhere in the United States, and non-Indian neighbors will only have an indirect say in the matter, by lobbying state governments to keep their interests in mind. The rights tribes claim in these situations derive from inherent sovereignty, a concept recognized by the United States in numerous treaties and Supreme Court cases.[9] At the same time, however, IGRA's provisions intervene in tribal sovereignty by regulating gaming, and they limit tribal decision-making powers by requiring Native leaders to attend to states' wishes and to reach accord with them in the creation of their casinos. If no legal precedent for bingo or for casino gaming exists in a given state, that state can reject a tribe's efforts to open such an operation.[10]

The most common result of a state-tribal gaming compact under IGRA is the construction of a casino on land already held in trust by the federal government for the tribe in question, that is, established reservation land. While Indian casinos on reservations, as the properties of sovereign tribal nations, do not pay state or local taxes, the compacts with states generally stipulate for specific contributions from tribal gaming profits to state budgets. Many reservations, particularly in the trans-Mississippi West, are located at significant distances from other centers of population; thus the emergence of a casino often enough makes relatively little difference in the lives of non-Indian neighbors. In the Northeast, however, as well as in California and in the Southwest, reservations are generally located closer to other communities where they have often met with indignation—in spite of the fact that casino compacts generally provide for substantial income to the states. Whether these objections are driven by issues of taste, class, or morality, or by the frustration that comes from having little or no say in the matter, the proximity of non-Natives to Native gaming operations has often resulted in enmity and litigation on both parts to determine whose interests should prevail.

In other instances, reservations have been established or expanded as part of the federal acknowledgment process.[11] In such cases, neighbors have found themselves living closer to casino operations than they ever imagined they would, as indeed happened when the Pequots began developing Foxwoods and a year later the Oneida of upstate New York started work on Turning Stone Casino.[12] Until recently, it was even possible for a federally recognized tribe to contract with a state to conduct a gaming enterprise without state tax obligations on land outside reservation boundaries.[13] In New York State, for example, the Seneca Nation operated such a casino in Niagara Falls under a compact signed with Governor Pataki that allowed the tribe to open two more such casinos.[14] Non-Native resistance to such developments has been active in New York and in Connecticut, where two years ago Senators Joseph Lieberman and Christopher Dodd introduced congressional legislation to put a freeze on tribal recognition while changes are made in the rules; the move was defeated in the fall of 2002.[15] More recently, the Supreme Court ruled in *City of Sherill v. Oneida Indian Nation of New York* that lands purchased by tribes outside their current reservations do not revert to sovereign tribal status, even if those lands are part of former reservations or homelands. This ruling leaves some very lucrative tribal casinos in New York State in the position of now having to pay state taxes or to go through the lengthy process of requesting reservation status for repurchased lands.[16]

The Mashantucket Pequots gained federal recognition in 1983, during a period when New England tribes were experiencing something of a legal renaissance.[17] While non-Native as well as Native supporters of the Pequots found historical justice in their federal acknowledgment, others have been indignant from the start at what they claim are the tribe's dubious origins.[18] These doubts have been exacerbated by the glitz and the supposedly un-Indian glamour of Foxwoods. In addition, since 1983, individuals and families claiming Pequot heritage have moved to the reservation from nearly every region of the United States. In order to gain tribal membership, applicants must produce evidence of direct lineal descent from someone whose name appears on either the 1900 or 1910 tribal rolls.[19] Apart from possessing these documents, many of the newer members of the tribe had little in common when they came to live at Mashantucket. They hailed from different parts of the country, from different social and professional classes, and they still maintain a variety of political and religious orientations. In addition to being Pequot, they present a broad range of ethnic backgrounds.[20]

Mashantucket officials have admitted that many of the newer tribal members had little knowledge of Pequot history or cultural traditions when they took up residence on the reservation.[21] Having grown to adulthood in non-Native cultural contexts, many only had a sense of the most recent phases of the tribe's history when they moved to Mashantucket. On-going projects for recuperating Pequot lifeways, language, and world views have thus been aimed at bringing the dimensionality of the tribal past into full view in order to address problems of individual as well as collective and public Pequot identity in the present.[22]

THE MASSACRE AND RESURRECTION

The tribe's most visible response to these challenges was the opening of the Mashantucket Pequot Museum and Research Center in August of 1998. The museum functions as an educational institution to demonstrate the group's historical connections to the seventeenth-century Pequots and, thus, to correct the somewhat common notion that the tribe had been extinct since that time. In large part, the museum's exhibits and narratives are the products of the twenty-year-old Mashantucket Pequot Ethnohistory Project. Since its inception in 1983, the Ethnohistory Project has literally dug up extensive material evidence of the Pequot past, from domestic and agricultural sites to burial grounds. In 1987 the project director, University of Connecticut archaeologist Kevin McBride, and his staff succeeded in "convincingly identifying the remains of the main Pequot village burned by the Puritans in 1637."[23] In this conflagration, the culminating moment of the colonialist action that came to be known as the Pequot War, more than half the tribe's population was slaughtered by John Mason and a band of Massachusetts Bay Puritans.[24]

In the aftermath of the massacre, the population is estimated to have been reduced to between two thousand and twenty-five hundred, from a prewar figure of around four thousand.[25] Within a few years, the legendary Robin Cassacinamon emerged as their leader, and in 1650 he was granted a five-hundred-acre tract of land in Noank for his community, known from this point as the Western or Mashantucket Pequots.[26] In 1665, the General Court of Connecticut assigned the Mashantuckets a parcel of about three thousand acres, including the current reservation, and the Noank property was eventually quit-claimed. Through the early decades of the eighteenth century, officially sanctioned incursions by colonists reduced the Indian land base to about sixteen hundred acres.[27] These reductions established a pattern for colonial and later state-sponsored appropriations of Mashantucket property.

Over the course of the eighteenth and earlier nineteenth centuries, colonial wars, trans-tribal Indian movements, and the demands of labor meant that Pequots left the reservation in increasingly larger numbers.[28]

In 1856, the county government auctioned six hundred acres of reservation land to the general public.[29] The tribal population and budget gradually diminished through the 1940s, when authority for Indian affairs in Connecticut was handed over to the state Department of Welfare. By the early 1970s, two elderly women resided at Mashantucket; their names and images have since become legendary in reservation public life and in the reconstruction of tribal identity. When Elizabeth George Plouffe and Martha Langevin Ellal died in 1973, they bequeathed to their descendants an intact Mashantucket homeland, which they had maintained for forty years in the face of great poverty and continuous threats of encroachment by non-Indian neighbors.[30]

In 1974 the children, grandchildren, and other kin of Plouffe and Ellal moved to reestablish a tribal council and a constitution. The following year, the now widely admired Richard Hayward, Plouffe's grandson, was elected council chairman. The tribe's goal of federal recognition was satisfied in 1983 with the Mashantucket Pequot Indian Claims Settlement Act, which extended tribal status and established a fund of $900,000 for the purchase of lands determined to have been formerly owned by the tribe.[31] The substantial extension of the reservation acreage and the commitment of the Bureau of Indian Affairs to subsidizing housing, health care, and education began the process of restitution for centuries of oppression and marginalization in Anglo Connecticut and the reconstitution of a modern—or perhaps the more appropriate term is postmodern—tribal community.

In 1987 Connecticut had passed a bill legalizing charity "Las Vegas nights" (play money blackjack, craps, roulette, and poker for door prizes only), so with the passing of IGRA, the Pequots were able to enter into negotiations with the state to offer high-stakes gaming in a full-scale casino.[32] In 1993 Hayward and his advisors negotiated with Governor Lowell Weicker to operate slot machines at Foxwoods, 25 percent of the profits of which would be donated to the state budget.[33] Reputed to be the fulfillment of a vision that came to Hayward, the casino has never closed since opening its doors in February 1992.[34] Earnings have made possible the development of the reservation infrastructure, including a health clinic, a police and fire department, a community center, and a child development center, all situated in elegant stone buildings that blend nicely with the woodland surroundings. The tribal council pays tuition

from the profits of Foxwoods for the education of tribal members anywhere they wish to study, from kindergarten through graduate school. In
addition, the Pequots have contributed substantially from casino profits
to the Native American Rights Fund and many trans-tribal educational
and cultural foundations. The annual powwow at Mashantucket is one of
the largest in the nation and brings many thousands of participants from
all over Indian country who compete for the largest prize money on the
powwow circuit, again from Foxwoods coffers. The tribe has also been a
prominent sponsor of the Smithsonian's National Museum of the American Indian and of local institutions like the Mystic Aquarium, the Connecticut Special Olympics, the Hartford Ballet, and the Old Mystic
Baptist Church.[35] Thus, the Pequots have emerged as a visible public presence in the corporate world, in inter-tribal circles, and in the public
sphere of southwestern Connecticut.

POSTMODERN/ESSENTIALIST
IDENTITY FORMATIONS

To a certain extent, Pequot history raises some of the questions concerning contemporary tribal identity that James Clifford took on in
"Identity in Mashpee," the concluding chapter of his widely read 1988
critique of Western ethnographic writing, *The Predicament of Culture*. In
Clifford's reading of the Mashpees' 1976 suit for federal recognition, neither the lack of evidence of a continuous Mashpee communal presence
in Cape Cod since the seventeenth century nor the patchwork, contradictory fashion of contemporary identity formation should have counted
against the Mashpee claim to legitimacy as a tribe.[36] Citing the difficulties that beset the Mashpees in their efforts at "negotiating . . . identity in
contexts of [colonial] domination and [intensive cultural] exchange" for
several hundred years, Clifford argued that tribal identity in this case
might best be construed not as a bounded entity but "as a nexus of relations and transactions actively engaging a subject." Representation of
cultural identity should not deny such interactions and "must then be
more complex, less linear and teleological."[37] Clifford's careful attention
to the Mashpees' efforts to satisfy the court's notions of a tribe as a stable
cultural entity enunciated a compelling and much needed critique of the
legal essentialisms the Mashpees and other Native communities have faced
in their efforts at gaining federal recognition. He quite openly proposed

the Mashpee case as a model for the study of the problematics of post-modern cultural identity in a broader sense.

Clifford's arguments, of course, have been taken up and expanded in more recent studies of postcolonial identity formation and in analytic frameworks that emphasize the dramatic shifts and protean shapings of cultural history generally. Although the Pequots' story has only been scantily addressed in academic writing, it could be quite effectively read with theoretical maps inspired by Clifford in "Identity in Mashpee." What are not substantially explored in such theoretical prospects, how-ever, are the claims often made by indigenous communities themselves that they are sustaining bounded, virtually essentialist identities.[38] Clif-ford himself acknowledges the centrality of these kinds of claims in the later essay, "Indigenous Articulations,"[39] and the Osage scholar Robert Allen Warrior notes in a complaining mode that "essentialist categories still reign" in American Indian self-representations in the public sphere. Warrior worries that "appeals to essentialized worldviews always risk an ossifying of American Indian existence" and that the preoccupation with "parochial questions of identity and authenticity" would better be ignored and replaced with attention to the "more pressing concerns" of Native intellectual traditions.[40] Trained in the intellectual traditions of poststruc-turalist and postmodern literary and cultural critique, Warrior joins Clif-ford and many others in the fields of poststructuralist anthropology and postcolonial cultural studies who recoil from the idea of a fundamental seed, somehow surviving through years of struggle, renegotiation, and near emptying out of any tribal profile to assert its continuing existence.[41] But if we take into consideration the anxieties of self-identification that surely come with histories like that of the Pequots', the inclination to assert what we might call a fundamental Pequotism becomes rather eas-ily understandable.

One familiar voice, speaking from the perspective of British cultural and communication studies, can help with some of these questions. A core Pequotism funding contemporary tribal activities, events, and state-ments might be said to serve as what Stuart Hall has called, in relation to colonial and postcolonial situations elsewhere, "a still point in a turning world," a grounded reference in relation to which any particular moment in Pequot history might be situated.[42] Hall recognizes that the fact of marginal peoples "coming into representation," as he puts it, constitutes

a virtual cultural revolution and a key feature of global, postmodern society.[43] The enormous weight, force, and speed of contemporary Western
circuits of capital and political power mandate the revision of conventional history by colonized peoples in order to resuscitate their own
"hidden histories." This is the moment of decolonization, according to
Hall, when history begins to not only include accounts of marginalized
peoples, but to be produced by them in various forms of self-representation. The process involves, as it has for the Pequots, the rediscovery of
origins in order to "return to some kind of roots . . . to snatch from the
hidden histories another place to stand in, another place to speak from."[44]
Although these places are hidden by the historiographies and material
pressures of colonialism, they can be reconstructed from memories, stories, bits of material evidence that suggest more than represent in a relation of part-for-whole an integrated field of cultural practice, ideology,
and belief. Historical memory in general is rarely accurate in any absolute sense.[45] "I do not think the margins could speak up without first
grounding themselves somewhere," Hall writes; and he quotes bell hooks
to ask the question, "Where would we be . . . without a touch of essentialism?"[46] In a widely cited essay in *Social Text,* Ella Shohat comments
that "the anti-essentialist emphasis on hybrid identities comes danger-
ously close to dismissing all searches for communitarian origins as an archaeological excavation of an idealized, irretrievable past."[47] As Hall sees
it, the pitfall lies in the possible emergence of an exclusivist structure of
self-identification that can propel forms of othering like those that have
become so threatening around the globe at the present time.[48]

The Pequots' assertion of kinship with their seventeenth-century ancestors and the tracing out of tribal history down the generations simultaneously marks out what Shohat calls the "communitarian origins" and
locates the tribe in a long history of Connecticut, such that its members
are indeed both Indian and American. The Mashantucket Pequot tribal
nation thus posits itself as having overcome its "outwaiting," to use Scott
Momaday's term, in the wilderness of the Anglo hegemony and deploying lessons learned during the outwaiting to conduct a business and a set
of self-representations in the shared public sphere.[49]

This relation of population to place provides Hall's "still point," and it
constitutes the possibility for what Frederic Jameson describes as "disalienation" and "the construction or reconstruction of an articulated ensemble

which can be retained in memory and which the individual subject can map and remap along the moments of mobile, alternative trajectories."[50] I would argue, then, that the concept of the essence of culture at Mashantucket is a heuristic that projects its sources retrospectively onto a revered past, built up in the present from shards of memory, archaeologically honored materials, and a great desire to *be as* Pequot among the present-day Anglo populations of New England.

The contradiction between a claimed Pequot essence and a narrative of history that complicates the very notion of essence does not render the assertion of a contemporary Pequot identity implausible. The history narrated at Mashantucket certainly makes the description of particular "traits" of Pequot culture difficult to establish, but that does not erase the possibility of any configuration at all of collective identity.[51] Indeed, the crippling circumstances that continue to this day as a result of the Pequot diaspora, including the lack of knowledge among some present-day Pequots about how ideas and practices of tribal culture produce meaning, are counterbalanced in part by the essentialisms that tribal leaders and spokespeople utter—to the tribe itself as well as to non-Native audiences who enter the tribal public sphere.

The immense project of drawing together a community of tribal members with shared interests of an order other than economic and more substantial than a nominal Pequot lineage from the disparate cultural experiences and styles of being among the population at Mashantucket has worked not by emphasizing differences, but by enacting similarities, not only between individual members but between the present collective and the Pequots of centuries ago. The formation of a functioning Pequot polity out of the present-day population's heterogeneous experience would not be best approached with an understanding of each Pequot subject or the tribal collective as "an immense discontinuous network . . . of strands that may be termed politics, ideology, economics, history," as Gayatry Spivak summarizes the conventional poststructuralist analysis of subaltern identity formations. Such a description would hardly serve the social or political imperatives of the Mashantucket Pequot Tribal Nation. The asserted Pequot cultural essence becomes an invisible backdrop, a protean core that must be re-imagined at the same time that contemporary identity formations presume to draw their terms from it. We might say, therefore, that this essence, like identity itself, is in process as much as contemporary efforts to recuperate and express it are. Call this postmodern essentialism or a form of postpositivist realism, the contradiction jars, but it has a clear pragmatic viability.[52]

In its role as benefactor of the project to rebuild a Pequot society, Foxwoods functions as a means to an end, precisely, a compartmentalized performance of global capitalism and corporate postmodernism as Jameson describes them in *Postmodernism, or the Cultural Logic of Late Capitalism*.[53] It is the mask of a familiar Las Vegas enterprise concealing an indigenous consciousness that looks intensely to the past and to the securing of a viable tribal future. At the same time, Foxwoods is the dynamic capital venture it appears to be, the hottest profit maker in town, a corporation among corporations, with a vision of even more accumulation of wealth in the future.[54] The Pequot community's acceptance of the contradictions that emerge in these self-representations bespeaks in itself a certain postmodern attitude, a willingness to exploit Western corporate methods and conventional U.S. casino styles combined with a recognition of the ironies and the difficulties of elaborating a Pequot identity at this moment in history. The tribe's claim to specificity is a claim to difference, made from a position within the global capitalist system of which it is a constituent.

In order to provide a closer view of these mappings of Pequot self-representations, it might be useful to take a look at the institutions themselves. The logics of relationship between the museum and the casino call for slow reading and close attention to details of space and design. On the assumption that most readers will not have been to Mashantucket, I begin the next section with descriptions of both institutions.

THE CASINO

If you take up the television advertisement's invitation and go to visit Foxwoods, the promise of woodland peace is made good for much of the drive along Route 2, a handsome country road that offers relief from the noise and congestion of Interstate 95. Eventually the traffic thickens, then increases dramatically. With the heavy summer foliage, it is difficult to see what lies ahead, even as you know where everyone is going. Abruptly the enormous complex comes into view. It looks like a glass castle, a shopping mall, the pleasure dome of Xanadu in Coleridge's fantasy, overwhelming in its size and elaborate design. The original casino-hotel

1-1. Foxwoods Resort Casino, Mashantucket Pequot Reservation

complex is painted purple and turquoise, trimmed in glass and marble. Behind it, like Mont Blanc rising over the Matterhorn, looms the newer and even bigger Grand Pequot Towers. The prospect is awe striking, reminiscent of Las Vegas and an anomaly amid the quiet, otherwise undeveloped woodland environment "where Mother Nature and Lady Luck Meet."[55]

Inside, an overwhelming array of portraits, video images, lights, and sounds assault the eyes and ears. Celebrities sing and dance on giant video screens posted outside the theaters. In the cocktail lounge, waitresses wearing Indian maiden outfits wait on customers from around the globe.[56] Tribal drumming music and mall-style Muzak compete with the clang of slot machines. The hallways are crowded with people looking driven, lost, gleeful, depressed.

As an advertisement for the casino suggests, and as visitors are continually reminded, the action at Foxwoods is defined as "Gaming in Its Natural State," the "Natural State" being illustrated by stands of fake, life-sized pines, maples, and oaks positioned between the slot machine halls. At the opposite end of the building stands a larger-than-life river scene, positioned somehow on a vertical axis with giant trout curling around imitation rocks and aquatic plants. The overt fakery of these woodland scenes inside the casino is all the more striking, given the panoramic views of the real thing through the casino's many enormous windows. Allowing for the vision of a different order of reality to penetrate the gambling environment, these windows seem to violate the conventions of casino design, but the synthetic woodland inside has the effect of drawing the exterior into its embrace, enlarging nature, polishing its surfaces and inflating its dimensions to a dream-like scale worthy of the most elaborate animated film.

References to Indian, sometimes specifically Pequot, history and culture attach themselves to the theme of "Gaming in Its Natural State" and become part of the spectacle. In the midst of one cluster of "trees" stands an enormous urethane statue of an Indian warrior, the locally famous Rainmaker, who kneels with a bow and arrow pointed skyward. The "ground" where the figure kneels is covered with a mixture of fake and natural mosses, ground cover, and shrubs. Every half hour, a scream, meant to sound like an eagle's cry, emits from the background, and the "sky" toward which the Rainmaker aims comes alive with lights, rain, smoke, and the sound of drums. A somber voice-over narration accompanies this display, testifying to the lifestyle of Pequots in their ancient homeland.

Yet other themes take up space in Foxwoods' labyrinthine corridors. Beside the plastic groves and cement rock beds, retail shops are arranged side by side in the manner of an old New England village. In particular, the quaint storefronts suggest nearby Mystic Seaport and Olde Mysticke Village—themselves designed to imitate, in differing degrees of authenticity, the historic past of the actual, functioning town of Mystic. These references seem to imply another motif, perhaps "Gaming in a New England Village," where the village, like the casino's sculpted natural scenes, lends some metaphorical morality to the practice of gambling.

The pastiche of cultural styles in Foxwoods, the plethora of signs and images quoted from already existing signs and images, the elaborate simulacra (of nature, most emphatically), and the bewildering labyrinth of corridors, halls, and passageways are much like the features of Frederic Jameson's exemplary text of postmodernism, the Westin Bonaventure Hotel in Los Angeles.[57] The overwhelming scale and density of decor, the ease with which you can get lost, and the channeling of movement along irretraceable passages have at least the momentary effect of diminishing personal agency and of catching one up in the spinning commercial energy of the place. The juxtaposition of stylistically unrelated elements leaves the impression that the design logic of the casino is not only plural but also a matter of chance, play, and anarchy. Foxwood's penchant for marshalling disparate icons and sound bites, with little thematic clarity to connect them, locates the design strategy in a postmodernism aesthetic of kaleidoscopic representation and testifies to the institution's participation in what Jameson has named "the cultural logic of late capitalism."[58]

THE MUSEUM

Over the past eleven years, the casino, this incongruous warehouse of styles and themes, has loomed into view as the most common— indeed, perhaps the only—signifier of the Pequots in general circulation. It is little wonder then that visitors, most of whom probably know little else about the Pequots, associate the tribe with the casino. Not far from Foxwoods, however, around a few bends in the road and further into the reservation proper, another impressive structure emerges into view, the Mashantucket Pequot Museum and Research Center. Enveloped among the trees, the curving sweep of the museum represents a different genre of Pequot interests. It aims to narrate and image the tribal past in a contemplative setting. Somber and graceful in its carefully conceived design, the museum does not so much extend an invitation to visitors as it permits you to approach. Unlike Foxwoods' Himalayan profile, the building angles and spirals downward, from the height of a solitary watch tower to galleries and research laboratories deep underground.

As the Foxwoods complex and profits have expanded, so too have efforts to revive Mashantucket political and cultural history, and the 308,000 square foot, $193 million museum is the tribe's most ambitious effort in this direction. Having opened its doors in August 1998, the museum is a relatively new addition to the reservation landscape, projecting an alternative image to the tribe's public profile as a gaming corporation. Inside, the prevailing themes link contemporary Pequots to earlier inhabitants of Mashantucket and stress the indigenousness of those people to the land and the regional environment. A sign near the entry reads,

1-2. Mashantucket Pequot Museum and Research Center, Mashantucket Pequot Reservation

"The stories of the Pequot people and our ancestors are preserved here in Cedar Swamp, a secluded place at Mashantucket where our people have sought refuge for centuries." The museum thus displays language, place, and people as inextricably linked and the present-day Mashantucket Pequot Tribal Nation as a distinct culture, the descendants of people virtually autochthonous in this location.

The entry consists of a long, slowly curving ramp leading downward from the lobby to the lower galleries. As the walkway descends, the walls on either side rise, so you feel like you're being admitted into a self-contained world situated within the very ground of Mashantucket. The permanent exhibit begins its narrative eighteen thousand years ago, "when a mile high glacier covered Mashantucket." An escalator takes you down through a pale green, dimly lit, simulated glacial crevasse, "complete with cold air and creaking ice."[59] Below the glacier stands the museum's trademark exhibit, a village designed to resemble what researchers imagine was an actual sixteenth-century Pequot village. The two-acre walk-through diorama features life-size manikins of Pequots going about activities of daily life—cooking, sleeping, hunting, farming, playing. Exacting historical research was done for every detail, from wigwam interiors and canoe design to the instruments and herbs for treatment of illness. Everything is arranged to look as it might have on a summer afternoon in 1550.

No attempt is made, however, to get visitors to suspend disbelief. The technology of the exhibit blocks such identification from the start, as you are handed an audio tour that guides you through the different sections of the village, with instructions to fast forward, rewind, and press numbers for specific information. Placards point to side galleries where photos and text explain how the village was produced, from research to construction and installation of all the sounds and smells. The differences between the world imagined and the one in which the imagining is done are plain to see, and that is part of the point: a particular set of practices and ideologies flourished here long ago, but through the inevitable processes of material change and colonialism's systematic destructions of tribal coherency these ideas and practices have been physically and socially buried over the course of generations. The great influx of wealth during the past seventeen years, however, has made possible the reconstruction of historical and cultural information to such an extent that contemporary Pequots can narrate their connection to that past, from the standpoint of their immense distance from it, and enact their felt responsibility for preserving its legacy.

Colonialism is, of course, the determining framework of modern Pequot history. Contemporary life is its product, however much influence recent wealth and recuperated lifeways may wield. But while the history of conquest is very much present in the story this museum tells, the more evident self-representation that the tribe projects highlights Pequot distinctiveness and the regained hold on culture, land, and authority at Mashantucket.[60] In a general sense, then, the museum represents the tribe as a distinct, historic entity with a stable core of being. In contrast to the stylistic pastiche of Foxwoods, with its implicit view of Pequot identity as inextricably mixed up in the popular culture of mainstream America, the museum projects the contemporary Pequots as inheritors of a distinct and viable legacy and of an errand to reestablish the cultural and material infrastructure for an essential Mashantucket identity.

THE NEIGHBORS

Responses to the two institutions have differed dramatically. At times, the tone of local public discourse concerning Foxwoods is redolent with resentment and even open hostility. While writers for the *New London Day* have honored Pequot history and efforts at cultural restoration, complaints published in the newspaper focusing on issues related to the reservation expansion and casino traffic imply larger tensions.[61] A theme emerges in which the Mashantucket Pequots and their casino are cast as a giant corporate entity with powerful connections in Washington and bottomless wealth to fund whatever projects they desire. Ledyard, North Stonington, and Preston, on the other hand, which surround the casino, figure as small, disempowered communities whose resources are only their voices and their Yankee integrity. Differences between the tribe and the towns in these accounts are sometimes cast as differences between tasteless commercial development and a simple, rural lifestyle. The towns are "learning to live in the shadow of a giant,"[62] as one *Day* headline puts it, but they are literally losing ground against developers of "the casino coast" in what an editorialist calls an "uncompromising transformation of a region into a [tourist] destination."[63]

Resentment of emergent Pequot power has been stimulated by visible evidence of the tribe's wealth in comparison with the towns' modest means. A *New York Times* reporter interviewed some of the neighbors in 1995 and described their feelings in response to "tribal leaders jet[ting] around the world meeting international leaders and . . . [m]embers of the tribal police patrol[ling] the reservation in new Ford Explorers, while officers on the town force ride in battered cruisers." The report concluded that "Foxwoods could finance the town of Ledyard's annual budget . . . on less than a week's gaming revenues."[64] The three towns tried to take a case to the Supreme Court in 2001 to prevent the tribe from expanding the reservation into township sections that would, if these efforts were successful, no longer provide tax revenues.[65] Del Knight, speaking for a group called Residents Against Annexation, confided that, "You can almost see how militias get started."[66] Images have emerged in the local press of the Pequots as latter-day conquerors who seek to overtake lands that properly belong to non-Indians. A North Stonington selectman once declared that there was nothing to stop the tribe from "buy[ing] up all of southeastern

Connecticut";[67] and a homeowner once claimed something like indigenous status himself: "We've been here for 30 years and our family was here
before us. Then these people came along, with all their money, and started
pushing people around. It's ridiculous."[68]

While Foxwoods has inspired such indignation toward the Pequots,
the museum has drawn extensive praise and has had something of a
sobering effect on the tribal public image. The museum's tasteful design
and seriousness of purpose have been honored in the local and regional
press as well as in academic commentary. In almost every case, these accounts highlight the contrasts between the museum and Foxwoods, emphasizing the museum's compensatory or corrective role in relation to
the tribe's gambling image. Michael Stoll, for example, writes that
"whatever the Pequot Museum does for understanding Native Americans, it will doubtless improve the public image of a controversial gambling enterprise that . . . has turned tribal members into millionaires."[69]

SERIOUS CASINO, PLAYFUL MUSEUM

What, then, can be said about the relationship between the museum,
as coordinator and manager of Pequot history, and Foxwoods, which ab-
sorbs public attention and has become the icon of the Mashantucket
Pequot Tribal Nation outside the reservation? For all their enormous differences, Foxwoods and the museum both serve as material ambassadors
of contemporary Pequot society to the tribe's multifarious publics. How
can both speak for the Pequots' desired public image as a legitimate,
identifiable American Indian tribe?

At the Mashantucket Public Relations Office and in the pages of the
New London Day, tribal spokespeople have often compartmentalized
Foxwoods in describing it as a means to an end and as an entity that was
never conceived as an expression of tribal culture.[70] The financial achievements of Foxwoods have come about through the Pequots' canny participation in the web of global corporate capitalism, but Skip Hayward and
other tribal leaders argue that they are sustaining these ventures in order
to fund the reestablishment of Mashantucket as a cultural entity.[71] Before
concluding, however, that the dynamics of compartmentalization explain
the contradictions between the different tribal images staged by these
institutions, we need to consider another matter that complicates things
further: their similarities.

Indeed, the casino and the museum have several things in common. According to a writer for the *New London Day*, the museum offers "a theatrical, time-travel experience where, like ghosts from the future, visitors can see, hear and smell the village—yet never break the dream by directly communing with the residents."[72] By this description, the museum's simulacrum of a sixteenth-century Pequot village recalls rather hauntingly the woodland scenes and New England villages inside Foxwoods. The giant, fake trees are like those that surround the casino's Rainmaker; and some of the manikins of Pequots in the diorama of life before the English came call to mind somewhat the figure of the Rainmaker himself. Michael Stoll describes the museum somewhat dismissively as "part Disney, part 'Dances with Wolves,'" but if his metaphors are insulting in the context of his argument, they are not entirely illogical.[73] Indeed, the manikin faces, modeled from contemporary Haudenoshone (Iroquois) people, the glacial crevasse leading to the Ice Age exhibit, the grinding and clashing sounds of colliding mounds of ice—these features invest the museum with a certain playfulness, an invitation to imagine how the past might have looked, and the imitations are manifest. Performances of the Pequot past in the museum's movie theaters and video displays call overt attention to the differences between the historical referents and the technologically sophisticated vehicles. One could argue that the old Pequot world portrayed here is a product of a twenty-first century Pequot imaginary, of global technology, and of historically documented, culturally specific styles of being.

At a recent conference on Mashantucket Pequot history held at the museum, Skip Hayward joked about an idea he once had to actually "Disnify" the institution by installing a ride where the escalator now takes visitors through the glacier. He described as well, half jokingly, a plan he has nurtured to connect the museum with Foxwoods via monorail.[74] A pamphlet published by the tribe several years ago pictures a sleek vehicle carrying passengers between Foxwoods and other sites in what is described as a complex that highlights "family entertainment and enlightenment," including the projected museum. If actualized, the monorail idea would function as a tidy metaphor for the aesthetic and conceptual ties between the two institutions.

The many installation pieces in the museum, including what might appear to be almost as many individualized video apparatuses as Foxwoods has slot machines, offer additional opportunities for experiencing the Pequot past; these pieces might be quite reasonably understood, as they appear to in Hayward's speech, as implements of fun, however heuristic their intended effects. From this point of view, the museum seems to highlight its own technological sophistication and its display forms—spectacles designed in the manner of contemporary advertising, film, and theme parks—as much as it concentrates on the representation of Pequot styles of being or landmarks of tribal history. The mixture of Pequot historical data and popular cultural forms, in addition to interrupting each other's differing generic purposes, produces a more dense representation than that seen in the earlier perspective. More than an account of a specific, limitable Pequot culture complicated by a historical narrative of the disruptions of Pequot society, this reading finds a contradictory, self-ironizing, and stylistically mixed account of a postmodern tribal formation.

Foxwoods, on the other hand, appears on further inspection to present a more coherent set of references to Pequot history and sense of place than it does at first glance. From this perspective, the casino seems a more consciously indigenous enterprise. Hanging prominently over one of the entrance lobbies to the casino is an enlarged photograph of Elizabeth George Plouffe. Stately and sagacious, wearing a plaid wool shirt, beads, and braids, she gazes upward, away from the camera, toward something outside the picture frame. Her calm and sturdy gaze seems fixed on a source of knowledge and inspiration beyond the scope of the photographer's view, beyond the historical moment when the picture was taken, and certainly beyond the immediate scene of Foxwoods, which nevertheless appears in this arrangement to have her blessing.

Details of the casino's decoration contribute to the impression that the institution projects a serious, historically grounded tribal self-representation. The basket and wampum designs embedded in carpet and wallpaper borders derive from older Mashantucket patterns, and the sculptures by Allen Houser and Bruce Lafountain that decorate the corridors are some of the finest examples of contemporary Native American art. Brochures highlight the "bright, airy, nature-conscious setting" and the fact that "the casino at Mashantucket is located on lands occupied continuously for thousands of years by the ancestors of today's Mashantucket Pequot tribal members."[75] Along the corridor between the Rainmaker

Casino and the new gambling floor in the Grand Pequot Towers stands a room identified as Mashantucket Pequot Museum. Here, in the midst of the clamor and rush of the gambling crowd, a narrative of tribal history with artifacts and photographs calls attention to the casino's origins and, presumably, its reason for being.

The implied relation of the casino to an older Pequot world seems at first glance rather strained. The Pequots' critics cite such efforts as well as the casino business itself as key evidence of the tribe's inauthenticity, but these complaints rest on assumptions about Indian styles of being that center heavily on notions of spiritual and environmental integrity drawn from Euro-American archives of knowledge, as Robert Berkhofer and Roy Harvey Pearce argued some time ago.[76]

These criticisms also ignore the fact of culturally contextualized gaming among earlier Native generations and some contemporary indigenous populations. James Fenelon cites several historians to emphasize that "we find ample evidence of gambling throughout traditional Native American societies, showing that gambling itself provokes little direct conflict with traditional lifestyles."[77] Paul Pasquaretta quantifies the point: "An estimated one hundred and thirty tribes from thirty different linguistic stocks played dice games of various kinds centuries before European settlement."[78] Pasquaretta and Fenelon list bowl and stone games among the Haudenoshone, the stick games of the Salishans, and Dakota bone games, dice, and carved plum pit betting. These were not simply recreational diversions, however. Early gaming was sacred in its origins, and outcomes were considered to be determined by sacred beings. Reuven Brenner writes that "the perception of acts we now view as games of chance were not viewed as such, but were part of a ritual where chance was not perceived as playing a role."[79] In a recent conversation, I learned that a well-known Native poet asserted not long ago that since gaming is a sacred practice which brings players closer to the gods, what tribes need to figure out today, in order to gain more respect for their gaming operations, is how, precisely, to make casinos sacred.[80]

Given the long history of gaming among Native peoples, arguments suggesting that the games at Foxwoods and other tribal casinos have nothing to do with indigenous traditions do not hold. Even if we agree that the secular, individualistic, and acquisitive context of gaming is a corruption of the older mode,[81] we should keep in mind that the end toward which the tribe often claims the casino is aimed—the reconstruction of and return to tribal culture—includes the sacred and the communal at its heart.

What is one to make, then, of the provenance of Native motifs at the casino? On the one hand, repeated references to indigenous environmental and cultural history and the somber, carefully wrought Native sculptures and paintings help identify the casino in terms of a specifically Pequot, intentionally Native, aesthetic. On the other hand, the Rainmaker statue, the drumming music, and the videos of Native dancing look very much like recycled bits and pieces of Indian stereotypes drawn from Euro-American popular culture and mirrored back to Euro-American customers—giving them, in effect, what they expect to see and hear from a Native enterprise.

Tribal spokespeople have never, to my knowledge, suggested or affirmed this intention, nor, for that matter, the distinctions I make here between more convincing, serious artwork and the reductive "Indian" motifs.[82] This is, after all, an American casino, where such kitschy decor might be expected. Yet it is hard to ignore the historical irony in the idea that such fragments of an iconography which has helped to foster the disempowerment of Native society since the seventeenth century are now being put to use in reverse order to redress the massive economic injustices of the past. In pointing out these ironies, I do not want to suggest that Foxwoods systematically ensnares its customers, seducing them into losing control of their money or their selves while tribal members stand by snickering. Nevertheless, these motifs can be said to implicitly critique their Western sources, insofar as they are part of a project aimed at reconstructing a society that similar components of a colonial discourse once helped reduce to the terms of Euro-American authority.

NATION BUILDING

Rather than reversing the binary of serious museum/playful casino, these observations imply that both establishments, in differing degrees, express both impulses. The deployment of historical realism in each of them keeps a relatively stable narrative of a specific past in view while the pastiche scrambles expectations of cultural clarity. The question arises as to whether the emphasis on historicity—on narrating to the public the

historical continuity between present-day Pequots and Robin Cassacinamon's seventeenth-century community—confirms the idea of a continuous cultural nexus or whether it sustains a counter-representation of a
continuously changing people struggling constantly to recompose themselves as a specific social entity named "Pequot." Does the current end-
point of the historical narrative, with its accumulated data of the past,
turn the present-day tribe more emphatically backward, toward Pequot
styles of being, inherited from earlier times, that made their way through
the turmoil of the years, or does the present moment locate them more
firmly among the mixed, postmodern populations where they unavoidably find themselves?

The work of keeping history alive at Mashantucket is part of what
Lawrence Hauptman has described as a project of "nation building":
"What may appear to casual observers as a Pequot 'edifice complex' is really a master plan, state-building in its grandest sense."[83] The photograph
of Elizabeth George Plouffe hangs in the entryway to Foxwoods, an inspirational figure for contemporary tribal leaders. Indeed, "Nanny," as
Plouffe is known among members of her extensive family, has been an
important reference point in tribal deliberations over membership, casino
operations, and reservation policy in general. As a crucial figure in recent
reservation history and as an elder, she carries a great deal of authority,
even in death. An emblem of *modern* Pequot traditionalism, she seems to
function as a precious bridge to what appears retrospectively as a classical
Mashantucket culture.

The difficulty of recuperating a Native style of being emblemized in
the portrait of Elizabeth Plouffe is recognized in its very display, as an
image positioned overhead, a figure of cultured being which contemporary Pequots revere but which sits at the center of an ever-receding horizon of memory. The ethics encoded in this image were spelled out by
tribal member Chris Pearson to Sioux Harvey for her study of what she
calls Pequot cultural reproduction: "1. Honor the tribe's heritage and
tradition, believing that balance must exist in all things. 2. Ask yourself
if this decision, act, or thought honors the Creator. 3. Ask yourself how
this decision will affect the next seven generations of Pequots." Honoring
heritage, the Creator, and the future of the tribe would certainly seem appropriate practices for building a sense of cultural identity through place

and lineage. As Harvey herself notes, "the challenge for the Pequot people now is to decide how they want to define their cultural ideology."[84]

Beneath the group photo at the entrance to the museum, the text reads, "In addition to being a tribal nation, we are also a newly revitalized community—one that has been realized by years of planning, hoping, and hard work." Nation and community building for the Mashantuckets is a collective effort at recreating a home as well as a public image as an authentic Indian tribe. Tribal member Judy Bell explained to reporters in 1993, "Its the rebirth of a nation, and you can't do everything all at once. . . . You're learning a little at a time, but unfortunately by having to unearth our culture, it's going to take us a while before we know as much about ourselves as other tribes know about themselves.[85] The museum placard and Bell's statement emphasize the unfinished condition of Mashantucket cultural formation, even as formal tribal assertions of a fundamental Pequotism frame the work-in-progress.

The Mashantuckets do indeed appear to be facing a porous field of cultural possibilities, a confusing, unstable array of associations, affiliations, and resistances to the larger culture. But to not conceive of themselves in terms of an ideal, bounded notion of identity toward which they are progressing, what Stuart Hall refers to as "a still point in a turning world," would be for them to forget one of the most deeply held notions of self, subjectivity and cultural identity in the West. We might see Pequot essentialism as a construction and invention rather than a return as such, but for us to assume that the tribe should or would be able to bracket such a claim would be tantamount to suggesting that they be more purely non-Western and perhaps more effectively postmodern than other cultural communities.

Images and stories of the tribe as group proprietor of Foxwoods stand in contrast to newspaper reports and exhibited plans of the work of curating Mashantucket culture and history. But taking into consideration the pragmatics of the "return to some kind of roots" in Hall's formulation, in order to establish an alternative place from which to speak, and Paul Gilroy's idea of the subaltern as linked to the metropolitan hegemony at the same time as he or she inhabits a separate zone of cultural identity, we could argue that the seemingly distinct activities at Mashantucket, represented by the museum and the casino, work in concert toward the recreation of the Mashantucket Pequot Tribal Nation as a culture that exchanges with as well as distances itself from "New England." Richard Hayward asserts that "all of the Tribe's activities over the past few decades have been conducted with the goal of preserving Pequot history and culture."[86] Perhaps these "preservations" will eventually serve as more obvious signifiers of tribal public identity than they currently do. But it is equally possible that the group will be known for this complex process of reproducing wealth, history, a population, and a culture from the nearly empty space of "Mashantucket," in the heart of the Connecticut woods.

CHAPTER 2

Displaying Loss at Navajoland

THE DRIVE TO NAVAJO NATION west from Albuquerque, New Mexico, on Interstate 40 and Arizona Highway 264 goes through some of the most stunning landscapes in North America. The vast expanse of Las Tuces Valley spans the southern horizon, bounded by the Zuni Mountains to the southwest. To the north, Mount Taylor, Mount Powell, and Hosta Butte stand in stately repose. At points the highway is enveloped by terrain that seems disturbingly enchanted: the Malpais lava beds, the Red Rock mesas, and the tumbling hills of the Hogback. Near the reservation boundary, Tse Bonito Wash parallels the road, its sagebrush and red sandstone outcroppings contributing impressively to the somber aesthetics. In late winter, the brown-rose earth, dotted with blackish green cedar trees, set against the huge, cream blue sky, presents an awe-striking introduction to Diné Bikéyah, the Navajo world.

The twenty-five-thousand-square-mile Navajo Reservation, the largest in the United States, extends from Window Rock, Arizona, in the southeast to Montezuma Creek, Utah, in the north and the Colorado River in the west. Before the arrival of Spanish and, later, U.S. agents of empire, the Diné homeland extended far beyond these boundaries to encompass the entire region marked out by the four sacred mountains: Blanca Peak to the east, Mount Taylor to the south, the San Francisco Peaks to the west, and the La Platta Mountains in the north.[1] The physical features of the landscape are indeed enchanted, for they are central to a local imaginary steeped in a spiritually charged, complex relationship with nature.[2] Klara Kelly and Harris Francis write that "Navajo creation stories describe the entire pre-conquest homeland as a hogan, with a sacred mountain in each of the four directions compared to a pole in the hogan's framework."[3] The geography encompassed by this "hogan"—the customary dwelling now used most often for ceremonial functions—makes up a crucial dimension of tribal ontology, since Navajo creation narratives invest it with living agency.[4] A few events from the creation cycle will give some sense of the sentient powers said to reside in these grounds.

As they emerged through three, in some versions four, worlds on the way to the present one, First Man and First Woman gave shape to Mount Taylor and the three other sacred directional mountains that mark the boundaries of the Navajo homeland.[5] Changing Woman, a central figure associated with Earth, who took over the work of creation from First Man and First Woman, journeyed from east to west across Diné Bikéyah, and particular sites are honored as her stopping points. Her sons, the War Hero Twins, set about making the fourth world safe for human beings and in the process kill an evil creature known in English as Big Monster, whose blood then coagulates to form the Malpais lava beds.[6] Other sites are identified as the body parts of the monster known as Travelling Rock, who was gradually chopped to pieces by one of the twins as he pursued him to the east.[7] In another story, the Zuni Mountains mark the home of a people who, in Navajo accounts, were created by a Navajo deity in the third world, the last one before emergence.[8]

While these stories are probably not familiar to most visitors, the living and storied landscape can seem uncannily anthropomorphic, and it constitutes an inescapable public presentation that easily inspires reverence, even as it gives away nothing about itself or the people who claim it. Jean Beaudrillard's musing on Monument Valley and other monolithic landmarks on the Navajo Reservation has some purchase here. Beaudrillard suggests that these structures look as if they had been "written," at least in the eyes of a mythically minded tourist; but he also makes the point that they are all the more mystifying for being unreadable. The Window Rock, Shiprock, and the Malpais shimmer with spiritual and cultural meaning, and yet apart from an occasional explanatory placard, these geological icons are nevertheless largely unintelligible to outsiders.[9]

Just outside Window Rock, the capital of Navajoland, a large sign appears beside the road displaying an image of the great mesas and pinnacles of the reservation in bright turquoise, orange, and yellow, outlined in broad, cartoon-like strokes. The caption reads, "Welcome to Navajo Nation: Enjoy Our Parks and Scenery." The brightly colored sign advertises the Navajo Nation as the welcoming host of a vigorous tourist enterprise. The contrast with the actual landscape, with its resonant silence, is

2-1. "Welcome to Navajo Nation" sign, erected by the Navajo Department of Parks and Recreation, outside Window Rock, Navajo Reservation

jarring. While the road sign identifies the nation as a constituent of the U.S. tourist economy and thus of mainstream American society, a host for whom outsiders are welcome visitors rather than strangers, the dramatic features of the landscape resist such openness.

Similarly incongruous public faces of the Navajo Nation stand side by side in displays and performances presented to off-reservation audiences in a range of open-to-the-public tribal institutions. The Navajo Nation Museum, which opened in 1996, and the Shiprock Northern Navajo Fair, the oldest of the several fairs held each year on the reservation, deploy the languages of historical and cultural instruction in their projects of tribal self-representation to set forth images of a religiously oriented, introspective society. At the same time, however, both enterprises deploy the methods of Western cultural display and invoke the terms and images of global popular culture to represent Navajo Nation as an inviting host of regional tourism and participant in the economic and social dynamics of the United States. Other tribal establishments might be cited that operate within similarly conflicting frameworks: Diné College has open-to-the-public seminars on Navajo culture and spirituality; the Tribal Council and the Navajo Nation president's office open their doors to tourism, with tribal politicians and the chambers of government portrayed as bearers of a traditional consciousness; and the Navajo tourism board, proprietor of the road sign at the entrance to the reservation, is part of the tribal Parks and Recreation Department, which conducts extensive programs of land and culture preservation, in addition to promoting tourism.[10] In their constructions of tribal profiles, the museum and the fair, respectively the newest and the oldest of Navajo for-the-public institutions, demonstrate overtly this pattern in Navajo public institutions of engaging outsider participation and simultaneously indicating the secluded status of objects and practices associated with privileged Navajo knowledge and custom. The museum and the fair model in particularly effective ways the mechanisms of tribal display that position Navajoland in the framework of the contemporary United States at the same time that they reaffirm the boundaries of cultural difference that help furnish modern Navajo tribal identity.

In the course of this discussion, I will argue that Navajo Nation represents itself in these venues as a present-day avatar of richly religious cultural pasts and as the inheritor of a long and violently disruptive process of colonization. The constant challenge of the historical and of the changing to the sacred and the constant in Navajo public identity attests to the powerful force which "the relationships that are articulated between words, concepts, and practices that constitute a particular . . . tradition" are capable of commanding in contemporary Navajo institutional self-representations.[11] Without attempting to resolve these conflicting accounts, I hope to demonstrate how the simultaneity of tribal self-descriptions which call attention to historical change through the experiences of colonialism and modernization and those that mark off a viable traditionalism constitutes an accepted contradiction in Navajo public rhetoric.

These conclusions are based on multiple visits I have made to the Navajo Reservation and on several conversations with tribal members at both venues. My intentions were not to discover occult data about the lives of contemporary Navajos—or Diné, in the tribal language—or to produce an ethnographic description. Instead, I took the position of an educated tourist and a reader of whatever information Diné institutions offered for public consumption about contemporary Navajoland. I have tried to avoid privileging personal experiences or perceptions as if they were unproblematic sources. At points, I was invited to attend certain ceremonies or participate in programs, which, because they are not generally open to the public, made my own tourist's status somewhat different from what others might experience. But I never left the role of visitor, even if an invited one; and so this story is told very much from the outside.[12]

CONTRADICTION, RESISTANCE, SCREENING

The gregariously commercial style epitomized by the road sign on Route 264 evidences the vigorous presence of Western tourism on the reservation, an industry that in off-reservation conversation gets blamed for the corruption of Native styles of being commonly associated with the authenticity and drama of the landscapes. The assumption seems to be that because Western practices are in use to such an extent on the reservation, little or no Native agency is at work in their deployment, and that the result, for all practical purposes, has been the irreversible compromising of Native styles of being. Some scholars of indigenous cultures and histories have gone even further by arguing that, because the material cultures and ideologies of Europe and European America have had such powerful, even overwhelming influence on Native North American subjectivities and social formations over the past half millennium, effectively, Native ways of being and knowing are virtually impossible to access, much less practice as genuinely different modalities from those nurtured by the West and modernity. In this view, efforts to reach back, to recover styles of being and knowing that prevailed before Europe appeared on the horizon, risk reinforcing the problem since what is recollected is surely to bear the imprint of these entrenched Western epistemes.[13]

As James Clifford, Joanne Nagel, Arjun Appadurai, and many other students of colonial and postcolonial culture would agree, however, the tropes and methods of Navajo communications of tribal identity directed toward non-Native audiences might well derive from Western archives, but they can nevertheless work to sustain effective forms of resistance to assimilation and to mitigate against the overwhelming of Navajo remembrance by the consciousness of the West.[14] In the process, these hardworking media elicit the recognition of Navajo Nation as a particular, indigenous society which, although determined significantly by the political and social dynamics of the United States, has been able to conduct itself, in daily as well as ritual life, in terms of a distinct cultural imaginary. Navajo blankets on display in the tribal museum, for example, are woven with artificially dyed yarn made by German chemists in the Northeast for an early twentieth-century Anglo market, as the discussion that follows explains in further detail. The exhibit keeps them at a distance, untouchable and certainly unusable, underscoring the dramatic ontological gap between the viewing subject and the inert object, an arrangement that materially manifests the Western philosophical regime operating in the very idea of the museum. At the same time, however, these objects and methods function as frontier devices, so to speak, ambassadors of Native knowledge in the form of the wisdom practice of weaving. As I hope to demonstrate below, the weaving display also exemplifies a form of resistance to assimilation in tribal self-imaging, a resistance sustained by repeatedly signaling the reverberant experience of loss at key moments in colonial history, an unassimilated loss, internalized in Navajo remembrance. Thus, resorting to the museum as a medium for the exposition of Navajo blankets and their spiritual contents, the tribe's agents not only publicize the long-lived contradictions of Navajo life since colonialism, but use the Western institutional form to, in effect, display the losses that came with conquest and cannot be forgotten, losses that, among far more dramatic effects, heralded the phenomenon of the tribal museum itself.

In addition, as if to respond to the incommensurability between the colonial history signaled in the orange and turquoise road sign and the indigenous spiritual presence exuded in the landscape, public self-representations at Navajoland often call attention to tribal concepts and practices while at the same time screening certain knowledge and custom from exposure. This screening effect lies in the representation's ability to reflect back what we have already seen and heard elsewhere and to render more privileged objects, practices, and ideas opaque. What is not shared outside the museum is not shared within it; what is felt to be private cultural property remains so.

How can an outsider know this? Attending to the rhetorics of tribal self-representation, one finds a motif, repeated references to precisely these withheld knowledges, unexposed to strangers. This practice of what might be called "displayed withholding" implicitly projects a difference and a bounding off from the dominant streams of being and knowing in the cultures of the United States. It is the point where the performance or display says, "There is more, but we choose not to show you." On the Navajo Reservation, as in many other contemporary Native American public displays and performances of tribal identity, the gesture points toward a dimension of being and knowing that cannot or will not be shared with visitors. In the Navajo Museum lobby, features of the interior design, including the sand patterns marking the four directions and the sacred mountains of Diné Bikéya as well as the hogan shape of the room itself, rehearse certain features of Navajo theology, but, without signage, these ideas are only held before us, as it were, unexplained. A seminar at Dine College offers instruction to Anglo guests in the multiple significations of the four directions and their reverberations in the tribal college curriculum, but the dean, a medicine man, makes clear that by participating in an introductory ceremonial event, guests should not think they have become initiates of tribal knowledge. At the tribal fair in Shiprock, a Nightway Ceremony is open to the public. We watch the dancers and see the patient being led out among them; but the sand paintings and the cure itself take place inside the hogan, walled from public view.

In her reading of Rigoberta Menchu's autobiography, Doris Sommer finds a similar pattern. Sommer explains that, in part, the displayed withholding demonstrates a resistance to identification with the reader for political reasons; and, in part, it designates a principled decision not to share information or knowledge with those who will not be properly prepared for it. In both cases, Sommer writes, "We are not so much outsiders as marginals, not excluded but kept at arm's length."[15] "Kept at arm's length" is a useful image of the distancing effect that displayed withholding creates. The phrase suggests that secrecy is maintained not by mounting a barricade but simply by performing a gesture, by keeping at bay that which is unavoidably near.

Such performances, implying a substance of authentic cultural autonomy, are continuously challenged by surrounding and contradictory tribal self-images that emphasize mixture, open-endedness, and shifting configurations of identity. Nevertheless, something of the old remains, even if invisible to alien eyes, that bespeaks the presence of distinct ways of knowing and being in the late colonial afterlife. As Aamir Mufti writes, "Modes of transition to modern forms of culture that have been mediated through the experience of colonial subjugation share the inability to produce narratives of cultural continuity that can absorb the dislocations of modernity. In such context, the question of tradition takes a distinct form, with the past appearing not exactly to be dead and buried, even if present in ghostly form, but murdered and still remaining, as Gayatry Spivak has suggested, inappropriately and insufficiently mourned."[16]

"Murdered but still remaining" suggests a haunting by indigenous pasts, by something that refuses to rest easy or relinquish itself to oblivion in a peaceful assimilation. Such remainders must be fiercely self-protective; and, indeed, I think we can assume that claims to such surviving older knowledges and practices are necessary for coherent resistance to the open-endedness of late colonial life and for the establishment of boundaries, however rhetorical or performative, around the always threatened interior, as it were, of Native ways of being.

N. Scott Momaday offers an example of this haunting in the context of his Kiowa inheritance in his memoir, *The Way to Rainy Mountain*. Momaday attempts to reconcile the facts of material loss with what he insists is an essential remainder. The haunting past must be acknowledged and reinterpreted, according to the speaker of his prologue and introduction, by contemporary Native's imaginations, for whom such work is both "the right and the responsibility."[17] In the process of making this assertion, Momaday claims alternatively that a core, fundamental "idea" of Kiowa being sustains itself through history and that the legacy is evanescent, there and not there for contemporary lives to engage. The idea of Kiowaness represented by "the way to Rainy Mountain," he writes, "has old and essential being in language" (4). But on the other hand, "what remains is fragmentary: mythology, legend, lore and hearsay" (4). Nevertheless, he adds to this list "the idea itself, as crucial and complete as it ever was. That is the miracle" (4). The contradiction in the idea being as tentative as Momaday suggests, and at the same time remaining intact and stable, speaks to the complexity of postmodern Indian cultural inheritance and identity. Funded by an undead past that cries for recognition and memorialization, the "way" that Momaday celebrates in his book is fueled by a productive understating of and living in loss. As he enters his grandmother's house, the sign of old Kiowa being and knowing, "there is a funereal silence in the rooms, the endless wake of some final word. The walls have closed in upon my grandmother's house. When I returned to it in mourning, I saw for the first time how small it was" (12). The house, like the woman herself, is not only a sign of the Kiowa past, but a part of it. In this double role of signifier and essence, Aho and her dwelling place are means of memorialization as well as identification for Momaday and what the Kiowa experience attempts to represent in the present. They stand for and as "a holy regard that now is all but gone out of mankind" (8). The "endless wake" that fuels the poet's relationship to Kiowa culture sustains a sense of loss which itself implies the memory of what is lost. What is lost and the continued mourning for it distinguish his identity from a more generic Americanness and particularly from the Anglo-European American society whose forebears appropriated all that his grandmother's house meant in the name of assimilation.

Inflected by history and contextualized by a postmodern mix of cultural materials, the privileged, private traditions make up a deferred but strategically essential category—in the sense of critically important as well as ontologically fundamental. Together with Western icons and institutions, this deferred stability serves as a tool for communicating a Navajo identity to the public and for simultaneously blocking the view, of showing and not showing and, in many cases, communicating that this block is in place.

THE MUSEUM

About a mile inside the reservation boundary, as Route 264 enters Window Rock, stands the Navajo Museum, Library, and Visitors' Center. Because it faces east, away from the traffic, the sprawling, dark red complex is only identifiable by a small sign posted on the roadside. The actual approach is somewhat confusing, as the drive leads past the museum itself, in what appears to be the wrong direction, before looping back to the parking lot. The entrance is obscured from view by the eastern orientation and by a brick wall jutting out from the northeastern end of the building. Standing before the doorway, a visitor might thus feel

2-2. Navajo Museum, Library, and Visitors Center, Window Rock, Navajo Reservation

rather as if they had found something for which they did not know they were going to have to look. It is not that you are made to feel that those who built the museum were deliberately trying to keep visitors away, an absurd idea on the face of it. It is rather as if the institution seemed simply not interested in attracting a lot of attention to itself. Like the Mashantucket Museum and Research Center on the Pequot Reservation, the Navajo Museum seems to allow visitors to approach rather than overtly reach out to them. The reserved posture speaks to the institution's serious, scholarly commitment to honoring Navajo sacred knowledge and to keeping tribal history.

The entryway is an opaque glass wall twenty-five feet high, framed by brick office wings extending on either side. The path to the door leads through a pavilion of red posts laid with turquoise beams across the top in a handsome geometric pattern. As if guarding the entry, an abstract metal eagle sits atop a pole beside the pavilion. A six-sided, slender glass tower angles upward from the center of the roof on graduated levels, looking to the north, out over the great extent of the Navajo reservation.

The fifty-five-thousand-square-foot museum opened in 1996 and has become an important site for the display of Navajo history and culture for tribal members as well as for visitors from off the reservation.[18] Inside, the lobby opens to a high, rounded glass atrium framed in sturdy, wooden vigas. The spaciousness and natural light of the reception area seem to hold and reinforce the quiet that lingers in the building.

When I visited in the winter of 2003, the spell was broken by the appearance of a genial staff member who had agreed beforehand to give me a tour. Commenting on the lobby's design, the guide pointed to a small "female" hogan outside, on the grounds in front of the museum, the rounded roof of which, she explained, has the curve of a pregnant woman's stomach. "We are always safe within the mother," she explained, gesturing upward toward the ceiling, which was shaped in the same manner as the hogan's. The glass tower overhead is the architect's interpretation of smoke exiting through the hole in the hogan's roof. The guide pointed to a circular frame on the floor, filled with cream-colored sand, in the middle of which stood a cluster of black, white, yellow, and red circles signifying the four sacred mountains and the four directions of Diné Bikéyah.

The spiritual and intellectual values associated with the four sacred directions in the geography of ancient Navajoland and the movement from east to south, west, and north in Navajo ritual are reproduced in the museum's interior design.[19] Visitors are directed to move through the space in a clockwise manner, as in most Navajo ceremonial arrangements. The pattern begins with the entryway, located in the east, the direction of the rising sun and the orienting point of tribal sacred geography as well as the starting place of any number of trajectories, from the life cycle to intellectual development. The exhibit space is located in the southern portion of the building, associated with midday and understood as the place of working and learning, while the offices are positioned to the west, related to evening and the place of reflection. The library is situated in the north, the zone of night and the place of knowledge.

These spatial interpretations derive from a key philosophical and ethical principle known as *sq'ah naagháí bik'eh hózhóón nishlą́ą naasháa doo.* The Navajo poet Rex Lee Jim writes of this concept, "[It] means to me the beauty of life realized through the application of teachings that work": "Literally, *są'* means old age, *ah* means beyond, *naa* means environment, *ghái* means movement, *bi* means to it, *k'eh* means according, *hó* means self and that sense of an ever-presence of something greater, *zhóón* means beauty, *nishląą* means I will be, *naasháa doo* means may I walk. This may be stated in the following way. 'May I walk, being the omnipresent beauty created by the one that moves beyond old age.' "[20]

In a prefatory note to this explanation, Jim makes clear that he is not providing a comprehensive account of the concept and that his readers should not assume from having studied his formulation that they might then have a secure understanding of it. "I do not offer a Navajo definition of the formula," he writes. "I simply share with you how I interpret and use the formula in my life. It is one Navajo's experience with sa'ah naaghai bik'eh hozhoon."[21] Indeed, the phrase is famously difficult to translate into English. John Farella, one of the more renowned Western students of Navajo philosophy, writes that it is "the key concept in Navajo philosophy, the vital requisite for understanding the whole." Farella offers, tentatively, "that which is whole or complete" and "continuous generational animation."[22] Earlier writers and oral philosophers emphasized the human model of spiritually and physically healthful old age, achieved by living in harmonious relation with other entities.[23] In less literal terms, it refers to a concept of order that implies beauty, harmony, health, and happiness—in the individual, the family or clan, the Diné world. By invoking sa'ah naagháí bik'eh hózhóón, the museum's architectural and interior designs refer to a sacred knowledge system which, we are invited to understand, serves as the existential spirit of the institution itself as well as of its collections and exhibits.

I had read a good deal about Navajo sacred thought but would clearly not have been able to read the concepts in the museum's layout without the assistance of the guide who showed me through the building. Any visitor might seek out a staff member and ask for information about the designs of the lobby or of the building's other features, but the stories and ideas reproduced there are not made readily evident. Not quite "secret," they are nevertheless components of a specifically Navajo world view that unlearned or unguided outsiders would not likely recognize. Thus, the museum offers this not-so-public, public representation that simultaneously displays and holds back its distinctly Diné meanings and values.

Even without this knowledge, though, a reasonably perceptive visitor might notice that the somber tones of the place and the sense of mourning permeating certain exhibits signal that something more than historical information and the display of cultural artifacts is intended here. A visitor might be surprised to see that the museum houses the offices of Miss Navajo Nation, the winner of a contest held each year in Window Rock that draws hopeful young women from all over the reservation. In the corridor that leads to her office, photographs are hung of Miss Navajo Nation pageant winners dating back to 1952. The contest has many of the trappings of the same sort of thing we still see in regional and national pageants around the globe: the queen is young and attractive; she wears a glittering crown and a silk sash bearing her title. She rides in parades on the back seats of convertibles and waves at the crowds. In her post as goodwill ambassador, she travels throughout the reservation and beyond, giving speeches about Navajo community values; and she helps charity organizations by associating her name and image with them. In the case of Miss Navajo Nation, however, the performance of these duties is expected to help foster a lived consciousness of the ideas and practices of Navajo styles of everyday life. A contestant's preparation for undertaking this role takes priority over good looks in the pageant. The official Miss Navajo Nation Web site explains that "unlike most beauty pageants around the world, the Miss Navajo Nation Pageant is of beauty 'within' one's self."[24] Hózhó, the final word in the phrase sa'ah naagháí bik'eh hózhóón, means, according to Harry Walters, professor of Navajo religion and culture at Diné College and director of the college museum, "I will walk in the beauty way."[25] The sense of beauty invoked in the term is clearly not synonymous with Western concepts that emphasize an exclusively visual appeal based on limited aesthetic criteria. Hózhó implies harmony as well as ethical and moral strength, which derive from a fluent relationship between the one who is hózhó and other beings in a social or spiritual environment. The title holder must exhibit knowledge of the Navajo language, customs, and certain ceremonials while at the same time presenting herself as a modern administrator capable of holding up her office as a delegate of the tribal culture, on and off the reservation. It is this concept of beauty which Miss Navajo Nation pageants honor.

Miss Navajo Nation for 2003 was Shaunda Tsosie, a biology major at Harding University. In public statements during her reign she expressed concern for the education of reservation youth and "the importance of maintaining their Navajo identity which will give them . . . self-esteem . . . [and] strength to succeed in life." She also worried about the health and well-being of Diné elders and focused much of her office on attending to hunger and malnutrition in the more remote areas of Diné-tah. Her published statements on the Web encouraged others to share in the work of "help[ing] comfort the pain of hunger and warm the hearts from the unbearable cold."[26] When I visited the museum in the winter of 2003, she and a helper were working on a quilt they were to take, along with several others they had made, to some of the tribe's elderly poor. She seemed modest, even diffident, when I was introduced to her but was very direct in explaining that the elders would need the quilts for the coming winter. Of course, wherever she goes, Miss Navajo Nation elic-its a good deal of attention, and her visits, even to the far corners of Navajoland, certainly draw crowds. I took her modesty as an indicator that her interests in these journeys were not in photo ops but in setting examples. In a quiet voice she told me that in her official capacity she also makes visits off the reservation. Rather than setting examples in these venues, though, her work is aimed at eliciting recognition of the Navajo Nation as a living and actively self-reproducing nation.

The Web site for the office of Miss Navajo Nation explains that "the role of Miss Navajo Nation is to exemplify the essence and characters of First Woman, White Shell Woman and Changing Woman and to display leadership as the Goodwill Ambassador. Miss Navajo Nation represents womanhood and fulfills the role of 'grandmother, mother, aunt, and sis-ter' to the Navajo people. . . . [S]he can speak as leader, teacher, coun-selor, advisor and friend."[27] Miss Navajo's mission is "to encourage every Navajo to assist in the preservation of Navajo culture."[28] This personage, who seems at first glance to be more related to the glamour and com-petitiveness of the society whose influences the museum attempts to thwart, turns out to be a substantial participant in the museum's projects of displaying Navajo styles of being. And like the museum itself, the Of-fice of Miss Navajo Nation operates within a definitively Western insti-tutional form to propagate Navajo knowledge and practices. In this, as in other functions and projects that appear derivative of Western practices (an exhibition of kids' and parents' paintings, for example, produced under the instruction of a tribal artist; a gift shop that sells jewelry,

T-shirts, tote bags, and books), the museum attempts to represent itself and Navajoland as conduits of a continuous Diné ontology.

THE NAVAJO MUSEUM'S MAJOR EXHIBITS, housed within this framework of references to a stable cultural legacy, have devoted a great deal of attention to Navajo history and particularly to the tribe's experiences with the United States. These histories, often emotionally evoked by resonant objects and images, speak to nothing so much as the colonial relation, the legacy of which continues to powerfully influence the horizon of economic, social, and cultural possibilities for Navajo Nation. Photographs, blankets, and legal documents of the nineteenth century in particular testify to forms of bodily, spiritual, psychological, and economic oppression that threatened Diné being as such at every level. Key phases of the colonial experience cut and tore into the fabric of Navajo cultural and political integrity, without destroying the memory of what had been cut away. Insofar as the museum looks back on and shows these histories from the standpoint of an inherited colonial legacy, it does its work in a context far removed from the epistemes that the building design and decoration attempt to invoke. Even as Diné creation narratives and sacred geographies are inscribed in the structure of the Navajo Museum, the installations and exhibits that focus on colonial experiences highlight the historical events that dramatically compromised the continuation of older, specifically Diné knowledges and practices referenced in the building itself. These contrasts speak to what might be called a divided tribal self-representation in which antithetical images of a living Diné traditionalism and of events that destroyed the conditions of possibility for that traditionalism appear to compete with and contradict each other. As I will argue, however, forms of mourning enacted by the museum's exhibits as well as certain methods of displayed withholding help make sense of the gaping differences.

Before turning to the installations, I want to explore these tensions further by thinking about them in terms of what David Eng and David Kazanjian identified as the differences between mourning and melancholia in the ways colonized peoples have often addressed the past. Eng and Kazanjian take a turn on Freud's familiar dichotomy of mourning and melancholia, where mourning is defined as a practice that puts the lost object of love to rest and melancholia as an unhealthy fixation that re-

fuses to let the lost object go. Eng and Kazanjian propose that to represent the losses of colonized peoples as resolved through mourning is to
consider history past, concluded, and dead, while, paradoxically, to represent these losses as unresolved allows for a productive, "ongoing and
open relationship with the past."[29] In a gesture that "depathologizes"
melancholia, the authors explain how this excessive engagement with
that which has been lost, in Freud's terms, produces "countless separation
struggles."[30] The museum's most prominent exhibits since its opening in
1997 have illustrated what Eng and Kazanjian analyze as the productive
richness of melancholic attachment to traumatic losses lodged in the past.
Productive attachment is particularly evident in the repeated focus in
these exhibits on what are perhaps the most emotionally central events of
modern tribal history: the infamous Long Walk of 1864 and the tribe's
captivity at Fort Sumner, New Mexico, from 1864 to 1868.

The Long Walk and imprisonment at Fort Sumner, known more
commonly as Bosque Redondo, are consistently regarded in narratives
of Navajo history, oral and written, as the most traumatic phase in the
tribe's relationship with the U.S. government. The Long Walk, a trek
which approximately eight thousand Navajo people were forced to make,
largely from Canyon de Chelly, in the center of the contemporary reservation, to Bosque Redondo, in southeastern New Mexico, covered a distance of over three hundred miles.[31] Hundreds died along the way from
starvation, disease, and exposure. The forced march was intended by U.S.
Army agents in the region to break the back of Navajo resistance to the
American presence and to transform the tribe into a disarticulated population of literate, farming Christians. As several historians have observed, the Navajo's land was desirable to the army as well as to Mexican
and Anglo settlers in the region. Removal of the indigenous people to
Fort Sumner would mean removal of any obstacles to the immigrants'
desires to overtake the Diné land.[32]

At Bosque Redondo, life was difficult at best. The parched terrain
was almost impossible to till, and flood ruined the meager crops. Hunger
and thirst, disease and hopelessness beset the people, as soldiers watched
over their daily affairs and forced them to work, in deep exhaustion and
malnutrition, to build the Anglo quarters and to sustain their own meager accommodations. Comanches raided the camp, killing Navajos and
stealing their firewood and food, and the Mescalero Apaches who had

also been driven to the site had to compete with them for the insufficient resources.[33] Fort Sumner was, by all records, indistinguishable from a prison camp, and the experience not only seared the minds of those who went through it, but left its stamp on Navajo self-representation to the present day. As Robert Utley notes, "for the Navajos, the four year exile on the Pecos River . . . remains the central event of tribal memory."[34]

I want to focus now on two of the Navajo Museum's major exhibitions, both of which engaged these histories and demonstrated how loss can be said to function as a component of collective, public identity formation. The museum's inaugural exhibition, "Woven by the Grandmothers: Nineteenth-Century Navajo Textiles from the National Museum of the American Indian," opened in the fall of 1997 and highlighted blankets, serapes, and dresses woven by Diné artisans during the captivity at Fort Sumner. The exhibit underscored the museum's commitment not only to displaying history but also, by highlighting contemporary weavers and offering demonstrations, to serving as a site of ongoing Navajo public culture. "The Navajo Treaties of 1849 and 1868," the most recent installation at the time of this writing, gave visual and material form to the Long Walk and to the Treaty of 1868, which ended the captivity period. Like the weaving show, the treaty exhibition emphasized loss and continuous mourning not only of precolonial styles of being and knowing, but of the event itself, the Long Walk, that precipitated the most dramatic phases of this loss.

As productions of the Fort Sumner period, the fabrics assembled for "Woven by the Grandmothers" were remnants of a collective experience that still signals collective pain. At the same time, it framed a narrative of survival and creative assimilation.[35] In many cases, weaving materials issued at Fort Sumner, like the bright, synthetically colored "Germantown" yarns, made in Germantown, Pennsylvania, were taken up by weavers, who preferred them to the merino wool which the Americans made available later, when the tribe had returned home, and which had a greasy texture that made it difficult to clean or spin. In terms of patterns, crosses began to appear, as well as serrated steps and diamonds found in the Mexican blankets distributed at the prison camp.[36] The blue yarn in some of the Fort Sumner weaving is said to have come from discarded U.S. soldiers' coats, the threads of which the weavers unraveled and wound into their own designs.[37] While indigo dye had been available for weaving since the Spanish colonists introduced it in the seventeenth century, it was generally not available during the exile itself.[38] Weavers often used the synthetic dyes and yarn offered at the camp, but they largely rejected the European methods and equipment that agency officials urged them to adopt, retaining their own instead.[39]

Thus the blankets, dresses, and serapes, with their regional and period specific designs, told a social as well as aesthetic history of the nineteenth-century Navajo. The works of the Fort Sumner period in particular demonstrate a noteworthy cultural resistance and creative adaptation of foreign styles. As Laura Jane Moore has noted, "weaving became a critical point of contact, valued by both groups but for different reasons." While the government in some cases perceived the practice of weaving as a sign of Navajos' resignation to their new situation and to the European American lifeways which the military agents were trying to propagate, weaving allowed Diné women to clothe their families, to continue the subsistence economics practiced in the homeland, and to avoid just that much dependence on their U.S. captors.[40]

The exhibition's displays of the pain of the loss of political sovereignty at Fort Sumner and of dislocation from the homeland and disruption of customary practices of daily life kept those experiences in view. As if to repeat the anguish of their ancestors and to internalize their losses, contemporary meditations on Fort Sumner and the Long Walk, like the museum exhibit, retain what Eng and Kazanjian would call the melancholia of the experience, its function as a continuously meaningful font of loss and as a frame for late colonial collective identity formations shaped by economic oppression, cultural deprivation, and political marginalization. This active remembrance in effect refuses closure to the history of colonization, refuses what literary scholars call narrative coherence to the sequence of conditions that have emerged since the Long Walk. Closure, were it accepted, would, in this sense, mean completion of the long colonial project to not only dominate but to maintain hegemony over the people of Dinétah.

This refusal of closure appears all the more justified, if one were not already convinced by the history itself, by the fact that the weavings now belong not to Navajo individuals or to the tribe, but to the U.S. government. The blankets were collected in the late nineteenth and early twentieth centuries, mostly by Anglo surveyors, military personnel, missionaries, and traders. The larger part ended up in the collection of George Gustav Heye, a wealthy easterner who made many buying trips to the Navajo and other reservations, in addition to acquiring Native materials from other adventurers.[41] With his holdings, he established the Museum of the American Indian–Heye Foundation, which merged with the Smithsonian Institution system in 1989. Scholars of all stripes have identified each of the textiles as Navajo, but because they are the property of the Smithsonian, the tribe, under the Native American Graves Protection and Repatriation Act, cannot reclaim them.[42]

The show was assembled in consultation with Navajo weavers and scholars; and it was prefaced by a workshop at the reservation, for which twenty-four blankets were shipped to the tribal college and local weavers were enlisted to identify the materials and techniques.[43] From 1997 through 2001, the exhibition traveled from the Smithsonian's National Museum of the American Indian in lower Manhattan to Window Rock, to the National Museum of Women in the Arts in Washington, D.C., to the Heard Museum in Phoenix, and to six Latin American countries.[44] The Window Rock show was thus one stop of an itinerant show which, while drawing national and international attention to the immense beauty of Navajo weaving, was not in the possession of the Navajo people themselves.

The Navajo curators' decision to host "Woven by the Grandmothers" for the tribal museum's inauguration in 1997 was a way of taking temporary possession of the blankets and shawls that had originated in Navajo hands. The fabrics were immersed in a tribal context where their religious values and relationship to the nineteenth-century material environment of the reservation were more evident than they had been in Manhattan. As in New York, they were wrapped around shoulder mounts to appear in their primary function as blankets rather than displayed on the wall as rugs or art objects, as such textiles often are in Western museums.[45] At Window Rock, the effect of this technique was to make them appear less like historical statuary and more like the worn clothing of grandparents and great grandparents, eliciting wonder in schoolchildren and tears in the elderly.[46]

The association of many of these textiles with Fort Sumner, itself the most iconic sign of colonial oppression in tribal public culture, and the fact that the exhibit objects are now owned by the U.S. government's flagship museum, clearly compromised their status as evidence of an ongoing Navajo cultural production separate from that of the larger, dominant society. This is not to say that the exhibit's curators were blind to the matter, or that they were implicated in their own marginalization in, for example, the way Patricia Hilden suggests when she writes that such communities, "the purported objects of . . . museological good intentions, have themselves sometimes ignored the ways in which participation with such museums collaborates in their own continuing colonization."[47] Hilden's argument risks assuming that the objects and institutions of a colonial enterprise will only be used for and have the effects of the intentions accorded them by the colonizers. Such an assumption denies the agency of indigenous and other colonized peoples who have a long history of what Achille Mbembe refers to (in a somewhat different context) as "creative assimilation" and Arjun Appadurai calls "indigenization" of First World processes and material conditions for indigenous needs and purposes.[48]

The fact that the materials are still owned by the Smithsonian and have not been returned to the Navajo Museum, I would argue, leaves the impression that, without exactly relegating the tribe to an "ethnographic past," the government's influential institution proceeds as if it did not regard the tribe as capable of owning and maintaining the collection itself.[49] Rather than expressing regret about the Smithsonian owning the textiles in "Woven by the Grandmothers," staff members at the Navajo Museum graciously explained that the National Museum of the American Indian staff had been helpful in setting up the exhibit, in terms of expert advice as well as funding.[50]

IF ITS INVOCATION OF historical memories of Bosque Redondo kept the pain of colonial relations in view as an inextricable component of contemporary tribal self-representation, the interpretations of spiritual knowledge in "Woven by the Grandmothers" at the Navajo Museum articulated a set of particularly Navajo collective experiences and memories. The show projected to non-Navajo visitors a history, specific to Diné people, that is also a significant component of the contemporary tribe's formal, publicly articulated identity, a narrative that distinguishes the Navajos as a society with a reproducible past and furnishes contemporary identity formations that might be recognized by Navajos and non-Navajos alike.

The show highlighted the immense spiritual and psychological values invested in the blankets and in the practice of Diné weaving generally. Unlike the Mashantucket Museum, where the restoration of tribal religious frameworks is an ongoing project and the task of claiming a specifically Mashantucket cultural identity is left almost entirely to the museum's rhetoric of historical realism, the Navajo Museum has a dense cosmology to cite in public self-representations, and weaving is a major text of that theology.[51] In her 1950 *Navajo Religion: A Study of Symbolism*, still a widely respected study (including among Diné scholars), Gladys Reichard wrote that Spider Woman "is a symbol of textile arts, having taught [human beings] weaving; she requires woven fabrics as offerings."[52]

Harry Walters, Navajo scholar and director of the Ned Hathatli Museum at Diné College, gives a detailed account of what this means in practice: "Navajo weaving is directly related to nature—dawn, day, twilight, and night, mountains, trees, animals, and insects; earth, air, and water. All of these are holy elements, and they are all present in Navajo weaving. These elements have power, and when we depict them in weaving, they have the same power. When a weaver is weaving a rug, she receives these powers."[53]

D. Y. Begay, a renowned contemporary Navajo weaver, gives a more personal interpretation of these principles in her contribution to the exhibition catalogue: "My weaving reflects who I am. It incorporates my beliefs, my family, and my community."[54] Before and after Fort Sumner, weaving was done while "caring for the families, homes, and herds . . . and remembering the sacred stories, prayers, and songs that 'go with weaving.'"[55] During captivity, weaving worked to invoke this dense context and became a means of literally restoring the quotidian behaviors of home and of enacting a connection with the ways of being and knowing associated with Diné Bikéyah.

Navajo curator Wesley Thomas explains how ritual utterances "go with weaving" in his essay for the catalogue: "The personification of textiles," he writes, "is activated by the weaver through construction. . . . By singing, praying and talking, weavers complete the process of personification."[56] In order to perform these acts in the process of weaving, or to understand that the blanket is composed of such utterances as well as of material yarn, one must know what the prayers and songs are like, what kinds of desires they might express.

Narrating the genealogy of weaving instruction in his family, Thomas demonstrates the exclusive transmission of weaving practices to which he himself was exposed. By describing the context of weaving in this way, Thomas's essay, like his contribution to the explanatory panels in the exhibit, gives outsiders an introductory account of the religious context but does not provide the content of those songs or prayers— other than to note that First Man and First Woman are to be thanked for bringing weaving to human society. The esoteric status of the utterances is thus marked; and the announcement of their existence serves to seal off a realm of cultural difference from the non-Native viewer to whom the world of weaving is being displayed. Similarly, at a conference at Diné College in the spring of 2003, Bonny Benally Yazee, director of the Eastern Crown Point Weavers Association, described the act of weaving as a combination of ritual and quotidian performances. "What goes into Navajo looms," she said, "are our songs, prayers, stories, taboos. Our whole minds, our feelings go into those rugs. You find yourself weaving those songs and personal thoughts from a recent ceremony." The material apparatus of weaving is understood as part of this psychological and spiritual ecology: "You give corn pollen to a plant first before picking it [to make a dye], and you don't take all of it. One bar of the loom is a sunbeam. The top tension rod is associated with lightning, so when it rains they put it away. Our grandmothers taught us all these methods." Finally, Yazee added, "There are a lot of things I can't tell you. I use it as a shield to protect myself."

The religious framework of weaving, which might have been immediately apparent to Navajo viewers of the exhibit, was described for the uninitiated in a series of explanatory panels that spoke of "meaning, process, and spirituality;"[57] but the acts of displayed withholding confirmed the impression that what "Woven by the Grandmothers" held up for view at the Navajo Museum, at least, was evidence of a living, particularly Navajo way of being and knowing, the visible components of which pointed to unarticulated and undisplayed zones of spiritual culture, as echoed in Yazzie's comment: "There are a lot of things I can't tell you. I use it as a shield to protect myself."

Given its very existence as a museum exhibition with a national and international audience, "Woven by the Grandmothers" helped the Navajo Library, Museum, and Visitor's Center take its place among contemporary Western, and particularly U.S., cultural institutions, and thus gained the tribe recognition as part of that sphere, sharing its vexed colonial history but now gaining recognition for that history. At the same time it represented the Navajo Nation as a continuing entity, distinct from other societies, even as the social, cultural, and economic dynamics of the United States long ago began taking hold in Diné life at all levels. The conflicting notions of Navajoland as simultaneously part of the fabric of contemporary U.S. postmodernity—because of the colonial past and its legacy—and a distinct linguistic, religious, and cultural society alternate with and challenge each other in a seemingly continuous, dyadic movement; but the dynamics of melancholia and of displayed withholding work to articulate a readable relation between the two.

SIX YEARS LATER, in the spring of 2003, the museum focused its attention directly on the experience of Bosque Redondo, which had hovered in the air of the weaving exhibit. A display of treaty documents from 1849 and 1868 between the Navajo people and the United States government emphasized the words which, on the one hand, established the conditions for forced removal and captivity and, on the other, concluded the notorious "experiment" of the Fort Sumner captivity.

The introductory placard read: "Today the Navajo-U.S. Treaties of 1849 and 1868 serve as legal proof of U.S. recognition of the internal sovereignty of the Navajo Nation. They also act as the legal foundation of the government-to-government relation between the U.S. and the Navajo Nation." The words themselves constituted the centerpiece of the exhibit. Key passages of both treaties, enlarged and mounted on poster board, hung beside the complete texts, each Xeroxed page enclosed in urethane protective casing.[58]

The very notion of a treaty implies a bilateral contract between separate, sovereign nations, a fact that explains the reverence of treaties in much Native public discourse. For an outside observer, however, a close reading of these pages might suggest that the political and social situations initiated by the treaties' performative words leant overt recognition of the authority of the United States by the Navajos as much as if not more than they guaranteed rights of recognition to the tribe by the government. But to understand their importance at Navajoland today, the treaties need to be considered in relation to the colonial context in which they were produced.

Formal, written treaties were struck between the United States and Indian tribes beginning in 1778, when agents of the Continental Congress settled with the Delaware at Fort Pitt.[59] Such negotiations were initially conducted on the assumption that the indigenous nations were independent, autonomous entities. So common was this idea that often, as Francis Paul Prucha writes, "tribes eagerly sought treaties in order to gain political recognition and not just to acquire the economic benefits that came from presents and from annuities paid for land."[60] Early in the nineteenth century, however, the Supreme Court began to whittle away at the concept of tribal sovereignty, even as rulings periodically emerged that upheld the concept in principle. In 1823, Chief Justice John Marshall, writing the decision in *Johnson and Graham's Leasee v. William McIntosh*, observed that Indian ownership of land was limited to occupancy and that indigenous nations could not sell the lands of which they had been the "ancient inhabitants." Marshall's infamous "doctrine of discovery" asserted that the European nation that first found a given territory in America maintained the ultimate rights to that territory, beyond the original occupants' right to occupy it.[61] Since, according to Marshall, British "rights [in regard to Indian lands] have passed to the United States," his declaration meant that the indigenous populations could only live on such lands; and only the United States government could sell them.[62] In 1831, writing for the Court in response to *Cherokee Nation v. Georgia*, Marshall coined another phrase that would resonate painfully down the centuries for the Cherokees and other tribes in their relations with Washington, "domestic dependent nations." In order to ascertain whether the Cherokees could sue the State of Georgia for encroaching on its lands, he first asked whether the Court had jurisdiction in the matter. Marshall concluded that it did not, since the tribe was not a "foreign state in the sense in which that term is used in the constitution." Denying the Cherokee identity as a "foreign state," Marshall's commentary attempted to enfold the tribe within the larger framework of the United States, with the ambiguous status of a nation, yet a "domestic, dependent" one.[63] Given the paradigm set forth in *Cherokee Nation,* Indian tribes throughout the United States came to be regarded as wards of the government. The ruling did not ignore the concept of tribal sovereignty but rather faced it head on in order to dismantle it. The Court's decision on the issues at stake in *Cherokee Nation* represented a distinct departure from the precedent set by the writers of the Constitution and prompted a rewriting of the official U.S. perspective on the status of Native nations. Nevertheless, in its self-appointed role as guardian to the tribes, Washington assumed duties and obligations which would continue until 1871 to be secured by treaties. Treaties articulated Native rights to the fulfillment of these obligations and to that extent empowered the tribes with the leverage to demand what was theirs. In practice, as is widely known, the treaties were continuously ignored, and sovereignty became a weakened principle in the view of the government, a principle that would have to be fought for again and again by Native nations and their allies, even in the present time.

The Navajos, like other tribes, operate from a Native legal perspective, which assumes sovereignty in a cultural as well as legal sense. At the same time, their repeated assertions of sovereignty in the public sphere are testimony to tribal perceptions that this, their proper political status, is continuously challenged and threatened by states and local governments as well as by Washington. The 1849 Navajo Treaty that was featured in the 2003 exhibit at the Navajo Museum was the second of seven negotiated between the tribe and the United States. It was struck one year after the Treaty of Guadalupe Hidalgo, the agreement that President James Polk concluded with Mexico in the wake of the Mexican War, which made Arizona and New Mexico, along with upper California and Texas, part of the United States.[64] The 1849 treaty with the Navajos therefore came at a moment when the United States was expanding its territorial reach and its imperial muscle. While the treaty allowed for the tribe's own "jurisdiction to charge, try, and punish members for violations of tribal law,"[65] it declared that the Navajos were "lawfully placed under the exclusive jurisdiction and protections of the government of the said United States, and that they are now and will forever remain under the aforesaid jurisdiction and protection."[66] In his summary of the treaty's provisions, Francis Paul Prucha notes that government agents "coerced one group of Navajos into a treaty . . . in which the chiefs agreed to recognize United States jurisdiction and to submit to the trade and intercourse laws, to return captives and stolen property and remain at peace, and to allow the federal government to determine their boundaries."[67] The federal government was also confirmed as the final arbiter in reservation affairs in the 1868 treaty, but while both treaties imply the recognition of tribal sovereignty on the part of the United States, simply by the fact of their existence, the 1868 accord is more prominently honored in Navajo public life.[68]

The Treaty of 1868 is indeed enshrined in contemporary Navajo tribal law because it provides for the exclusivity of the reservation and the legal basis for Navajo rights of individual land ownership, protection from crime, education, and an annual allotment of goods. According to the treaty text, the reservation is "for the use and occupation of the Navajo tribe of Indians, and for such other friendly tribes or individual Indians as . . . they may be willing, with the consent of the United States, to admit among them."[69] It was drawn up at the conclusion of the captivity at Fort Sumner. The nightmare of captivity had ended when two highly revered chiefs, Barboncito and Manuelito, went to Washington to plead with the commissioner for Indian Affairs to allow their people to return home. The patent failure of Bosque Redondo, together with the huge expense of the experiment, swayed officials to settle with the Navajos and to allow them to leave Fort Sumner for the sacred mountains again. William T. Sherman, in 1868 commander of the U.S. Army in the plains, was sent to Fort Sumner to arrange the treaty. As the means of closure to the captivity episode, the treaty gives narrative coherence to events that began with Kit Carson's surrounding of the Navajo in Canyon de Chelly and driving them from their home. By means of the story in its numerous parts and versions, the agony of the experience and the honor of the treaty are kept alive in the memories of descendants of the victims of exile, and they both have priority in expressions of tribal collective identity, as the museum exhibit emphasizes.[70]

Thus, while the Treaty of 1849 displays the implied recognition of sovereignty, it stands in contrast to the 1868 agreement not only by virtue of the pronounced authority of the United States in tribal affairs articulated there but by the lack of substantive rights and privileges for the Navajos. The fact that both treaty texts were displayed in the exhibit, side by side but without overtly indicated comparisons, gave rise to several observations. First, to the extent that both were held up as honored documents, the exhibit demonstrates that sovereignty recognition is of paramount importance, whether the rhetorical frameworks where it is reiterated are in other ways supportive of tribal interests or not. Second, the contrasting tribal profiles that emerge in the two treaties point once again to an apparent contradiction in public identification of the tribal collective, in the past as now. The Navajo Nation figures, on the one hand, as a distinct, unassimilated corporate cultural body and, on the other, as a group that articulates itself to the American social economy. The 1849 text describes the Navajos as a people living under the domination of the United States precisely because of their difference and thus underscores the separateness of the tribe from the cultural, social, and political dynamics of the colonial power. In the Treaty of 1868, however, the tribe is a party to a contract in which rights and obligations are exchanged between signers, a status that puts the Navajos in a relationship of exchange and dialogue with the United States. The fact that both are positioned in the exhibit as exemplary texts of treaty history, I would argue, speaks to the ambivalence on the part of contemporary Navajo agents about their relation to the United States, an ambivalence that simultaneously asserts the tribe's separateness, by virtue of marginalization as well as by culture, society, and economics, and acknowledges its participation in a postmodern relation of exchange that allows for multiple, tactical positioning of tribal identity.

While the privileging of the 1868 accord in the exhibit gave prominence to the words which confirmed Navajo rights and the freedom to return to and possess their reservation, other objects included in the show in a sense acted out the pain of banishment which the treaty in part resolved. In a corner of the room, propped against the wall and roped off from the visitors' space, stands a display of the rough work clothing of the sort that would have been worn at Bosque Redondo, as well as some of the tools that were used for digging, hoeing, and brick laying. The display was intended, as one of the staff members explained, to enliven the exhibit by showing some of the actual materials of the hard work of daily life at Fort Sumner, things that might bring the experience into closer focus.

Just as the blanket exhibit called attention to the experience of Fort Sumner by focusing on weaving styles initiated there, the treaty exhibit kept the events that marked the most resonant losses of the colonial experience in close view, close to the heart, so to speak, of Navajo tribal memory. The repeated reference in Navajo public discourse to the separation from the fullness of Diné life that preceded Fort Sumner and the official articulation of Navajo Nation within the dominant, imperial power of the United States might be described as a "productive" anguish, to use Eng and Kazanjian's term, that helps resist assimilation by internalizing loss, even as these particular representations were staged in the Western format of the museum.

On a wall adjacent to the treaties themselves, photographs were arranged in such a way as to provide "a comparison of living conditions between captor and prisoner." One of these featured a landscape of flat, hard ground, with rough mud houses and tents in the background. In the foreground, Native people were at work in the fields. The photograph beside it showed a town-like structure of comfortable-looking adobe houses with windows and chimneys. Trees dotted the neighborhood. In the doorways, European Americans in good street clothes stood chatting. The caption read, "Though sometimes in tents, the soldiers still had acceptable quarters, while the Navajo used whatever they could find to make a home." Another explained, "Under armed guards, the Indians . . . were forced to help build the Army's fort." Near the end of the exhibit, a group portrait showed twelve somber-looking Navajo teens, young adults, and children standing before the porch of a large, comfortable house. Behind them, a white man in a suit and starched shirt, perhaps a teacher or minister, sat in a relaxed posture, gazing out over the heads of the Indians with a benign half smile, clearly in charge. The caption read, "It was probably in this way that the people returned from their prisoner of war days at Hwéeldi [Bosque Redondo]." It is hard to know whether the phrase "in this way" referred to the despondency and shabby dress of the Navajos or to the social situation reflected in the photograph. In any case, this and the other images were clearly documents of the classic colonial paternalism, with the Navajos reduced to the status of servants and children while the white masters lingered in the foreground, lazily enjoying the safety and health of colonial power.

The photographs gave visible testimony to the severe oppression in the past, and their presence in the exhibit evidenced as well the curators' critical view of the overtly colonial relationship. But a small note reading "Courtesy of the Navajo Gospel Mission" pointed to the legacy of that relationship in the present time. The mission, now known as the NGM Indian Tribal Outreach, has been operating on the reservation since 1868 and owns most of the photographs in the exhibit. While they were freely loaned, these telling records of the Navajo Nation past nevertheless remain the mission's property. Like the blankets in "Woven by the Grandmothers," which are owned by the Smithsonian, and the original treaty texts, property of the National Archives, the photographs were made possible by Navajo subjects, created at Navajoland, and constitute important documents of tribal history; but they could only be borrowed, and they resided in the Navajo Museum temporarily. Neither the Smithsonian nor the National Archives nor the Navajo Gospel Mission has seen fit to return these objects to the Navajo Museum. Even as the exhibit ostensibly celebrated the recognition and demarcation of the Navajo Reservation, it implicitly demonstrated how the entire experience of Bosque Redondo and the history it set in motion continues to have effect in the alienation of powerfully meaningful Navajo historical materials that can only be borrowed by the tribe for the exhibition of its past. In this sense, the exhibit itself, like the weaving show, demonstrated the living legacy of colonization in ways that dramatically supplemented the narratives of loss and the displays of melancholia, seared in public memory and displayed for all the world to see.

If the objects that stand for the larger meanings of the Long Walk and Fort Sumner do not belong to the tribe in a material sense, the narratives of the traumatic experiences certainly do. They are put forward as intellectual property, so to speak, as stories central to the late colonial social psychology of the Navajo Nation. Enlarging the words of the treaties themselves and imaging the deadly daily-life experiences of Navajo people at Bosque Redondo, the exhibit magnified the tribe's painful history with the U.S. government and its agents. It underscored, somewhat paradoxically, the place this narrative occupies in contemporary identity formations. The systematic, ritualized remembrance of the Long Walk and Fort Sumner might reasonably be said to function as a form of "melancholia," in Freud's lexicon a "pathological form of mourning [in which the mourner is] unable to 'properly' grieve the loss of an object." In Eng's rereading of Freud, the melancholic not only "repudiates the finite process of mourning, languishing instead in the refusal to [properly] grieve," but "is so militant in his or her denials that the lost object is finally incorporated into the self, turned into the shelter of the ego, and preserved as a form of ghostly identification."[71] The point is neither to repress nor to "get over" the loss or the pain attendant upon it, but to keep both in view as healthful, useable, and, in Acoma poet Simon Ortiz's words, "significant and realized in the people's own terms."[72]

Insofar as tribal political identity is historically associated, in the museum exhibit as elsewhere, with the government's attempts to obliterate the Navajos' patterns of daily life and ritual practices, that political identity arguably doubles as a cultural identity. But because this narrative depends for its logic on the intricacy of relations with the U.S. colonial regime, it does not openly assert the sort of tribal essentialism apparent in the Mashantucket Pequot Museum. The treaty exhibit displays oppression as a process that nearly exhausted Navajo physical and cultural resources, and as a traumatic experience continuously revisited in public discourse in order to prevent the "hard experience of the Euroamerican colonialization," in Ortiz's words, from being "driven into the dark recesses of the indigenous mind and psyche."[73] Keeping the memory of the Long Walk and the more violent colonial experiences it symbolizes before its visitors, then, the museum does its part in upholding the event as a permanent, consciously recalled feature of Navajo history and tribal identity. The loss and regaining of the reservation necessitated the reconstruction of daily life and a Navajo episteme in the light of Bosque Redondo. The process would be repeated in later cycles of oppression that, with the exception of the forced livestock reduction in the 1930s, did not approach the violence of the Long Walk and Fort Sumner but nevertheless always recalled and reconfirmed their pain. Thus, the work of rebuilding the Navajo Nation since the late nineteenth century has meant reconstituting Navajo cultural practices and knowledges as distinct forms, even as they have always been threatened by colonial cultural and political pressures.[74]

Can we reconcile the apparently contradictory Navajo self-representations in the museum as simultaneously a tribal entity ruptured by history and one that continues to know and honor older concepts and values? Given that the latter are perceived and enacted from the point of view of a belated historical moment, can they indeed be properly understood as "older," or are they inevitably constituted out of the needs and anxieties of the present? While the exhibits allow such questions to arise, and in a sense call attention to them, the simultaneity of historical and contemporary negotiations of Navajo being and knowing bespeaks the familiarity of these contradictions; and, indeed, Navajo public rhetoric directed to outsiders often calls attention to them, thereby informally and undramatically displaying the constructedness of tribal identity, as if the accumulated ironies and contradictions of the long colonial experience were simply to be expected. The museum, a Western institution, exhibits the displacement and severe challenges to Navajo being, while the creation narratives and the Navajo spirituality referenced in the building's design perform a continuing, distinctly Diné modality that survives the renegotiations of Navajo styles of being and knowing mandated by history.

Eng and Kazanjian suggest that melancholia, as a mechanism for marginalized and colonized peoples dealing with cultural and political losses, fosters "continual avowals of and attachments to loss [which] produce a world of remains as a world of new representations and alternative meanings." In their continuous attachment to the past and the traumatic events that resulted in loss, Navajo and other Native cultural leaders and their constituencies retain those losses as ongoing experiences that nevertheless acquire "new perspectives and new understandings of lost objects" and "creat[e] a vast number of disparate bodies, places, and ideals comprising the symbolic world."[75]

In several ways, visitors to the treaty exhibit from the reservation did not limit themselves to spectatorship in the museum but engaged in secondary displays or performances by which they participated in or revised the projects of tribal self-representation there and thus enacted precisely this kind of ongoing experience of loss. At the display of work clothing from Fort Sumner, for example, dustings of cornmeal began to appear, strewn on the cloth and the shoes, shortly after the exhibit opened. Corn, a central figure for life itself in Navajo discourse, is referenced in any number of religious designs and performances. Cornmeal is customarily sprinkled on the ground at dawn when one rises and in the evening before retiring; it is also placed on animals killed in hunting and on the bodies of patients being treated for disease in a number of ceremonials. Coins were also tossed in the middle of the tools and garments, as if to substitute for the cornmeal in a distillation of the same process. Thus the clothing and tools had been supplemented with personal, emotional value and transformed from their framed, isolated status as illustrations into relics of a beloved community with which the viewers identified. By thus "indigenizing" the exhibit, the unnamed Navajo visitors showed their unbroken attachment to the pain of Bosque Redondo, leaving signs that subsequent visitors might read as evidence of the open-endedness of this melancholy history.[76] The staff had been surprised to discover these improvised contributions to the display but decided to leave them in place, in recognition of the visitors' remembrance of Bosque Redondo and their desire to mark the relics with a small, ritual performance "for their ancestors."[77]

In another instance, during the installation, the staff member with whom I talked had been hanging a third-phase Chief 's blanket, a beautiful piece woven in the familiar black, white, and red colors of this particular style. Paralleling some of the horizontal rows, however, are strips of a deep, indigo blue. She explained that as she was installing the display an elderly Navajo man approached and asked if she knew where the weaver would have acquired the blue dye. Not wanting to preempt the elder's authority, the staffer asked if the man himself knew. He did indeed: in his youth, his grandmother had told him her grandmother's story about the women at Fort Sumner somehow acquiring U.S. soldiers' jackets and actually unraveling the blue thread to weave it again into their own patterns. The man seemed pleased, the staffer told me, to tell her of the origins of the blue yarn and to, in a sense, contribute to the knowledge that the museum was storing.

The Navajo Museum staff member who showed me around was keen to point out these impromptu contributions to the exhibits on the part of Navajo visitors. It was clear that a good deal of effort had gone into making the institution a living cite, continuous with the reservation community. As James Clifford noted in regard to the museums of his "Four Northwest Coast Museums" essay, these performances are components of the Navajo Museum and contribute to its function as a "continuation of indigenous traditions of storytelling, collection, and display."[78]

IF THE MECHANISMS OF melancholia work to restore meaning and value to loss, the museum maintains yet another means of resisting assimilation to the consciousness emblemized by its own ostensive institutional mission. Down the hallway that bisects the western half of the building, behind one of the staff offices, is a spacious vault where, since the museum opened in 1997, the collection is gradually being moved from a storage space in a nearby building. Among the objects stored in the vault are rugs, pottery, and baskets, many of which are ancient. Having been warehoused in cramped quarters for many years, they have to be treated carefully when moved to the museum. Once there, each object is frozen three times and then vacuumed to eliminate vermin and dirt. Then they are wrapped and placed on a shelf, labeled, and recorded. The room is dark and kept at a continuous, slightly cool temperature. One of the walls in the vault has a large window through which the museum registrar can see the objects. The gingerly handled, treasured possessions may one day become part of the museum's permanent collection. But for now, they sit in the depths of the museum, highly valued, even sacred objects that are part of, not different from, the tribal legacy and presence they signify. Some of them will never appear in public, and the ongoing deliberations over the makeup of the permanent exhibit are to determine which ones will be least diminished by being displayed. The very fact of this committee and its task attests to the privacy of the collection and to the reverence with which it is held. Whichever pieces do go on display will nevertheless make reference to those still in the vault, the ones not seen. The staff member who showed me around the museum included the vault in her tour. She turned on the lights and let me look from a vantage point just inside the door. The silence in the room, the absence of human activity, was palpable, as if these things had lives of their own, some kind of agency, and preferred to remain where they were. Many will. No one but certain tribal members will be able to see them, but they are there, part of the museum, part of the Navajo world the institution contains. Their absence from public display both points to and guards the dimensions of Diné knowledge and experience that will not cross the boundary into the dynamic space of other-world negotiations.

THE SHIPROCK FAIR

Some ninety miles north of Window Rock, in the northeastern sector of the Navajo Reservation, the dramatic rock formation Tse Bi'it A'i juts out on the horizon, rising seventeen hundred feet above the plain. The name translates into English as "the winged rock," but the landmark is known commonly on and off the reservation as Shiprock, a term coined in the early twentieth century by a government agent because the high pinnacle looked to him like an ocean-going vessel. The name has stuck, in spite of the fact that the rock rises out of some of the driest landscape in the American West. Perhaps the agent's vision was influenced by the rhetoric of U.S. frontier writing, where prairies, deserts, even mountains of the trans-Mississippi region are imaged time and again as features of some vast sea. The metaphor expresses a commonly held assumption among nineteenth-century European Americans that the entire zone was empty, geographically formless, and its indigenous populations as fluid and unshaped as wild ocean waters.

Navajo people use both names today, at least in public discourse, even as "Shiprock" calls to mind the living colonial legacy. But locally the landmark has different histories. According to the roadside scenic marker posted by the tribal tourism office, the limestone rock was "the great bird" that flew the Diné people to their present location from an ancient homeland far to the north, delivering them from hostile neighbors and in fact saving them from extinction.[79] Another story describes Tse Bi'it A'i as the home of a giant, murderous female bird that fed on the people of Diné Bikéya in the distant past. The hero twins slayed her with arrows made from lightning and thus freed the people from her tyranny.[80]

The iconic landmark thus bears a complex, contradictory set of associations, not unlike the features of the reservation's southern landscape or of the exhibitions at the Navajo Museum. In this case, though, rather than thematizing the losses and other implications of colonialism in a controlled, intentional environment, Tse Bi'it A'i/Shiprock and the town it names now "fly" the effects of Americanization into the practices of daily life. At the same time, references to reservoirs of tribal culture, to a distinct, self-reproducing system of being and knowing, counterpoint familiar scenes of troubled consumerism in an array of seemingly accepted contradictions.

The town of Shiprock itself lies some ten miles to the northeast, in the same high desert plain, but it has little of its namesake's majesty. Unlike the overdetermined landmark, distanced from the main road by some five miles, the town isn't so difficult to read. The banal street plan and dusty air could be mistaken for any border town, or, perhaps more accurately, for any middle-America strip zone. A large Kentucky Fried Chicken sign comes into view as the road bends around a curve, then Taco Bell's, Thriftway, and a garish used car dealership.

Shiprock has the largest population on the reservation—9,129 according to the 2000 census—and unemployment has held at about 50 percent for the past five years.[81] The only jobs besides those at the Bureau of Indian Affairs and tribal offices are at fast food and retail stores that line the main road—all minimum-wage positions with no benefits or job security. An unofficial economy based on drugs, bootlegging, and theft keeps cash flowing through the town. As in other urban sites of the reservation, gangs have thrived here for at least a decade.[82] The spirit of Shiprock, to an outsider approaching it for the first time, seems grim.

In mid-autumn, past the string of chain stores and the half-abandoned Tse Bi'it A'i Shopping Center, the Shiprock Northern Navajo Fair opens its gates to streams of people pouring in from all directions. Every year the traffic gets backed up for miles as crowds of Natives and non-Natives, estimated as large as one hundred thousand in 2002, converge on Shiprock for the week-long event.[83] Originating in an annual seed exchange, the fair was established in 1909 by William Shelton, a notorious local superintendent for the Bureau of Indian Affairs (BIA), as one of his many efforts to act on the bureau's assimilation policy.[84] Shelton's agency offices, storehouse, jail, and clinic, in fact, constituted the beginnings of the town itself. Shiprock as well as its fair are thus the creations of the U.S. government in its efforts to make the Navajo people live and think like "Americans." The fair is, indeed, still in many ways a Western-styled event, as the descriptions below make quite clear. But I will argue that the annual event illustrates Shiprock's work over the past hundred years to reverse the impulses of assimilationism. The unidirectional focus and the ruthlessness that often characterized the BIA's policy as it was pursued in the early twentieth century generally, and particularly under Shelton's tenure, fostered many intelligent, often effective forms of psychological as well as social resistance across Diné Bikéya.[85] In any case, the greater percentage of Navajo people in the area of Shiprock, as elsewhere on the reservation, have never been able to truly assimilate to the forms and styles of the solid working-class model Shelton and his superiors had in mind, for poverty, crime, and illness have permitted most of the population to adopt only the desires, not the materials, of a safe and productive American lifestyle.[86]

While Shiprock has indeed been converted into a market for the chain stores on the main road into town and for other corporate giants, profits from the fair have helped the local economy and the chapter government. The town, under Navajo management and authority, has grown a world for itself from Diné ideas and practices existing side by side with the concepts and customs of global consumerism and competitive individualism exemplified by the strip zone in which much of Shiprock is set. These conflicting discourses and images, alternating with each other in a seemingly continuous dyadic movement, do not, I would argue, herald the inevitable hegemony of Western styles of being in some near future. What Shiprock and other Navajo towns demonstrate in this sense is the social structure that Ranajit Guha named "dominance without hegemony." Guha refers to Antonio Gramsci's "hegemony" as a form of power secured through persuasion and coercion such that those who are dominated become convinced, to one degree or another, of the plausibility of the social arrangements and ideologies of the powerful.[87] Dominated by means of violent oppression and left out of the economic and political mainstream of American modernity over the course of the nineteenth and early twentieth centuries, the indigenous population was not "persuaded" to embrace the world views of U.S. ideology or its military, political, and social practices. Much was lost under the pressure of occupation and under colonial oppression generally, but the exclusion from economic development meant that older modes of exchange continued to prevail, as did the forms of being and knowing that gave them legitimacy.

Many exceptions in the past complicate this picture, of course; and in the present, television and advertising, which saturate this and other reservations with images and ideas of the dominant society, do much of the work of extending hegemony. But through the nineteenth and much of the twentieth century, Native America lived beside more than within U.S. modernity; and even now tribal societies, having inherited the legacies of economic disenfranchisement and political marginalization, are in many ways determined by the capitalist culture of mainstream America and are framed by its institutional structures, while they are rarely imbued with means by which to reproduce its wealth. Without this deeper inscription in the modern, European American state, tribes continue to exist apart, sustaining a familiarity with the modern and certain means of addressing it, but the lack of hegemony means that difference itself is ineluctably sustained.

The Navajos, like other tribal people located in the United States, have not had sufficient access to the economic engines of modernity for comprehensive assimilation or hegemony to occur, for the differences to be forgotten and left aside. Older styles of collective life change with the powerful pressures of colonialism, but they remain, nevertheless, the major means of dealing with those pressures, in addition to constituting one of the major effects of having been left out of "the American century." David Eng and David Kazanjian's theory of melancholia as an unresolved form of mourning that sustains the phenomenon of loss as a means of resistance to assimilation would appear to contradict Guha's "dominance without hegemony." The loss central to Eng's and Kazanjian's theory would appear at first glance to imply the erasing effects of hegemonic influence. But what these writers emphasize in their deployment of melancholia is, somewhat paradoxically, the refusal to accept loss, the refusal to "get over it" and absorb the experience into a consciousness that develops around the wound, allowing it to heal, which, as Freud suggests, comes with proper mourning. Keeping the gaping hole of loss in view as a practiced memory of everyday life both keeps the history of colonial oppression in view as such and functions as a lived refusal of assimilation, of, in other words, hegemony. The difference between melancholia and dominance without hegemony might appear to be the difference between intentional and unchosen postures of exclusion, but both of these writers convincingly describe the means by which the experiences of colonization produce both exclusion and forms of resistance based on just that exclusion. In both arguments, the need to move in the older as well as the newer worlds is unavoidable, as is the pressure of living with the contradictions.

It is in this sense that specifically Diné ways of being and knowing are not simply "residual" in contemporary life. They are taught in tribal schools, espoused in the curriculum of Diné College, articulated in tribal politics and journalism. One might argue that the systematic nature of such programs bespeaks an anxiety among tribal leaders and Diné culturalists, a wafting fear that Diné identity is in fact threatened. But if this anxiety is indeed at work in culture programs at Shiprock and elsewhere on the reservation, it does not obviate the firmer fact that Navajo knowledges and practices are alive and present, there to be taught, shown, and reproduced in the public sphere for all the world to see. At events like the fair, where outsiders are openly welcome, identity—anxious and not—is the central idiom, and "Diné" is its key term, even as American methods and the signs of global input are everywhere apparent.

In 1997, the opening-day parade featured a team of "hog riders" on Harley Davidson motorcycles bearing the American flag. Floats and marching bands representing communities from all over the reservation followed in a very familiar format, with beauty queens and rodeo riders proudly waving to the huge crowds. Inside the front gates, vendors sold junk food, T-shirts, and baseball caps in booths that lined the fairway. Beyond, crowds lined up for the roller coaster and the Ferris wheel. At the northern end, a barn converted to an arts-and-crafts hall displayed homemade clothing, jewelry, weavings, and beadwork alongside baked goods and prize-winning vegetables. Sheep, goats, rabbits, and chickens were exhibited outside the agricultural hall, just as they are at county fairs across the United States. At the same time, educational exhibits of class projects from Navajo elementary schools demonstrated the efforts underway to teach children to identify with the principles and practices of Diné life, a project named in the fair's theme for 1997, "A Harvest of Diné Cultural Achievement."

The agricultural metaphor emphasized the rural nature of much of northern Navajoland in the perimeter of Shiprock. But the "harvest" was more explicitly intended to suggest the efforts made in recent years by the Shiprock Chapter and the Navajo Nation government to cultivate Diné knowledge and practices among the tribe's youth. As much as the material culture of European America was clearly in evidence, the fair's theme singled out the achievements of a specifically Diné cultural harvest.

Serving as a kind of bridge between the American popular cultural styles of the fair and the older Navajo ceremonial events held there, a series of dance competitions at the fair's powwow arena was billed as "open to the public," and, it seemed, this meant anyone who wanted to could participate. Indeed, the stands were filled with Anglo observers, sitting beside Indian families and milling about among them. In the next chapter I will address the gregariousness of the powwow as an institution that in recent decades has become increasingly common throughout the United States. For now, it is worth noting that the dances, the spectatorship, and the give-aways of powwows serve as opportunities for outsiders, Native and non-Native alike, to approach the host tribe in a ceremonial scene more related to tribal life than the more commercial features of the fair are. The festival atmosphere and the congenial reception of outsiders at the Shiprock Fair powwow meant that non-Natives could "mix it up" with Navajos in the inter-tribal cultural forms of powwow dance, either by dancing or by watching from the stands. The organizers thus allowed for a public encounter somewhere between the scenes of familiar, global forms of consumerism in the fair's midway and the more esoterically Navajo ceremonial events at the other end of the fairgrounds.

Indeed, if the midway, the agricultural exhibits, and the powwow arena were sites of open sociability to which anyone was invited, the Nightway ceremony, in spite of the fact that it too was officially open to the public, offered much less readable signals to observers from elsewhere and was a much more difficult scene to enter from "outside."

The Nightway ceremony is the enactment of one or more of the many episodes in the experience of a figure known as the Dreamer or the Visionary, as Washington Matthews, the celebrated late nineteenth-century ethnographer of Nightway, called him.[88] The Visionary has a series of encounters with the *yei,* or Holy People, from whom he learns the precise details of the ceremonial that gets enacted as Nightway.[89] The reenactment of the Visionary's experience in this highly honored ceremonial event is a healing performance, intended generally to address paralysis, deafness, and other illnesses originating or located in the head.[90] The Nightway process is intricate and elaborate. Each movement, each prayer, and sand painting must be executed correctly in order to draw the attention of the yei to the ceremony and to the illness it is intended to cure.[91]

When I attended, a crowd of about one hundred people gathered to watch the ceremony. Three other Anglos, or *bilagáanas,* were standing, like I was, in the back row. As time passed, they drifted away. While publicity for the fair had specifically indicated that anyone could attend the ceremony, I began to feel intensely self-conscious about my presence. William Overstreet has commented in precise terms about this experience: as a bilagáana at Nightway "you don't feel unwelcome here, but you can't help feeling apart, an outsider at this healing ceremonial."[92]

Before traveling to Navajoland, I had contacted one of the local tribal chapter leaders at Shiprock to confirm the public status of the ceremony. She responded unambiguously that indeed it was and invited me to contact her when I arrived. Once in Shiprock, I called her, but no one answered the phone, and the tribal chapter headquarters, where her office was located, were closed. It only made sense, of course, that officials wouldn't be at their desks during Shiprock's biggest event of the year. Even so, it already seemed that this was going to be a very different kind of for-the-public tribal event from the exhibits at the Navajo Museum. Public and not so public, part of the popular culture of the fair and an esoteric performance, the Nightway at the Shiprock Northern Navajo Fair seemed to beckon and, simultaneously, turn away from interested strangers.

I was happy, then, to find people willing to talk to me at the ceremony. While we waited for the dancing to begin, a man standing next to me struck up a conversation. He explained that although his father had been a Nightway dancer, he himself had only witnessed the ceremony a few times. He asserted that he was proud of his heritage and actively interested in seeing the Diné language and religious traditions "kept alive," as he put it. He was particularly concerned for his son to have the opportunity to see the ceremony while he is young. The son, however, was not there. Later in the evening, a woman and her husband expressed similar concerns to me. Taking their children's interests in gang styles of dress, speech, and music as serious threats to their Diné upbringing, they described themselves as worried about the future of not just their own families, but the tribe as a continuing entity.

Certainly, the event itself might have prompted these conversations, given the increased consciousness of the very idea of traditionalism and its presence or absence in everyday life, but the fact that people were willing to share these concerns with a stranger was somewhat harder to understand. As if mourning in advance what they feared might be lost, they seemed to attach themselves to the language and ceremonial consciousness so richly present and to reiterate intentions to protect them. This valuing of and identification with the potentially threatened Navajo ways of being seemed to frame what was before us with a special luster and to muster a commitment to support its reproduction and performance in the future.

It was also rather noticeable that apart from their welcoming of me and their open discussion of traditionalism and inheritance of Navajo language and styles of being, none of these people talked about the ceremony itself before us—its movements, characters, or purposes. As the public part of the event finally got under way, the announcer intoned in English and Diné over an aged PA system that there were to be no pictures taken or recordings made of the ceremony. This censure, common after all to many American Indian ceremonial events and exhibitions involving sacred references, seemed to echo my interlocutors' silence about the event before us. The restrictions indicated as well the hosts' desire to limit reception of the event beyond the immediate public, even though much of the ceremony took place inside the hogan, hidden from our view.

After perhaps an hour had passed, a group of blanketed dancers emerged from the hogan, striding purposefully toward the brush that had been set up at the far end of the dance ground. One was the personator of Talking God, grandfather of the deities or yeis, in Gladys Reichard's scheme a "persuadable" hunter deity. In most accounts, he is the son of Changing Woman and a leader among the Gods, for whom he is often mentor; he is helpful to humans, modest and compassionate.[93] The personator assumes the subjectivity of Talking God, wearing his dress and mask. Returning from the brush without the blanket, he came forth uttering his high-pitched, staccato call. Together with other yeis, he approached the patient at the hogan door with rattles, pollen, and herb bundles. They danced about him, emitting calls. The dancer who is Talking God must be especially careful not to speak when personating the yei, even though the god speaks in the narratives. His calls cannot be translated into words in performance, for, according to Reichard, "to speak while wearing his mask is tantamount to suicide."[94]

Initiating the transition from social to ritual scene, the appearance of Talking God rendered most of the audience still, except for a few drunks hovering in the background, imitating the call. There was something obscenely comical about these jeering voices; faces in the crowd turned to look, amused but a little ill at ease. Humor is clearly a common feature of the Nightway ceremonial, and the clown known as Water Sprinkler offers a good example of this point, as he chases after other dancers, caricaturing their formal, ritualized motions, and makes fun of Talking God. The similarity of the drunks' behavior to that of Water Sprinkler was striking and perhaps might explain the crowd's tolerance of them. But many spectators were visibly uneasy, and none laughed openly at the drunks' antics like they did in response to Water Sprinkler. If the insult could, in some sense, be contextualized by the model of the clown's actions, it was also, obviously, an instance of a social problem so common at Navajoland that it could intrude in this highly privileged event without serious sanction.

The large audience on this last night of the Nightway included an impressive number of children and teenagers, brought along by parents and other elders. The youths' interest in the event, if it could be justly read from facial expressions, body movements, and chit chat, registered about the same amount of patience I would have expected to find in any young teenager: some, but not a great deal. They seemed like good kids, nevertheless, dutifully attending an event which with their parents, grandparents, and community leaders wanted them to be familiar.

Other dance groups followed the first one, each wearing slightly different costumes but performing the same movements with Talking God, Water Sprinkler, and the other yeis properly masked. What I saw at the Nightway ceremony is, as Overstreet notes, "as much of the Nightway . . . as most Anglos ever see."[95] Indeed, pamphlets for the fair stipulate that "the public is welcome to view parts of the [Nightway] ceremony during the fair."[96] The healing takes place inside the hogan, even though the presence of the audience, including outsiders, is important to the ceremony's ethic of sharing good will and good health within the community and beyond. To participate in the events inside the hogan, that is, to perform as a medicine person, requires years of study. In this sense, many of the Navajo observers among whom I stood were as excluded from the details of the Nightway as I was. But their understandings of the yeis, of the sand paintings that attract the yeis to the ceremonies, and of the language in which the sacred rites are conducted are beyond my ken, even if I had had the opportunity to spend many years at Navajoland. And little has been published on the narratives that inform or accompany the dances, gestures, calls, and sand paintings.[97] One might study them closely, but as James Faris insists in his history of Nightway documentation, it is the ceremony, the action of its performance by medicine people and patients and of the attentive presence of the audience, that matters in Nightway: "The activity itself is paramount, the ceremony—the action—carries significance, not the product [of the sand painting]." The sand paintings themselves are destroyed shortly after the ceremony, since the function of the image itself is to attract the Holy

People to the occasion. Further use or display runs the risk of exposing supra-human power in contexts not designed to effectively manage it.[98]

James Faris and William Overstreet claim that most Navajo medicine people recite or refer to selected incidents in the experience of the Dreamer, and very few "know" the entire narrative as it was reproduced in print by Washington Matthews, Edward S. Curtis, Mary Wheelwright, Edward Sapir, and a few others in the early twentieth century.[99] Overstreet explains that as such, "the Nightway narrative does not belong to the Navajo oral tradition . . . [and] the totalizing character of the [recorded] text[s] . . . sets them apart from this tradition."[100] If the Nightway cannot be comprehended in written narrative and is not in its totality represented in oral narrative, and if outsiders are excluded from the central events of the performance, then the "open to the public" status of the Nightway ceremony at the fair clearly had its limits.

Public events like the Shiprock Northern Navajo Fair represent the tribe as a nation that welcomes foreign visitors, not just as a market for Navajo goods but also as participants in activities that mark Navajo identity. The invitation to observe and dance at powwows and to attend Nightway ceremonies opens the possibility to outsiders to witness Navajo ritual and aesthetic styles and thus garners recognition of a particular Diné world view and social body. The Nightway itself demonstrated the vibrant presence of a very old ceremonial practice, which in turn elicited recognition among strangers and Navajos alike of the living presence of Navajo styles of being and knowing as components of a distinct, different cultural order existing within the boundaries of the contemporary social landscape of the United States. To the extent that anticipatory mourning of the Navajo knowledges represented by Nightway was part of the presentation, it evidenced a need to protect the cultural imaginary of Diné Bikéya from dissolution, given the perceived threat of a different kind of loss that comes on the wings of postmodern, global, American popular culture, "flown" to the reservation by any number of media. A key means to securing that protection was the overt display of the limits of demonstration, the showing of boundaries that sealed off the perception of Navajo sacred knowledge from outsiders' eyes.

CHAPTER 3

Wind River Lessons

THE WIND RIVER RESERVATION stretches across thirty-five hundred square miles from the base of the majestic Wind River range in south-central Wyoming. The reservation is home to the Eastern Shoshone and Northern Arapaho tribes, each of which has proprietary rights over roughly half the land and its resources, including the significant gas and oil reserves that fuel their respective, struggling economies.[1] The two tribes once considered each other enemies, but in 1878 the U.S. government assigned the Arapahoes to Wind River as a purportedly temporary home.[2] The boundaries of the reservation were established by the 1868 Treaty of Fort Bridger ten years before the Arapahoes arrived, but this had reduced the Shoshones' earlier, far greater reservation described in the Treaty of 1863, and it included several white settlements within its boundaries.

Over the course of the late nineteenth and early twentieth centuries, the government, in spite of the legal commitments outlined in the document, repeatedly diminished the reservation described in the Treaty of 1868. In 1872, the Shoshones were pressured by Congress to exchange seven hundred thousand acres in the southern sector of their reservation for less valuable land to the north—land which they recognized as Crow territory. Under these constraints, the tribe opted to sell the southern portion to Washington for twenty-five thousand dollars. In 1906, an Executive Order of the U.S. President "opened" 1.5 million acres of reservation land north of the Wind River as an irrigation district for non-Native homesteaders, with a section set aside for a town site.[3] Hundreds of potential settlers turned up at what is known as the "Big Bend" of the Wind River to draw lots for the opportunity to purchase parcels extending northward to the town of Thermopolis. Riverton, the new town that developed on the site where the lottery took place, quickly became a large and prosperous European American community, surrounded by impoverished Native villages and farms.[4]

Despite the fact that their homeland as well as their political and economic sovereignty were so systematically diminished from the late nineteenth through the early twentieth centuries, the Eastern Shoshones of Wind River have often, in the past as well as the present, represented themselves in public discourse as living on relatively friendly footing not only with the Arapahoes but with the United States and its non-Native citizens. Indeed, as early as 1849, John Wilson, the first agent of the Indian Office to work in Wyoming Shoshone territory, described the tribe as "an honest and sober people, decidedly friendly to the whites."[5] When the Treaty of Fort Bridger was struck in 1868, the Wind River region was already populated by a mixed society of Shoshone, Bannock, and Anglo hunters, farmers, trappers, and traders. In his study of this world, Henry Stamm describes it as a community in which "Americans, Indians and whites, frequently interacted with each other in friendly relationships based on marriage, trading partnerships, and military alliance against common enemies."[6]

In present-day Wind River, Shoshones, like Arapahos, come to Riverton to work, shop, enroll in university courses, and conduct business. Non-Indians visit the Native villages of Fort Washakie, Crowheart, Ethete, and St. Stephens. At powwows, church services, and events in Riverton City Park, one sees Natives and Anglos watching the same spectacles, applauding and ignoring the same achievements. The amicable relations among the differing ethnic groups is illustrated by the events of Martin Luther King Day in 2003, when seven hundred residents representing the spectrum of valley ethnic groups—Native Americans, Hispanics, African Americans, and Anglos—came together to protest plans of the so-called Church of the Creator, a white supremacist group, to establish its headquarters in Riverton. Organized by high school students from the reservation, the demonstration sent a message to the Church of the Creator that their radically racist policies were not welcome. By the summer of 2003, the supremacists had decided not to locate there.[7]

The Eastern Shoshones today cherish two tribal icons that image their benign relations with the United States: Sacajawea and Chief Washakie. Images of these historical characters appear regularly in tribal public self-representations. Sacajawea was the young Shoshone woman who aided the Lewis and Clark expedition from 1805 to 1806, and she is remembered as such at Wind River in statuary and in much historical documentation. Washakie, principal chief of the Eastern Shoshones from the middle of the nineteenth century until his death in 1900, saw his people through the invasions of Wind River country by whites with as little hostility as possible. In modern public iconography at Wind River, Sacagawea and Washakie have become familiar references and perhaps the most central vehicles for the tribe's social recognition in the larger public sphere. The simple fact that these two names and images turn up in Shoshone public discourse as often as they do today suggests that the amicable tones they project still prevail.

But other dimensions of the past are evident in histories of the Wind River Reservation and complicate this picture. Stamm concludes his description, quoted above, of the benign multiculturalism of the 1868 community with the qualifier that "underneath this veneer of mutual goodwill . . . lay radically different understandings of the world."[8] These differences and the tensions they provoked as well as the negotiations that allowed for what amicable relations did exist at Wind River between whites and Indians are central in representations of tribal identity on the reservation today. Indeed, more complex features of their individual profiles shade the emphasis on congeniality and collaboration in the careers of Sacagawea and Washakie narrated at Wind River. Tribal self-representations that invoke their memories reflect this shading of the more overt images and narratives.[9] Biographies of Sacagawea and Washakie help to show how it is that these iconic personages continue to inspire the subtle delineation of difference between Shoshone ways of being and knowing and European American interests.

This chapter looks at the functions of Sacagawea and Washakie in representations of Eastern Shoshone historical and contemporary identity erected at the tribal museum. In addition, it studies performances of Shoshone tribal culture at the most well known annual public event in the contemporary scene, the mid-summer Indian Days Powwow. The museum and the powwow in their distinct ways evidence more ambivalent interpretations of relations between the Shoshones and the United States, interpretations that challenge those offered in formal accounts where friendship and shared interests are emphasized. Even as histories of Sacagawea and Washakie offered at the museum help to image benign working relationships between the tribe and the United States, these histories have become the means for telling stories of Native difference and of tribal departures from the ideals of the larger culture. So too, while advertisements and arrangements for the powwow extend an invitation to outsiders to join in the dances and other events, Indian Days is distinctly an occasion for enacting cultural distinctiveness and for demonstrating how the substances of cultural knowledge are withheld from public view.

By contrasting exogenous, friendly representations of tribal identities at the Wind River museum and the Indian Days Powwow with those that image more enclosed and indigenous styles of collective life, the chapter argues that Native exclusivity operates beside hospitality in a complex relationship. The ambivalence in this dynamic of public interaction, I will argue, allows the Eastern Shoshone tribe to conduct its public self-representations in several different ways simultaneously. Both the museum and the powwow venues attempt to locate the Shoshones within the more dominant economic circuits of the United States after a long history of disenfranchisement from those resources. In addition, they work to elicit the larger society's acknowledgment of the Eastern Shoshones as a distinct tribal society with a particular cultural identity and political sovereignty. At the same time, the various displays and performances of tribal difference express the living memory at Wind River not only of a continuing cultural legacy, but of the pain that continues in the memory of loss of land and autonomy, a pain that, like economic marginalization, appears to have kept the Eastern Shoshones from assimilating in any totalizing way to U.S. cultural hegemonies.

SACAJAWEA'S GRAVE

Among the small frame houses and government buildings clustered together at Fort Washakie, a village of seventeen hundred on the western edge of the Wind River Reservation, stands a white Victorian structure that houses the Eastern Shoshone Tribal Cultural Center. The building looks different from the prefabricated homes and corrugated sheds that surround it. More delicately designed and aged, it seems a misplaced image of domestic elegance whose height and architecture speak to its importance as vault of tribal history and museum of contemporary culture. But there is a certain shabbiness about the house—the porch sags, the screen door needs to be replaced—which suggests that the history

3-1. Eastern Shoshone Cultural Center, Fort Washakie, Wind River Reservation

and culture displayed there aren't, after all, accorded much priority at Fort Washakie.

The idea of a "cultural center," located in a particular place and displaying objects for a spectator's curiosity, is in many ways antithetical to traditional Shoshone methods for maintaining history and culture. Oral narratives, ceremonies, and dances performed those functions in the past, and they still have that authority in contemporary life, as the discussion of the Eastern Shoshone Indian Days Powwow below demonstrates. But this museum-archive makes available to non-Indians, in ways that are familiar to them, the elements of Shoshone culture and history that the tribe is willing to display in public. In this sense, the Shoshone Cultural Center presents neither a gateway nor even a vestibule to the inner sanctums of a more private or sovereign tradition but a sampler of historical material that mutually situates Shoshone and European American cultures in the history of the United States. The displays of tribal culture and narratives of history offered to the public at Wind River seem to assert a place for Eastern Shoshones in the larger picture of U.S. cultural development, but at the same time these self-representations work to seal off

Shoshone identity as something shaped in a parallel, distinct formation that contests the idea that the tribe has conducted itself "in harmony" with U.S. interests.

One of the most extensive collections in the Shoshone Cultural Center's archive consists of a series of articles and essays devoted to Sacajawea.[10] Born to the Lemhi Shoshone of what is now southern Idaho in about 1790, Sacajawea was abducted in her early teens by a group of Hidatsa hunters and taken to their villages along the northern bend of the Missouri River. Subsequently, Sacajawea came to be in a liaison with the French trapper Toussaint Charbonneau, who very likely bought or won her from the Hidatsa captors.[11] During the autumn of 1804–1805, Charbonneau enlisted with the Lewis and Clark expedition, then quartered near the Mandan villages just south of Hidatsa country. Sacajawea gave birth to her son with Charbonneau, Baptiste, the following winter; and in the spring, when the expedition set out again to find the sources of the Missouri River, she and the child were among the personnel. Her familiarity with the area of the Missouri headwaters was useful to the expedition, and her knowledge of the Shoshone language significantly aided the explorers' negotiations with the people there, who made their portage through the Rocky Mountains possible.

The written materials at the Shoshone center offer various details of Sacajawea's contribution to the expedition, but many of them focus particular attention on the narrative of her life afterwards. The course of that life is much debated. One argument has it that she lived for only a few years after the expedition, died in 1812 at about the age of twenty-four, and was buried near Fort Manuel, a short-lived trading post on the border of North and South Dakota. This account is for the most part subscribed to by European American historians, whose evidence comes from contemporary diaries and letters of trappers and traders who encountered Charbonneau in St. Louis and at Fort Manuel from 1811 to 1812.[12] The other argument constructs a very different story of Sacajawea's life by claiming that she died in 1884 at Wind River, after having lived there for many years as a highly respected member of the community and thus an important figure in local history.

The Eastern Shoshone Tribal Cultural Center as an institution supports the latter account. Several European American writers whose commentaries make up part of the center's collections also subscribe to this

3-2. Statue of Sacagawea outside Fort Washakie, Wind River Reservation

story, but the 1812 argument is represented as well in the archival materials. Asked if the argument that runs contrary to the center's own position ever tempted local readers to think differently on this question, a Shoshone researcher told me that no one at Fort Washakie was ever bothered by it, because they knew Sacajawea was there, buried just outside the hamlet.

Indeed, Sacajawea, like Washakie, presides over what might be called a pervasive funereal tourism at Wind River. A short drive to the outskirts of Fort Washakie leads to Sacajawea Cemetery, in the midst of which stands a large gravestone, marked with the epigraph "Sacagawea, A Guide With the Lewis and Clark Expedition, Identified By Reverend J. Roberts Who Officiated at Her Burial." Those who maintain she died at Wind River in 1884 believe it is in fact Sacajawea who is buried here; and this is important enough for them to have named the cemetery after her. In the spring of 2003, the tribe commissioned a bronze sculpture of Saca-jawea, which now stands on the upper slope of the cemetery, facing east and out across the reservation. The sculptor, L. M. Boller, who is part Shoshone and lives in the off-reservation town of Dubois, depicts Saca-gawea gazing with happy curiosity at a sand dollar, a copy of one she reputedly gave to Chief Washakie and which he wore as a necklace. It is an image of the young heroine as *voyageure,* having arrived with her fellow crew members at the expedition's goal, the Pacific Ocean and the mouth of the Columbia River. The statue is enormous, nearly eight feet high, and stands prominently amid the nearly treeless rolling hills, against the background of the Wind River peaks. It is, indeed, a figure of tribal pride in Sacajawea, a formulator of American history and a remembered Shoshone woman.

Oral histories related by tribal elders in the early twentieth century to the European American researcher Grace Hebard serve now as textual evidence for the identification of the Sacajawea who lived at Wind River in old age with the woman who accompanied Lewis and Clark.[13] Their stories are supported in a statement written in 1935 by John Roberts, an Episcopal minister at Wind River from 1883 until 1945.[14] Roberts explains that the woman he knew as Sacajawea had through the years related to her family incidents of her experience with the expedition, and that this information came to him via the Indian agent who took down Sacajawea's history from her adopted son, Bazil. The epigraph on the gravestone indicates that Roberts himself officiated at her burial in 1884.[15]

In both of these accounts, it bears noting that Sacajawea is considered a brave, generous, and intelligent person whose contributions to the expedition were estimable and whose place in the historical record is highly valued. As an actor in the chronicle of the American nation,

Sacajawea has achieved a good deal of popular recognition; and through her the Shoshone people have been acknowledged in mainstream history more than they otherwise might have been. Since her first appearance as a central figure of the Lewis and Clark expedition in Eva Emery Dye's 1902 novel *The Conquest,* she has become the subject of much popular fiction, a virtual icon of U.S. romantic nationalism.[16]

In such a role, Sacajawea might seem to present a figure of ambiguous cultural value among Indian people, since the expedition spearheaded a Euro-American settlement history that overtook the spaces and resources of all Native American peoples in the trans-Mississippi West. One historian—the daughter of John Roberts, the missionary who gave firsthand testimony to Sacagawea's life and death at Wind River—writes that Sacagawea herself tended to keep her experiences with the expedition secret since "if the fact should be published about her leading the expedition of White explorers across the Indian hunting country, it would have brought only reproach and scorn from the members of her tribe."[17] Sacajawea's sisters in hemispheric expeditionary fame, Pocahontas of the Virginia Powhatans, who assisted John Smith at Jamestown, and the Aztec-born La Malinche, translator and mistress to Cortes in Mexico, have both acquired complex reputations as sensitive diplomats and exceptionally canny women who at some level betrayed their people. Certainly this is more apparent in the case of La Malinche, but the complications of Pocahontas's and Malinche's roles as negotiators and interpreters between indigenous leaders and white political-entrepreneurial missions are evident in the extensive scholarship and popular writing on both.[18]

But the potential opprobrium that Roberts's daughter assumed was the cause of Sacajawea's silence about her role in the expedition has not emerged in overt reservation public discourse. It is more than clear that most Wind River Shoshones want to claim her as their own. Indeed, the iconic image of Sacajawea with wind-blown hair and babe on her back, a "Noble Savage" pointing the way west, is affirmed not only in white statues and story books,[19] but in the writing of one of the most influential Native American cultural analysts and poets of the present day, Paula Gunn Allen, a radical feminist who celebrates Sacajawea's strengths in the following terms: "When Eva Emery Dye discovered Sacagawea and honored her as the guiding spirit of American womanhood, she may have been wrong in bare historical fact, but she was quite accurate in terms of deeper truth. The statues that have been erected depicting Sacagawea as a Matron in her prime signify an understanding in the American mind, however unconscious, that the source of just government, of right ordering of social relationships, the dream of 'liberty and justice for all' can be gained only by following the Indian Matrons' guidance."[20] To support her position, Allen quotes from a 1905 speech, by the suffragette Anna Howard Shaw, which begins, "Forerunner of civilization, great leader of men, patient and motherly woman, we bow our hearts to do you honor."

Allen's praise assumes much about Sacajawea's abilities to make choices and decisions in her role as Charbonneau's bought wife and as figurehead of the Corps of Discovery.[21] But this and other hagiographies of Sacagawea, including those in the Shoshone Tribal Cultural Center, beg some critical inspection, for they ignore much historical scholarship on the topic of her death and leave unaddressed the awkward political implications of her cooperation with Lewis and Clark.

In their representation of Sacajawea, the Tribal Cultural Center's staff and most of the Shoshone people living at Wind River would seem to subscribe to the dominant culture's valuation of her and, in the process, identify the Shoshone people with those values by according her such a central position in their own history. Perhaps one of the more patent indications of this fact is that the well-tended grave at Wind River, which is dedicated to Sacagawea, includes near the bottom, in small print, the notice "Erected by the Wyoming State Organization of the National Society of the Daughters of the American Revolution, 1963." At the foot of the grave appears a pair of American Legion medallions. Beside these ritualistic monikers of American national culture lay a number of more humble and less readable tributes: a milk pitcher and a vase, a Bunsen-burner candle, plastic dolls, a basket ball, shells, stones, beads, a rock engraved with a peace sign, a small coyote, a scallop shell with a dream catcher woven inside, a toy car, a disc of wood reading "Wooden Nickel."

The wooden nickel and other ambiguous objects at the grave might suggest that for some visitors—and we don't know whether they were Native or not—Sacajawea figures as a collaborator whose legacy is more questionable than that upheld at the center. There are other ways of looking at this picture, however. The first thing to reconsider is the neglect of the evidence for Sacajawea's death in 1812. In my own experience of studying the characters of United States expeditionary narratives, the 1812 death has always seemed the more compelling: passages from journals are cited, with dates, names (though not Sacajawea's), and places indicating where Charbonneau was seen with his "Snake," (an Anglo term for the Shoshone, commonly used in the early nineteenth century) his Indian wife, who had participated in the Lewis and Clark expedition. These journals were kept by travelers whom contemporary historians can identify by occupation and origin; indeed, their names ring with familiarity: Brackenridge, Bradbury, Luttig.

But after speaking with people at Fort Washakie, studying the archival material at the Shoshone Cultural Center, and visiting the Sacajawea Cemetery with its solemn, indeed, sacramental, argument for ownership, I found myself drawn to the center's story. One thought in particular disrupted the clarity of my earlier position: the fact that everyone involved in this debate admits to Charbonneau's having been a profligate lover, marrying what Harold Howard calls "Indian girls" all over the western country until he was an old man.[22] Any wives he had before 1811 might have accompanied him from St. Louis to Fort Manuel. The researchers at the Shoshone Tribal Cultural Center explain that people who claim to be Charbonneaus, and who wonder if Sacajawea might have been their ancestor, approach them continuously, in the mail and over the phone. This fact is not necessarily testimony to the multiplicity of Charbonneau's amorous connections, but it does point to the difficulty of establishing secure identities in such a case. Moreover, as Howard has indicated, there is a good deal of contemporary oral evidence of Sacajawea's presence after 1812 in what are now Wyoming and Montana, in which she is identified in the same terms as those used to describe her in the journals of Brackenridge, Bradbury, and Luttig. She is the former wife of a "Frenchman" or of someone whose name is spelled something like "Charbonneau"; and she once accompanied Lewis and Clark to the Pacific.

The significance of this debate in a sense calls for reconsideration of the second objection to the account of Sacajawea's life propounded at the Shoshone Cultural Center: the lack of commentary on the politics of Sacajawea's cooperation with Lewis and Clark. We have no evidence to indicate that Sacajawea was in any position to make choices or decisions in joining the expedition or in determining any of its activities, other than to advise certain geographical directions. The problem arises when one considers the fact that the Shoshone people have embraced her for having had this experience. How else, after all, would she even be known in the historical record; what, one might ask, is there about Sacajawea to appreciate besides this role? I think an appropriate response is simply that she is recognized. Several posters and pamphlets at the Shoshone Cultural Center label her "Sacajawea, Recognized Shoshone Woman." As caretakers of her legacy, the women who manage the museum and, indeed, all the Shoshone people of Wind River are directly associated with her. Sacajawea's recognition is not theirs, but it is as close as they are likely to come to substantial acknowledgment by the American public sphere, and that is no small effect of Sacajawea's influence. While it is true that the center indirectly connects its values with those of the dominant culture's historiography by affirming Sacajawea's heroic status for having assisted Lewis and Clark, the fact that the expedition served to raise her name to national fame seems far more significant at Wind River than the broader ideas or aims which the expedition was intended to actualize.

Yet another perspective on Sacajawea's character and destiny in local oral commentary further attests to the way in which the Wind River community asserts its possession of her memory, apart from the roles she occupies in the more widely accepted narrative. As one of the women who work at the center told me, many people at the reservation now feel that she should have left Charbonneau rather than accompany him on the expedition. His womanizing and ill treatment of his wives seem deplorable by their contemporary standards; and the retrospective advice, or admonition, to Sacajawea effectively separates her from him by prescribing her proper action, even if that action never occurred.

On the other hand, the comment made to me by the woman at the center would also seem to imply that Sacajawea's participation in the expedition was not a matter of her choice, but part of the generally "bad deal" she had in being attached to Charbonneau. And this seems quite plausible. Most accounts of her life agree that after childhood—when her father had reputedly promised her to a particular man—Sacajawea spent a good part of her youth in captivity. Taken together with the fact that she was most likely bought or won by Charbonneau, these conditions of her life suggest that she acted, at least in the episodes recorded by Lewis and Clark, not so much as a strong-willed or determined woman, but rather as one whose own desires are quite unreadable, in that her actions are so evidently determined by the series of men in her life.

The expedition was designed and controlled at a distance by the "Great Father" in Washington, as Lewis and Clark referred to President Thomas Jefferson in the orations that they periodically delivered along the way about the new nation and the Indians' part in it. The bad deal that they offered, and that the Indians could not refuse, is writ small in the deal offered to Sacajawea herself and to her descendants, who today look to her for recognition within the larger culture. In her capacity as guide and interpreter, however, Sacajawea acts and speaks for the interests of Lewis, Clark, Jefferson, and the mix of European enlightenment and romantic national ideas for which they stood. From the evidence of the expedition texts, she never speaks for herself.

By claiming Sacajawea as their ancestor and at the same time imagining her separated from the man who connected her with the activities through which her recognition and very likely their knowledge of her comes, the people at Wind River mark their own minor recognition in the narrative of U.S. history while also critiquing that narrative in posing an alternative one. The critique is aimed not only at the facts of the 1812 story but also at the set of patriarchal relations which kept Sacajawea in a compromised situation. An indirect connection links that patriarchal structure to the national project in which she and Charbonneau participated. The irony, of course, is that if Sacajawea had cut her connection to Charbonneau, she presumably would never have participated in the expedition and thus never have been represented in mainstream history.

In the account of Sacajawea's longer life, ending in 1884, she does in fact leave Charbonneau several years after the expedition, when he has taken another, younger wife whom he demonstratively favors, to the disadvantage of the increasingly mistreated Sacajawea.[23] By the time she arrives at Wind River, she is rather appropriately renamed Wadze-Wipe, or Lost Woman. Disconnected from any sort of tribal or marital relations, she is on her own, a figure of womanly independence who still does not speak and is thus still rather unreadable to history, but who finally opts for life among her people rather than for association with the white culture of whose history she is now a part.

In this position, Sacajawea's character as expedition participant and the potential charge of collaboration that it bears are revised as she is written out of the earlier histories and resituated in that of Native Americans.

In subscribing to this narrative of Sacajawea's life, the Shoshone people at Wind River claim her participation in that project as well as her distance from it. To understand Sacajawea in this way is to accord her neither the role of grand matriarch of Native American female strength nor that of heroine of U.S. colonialism. Rather it is to portray her as one who turned away from the white history in a complex refusal of recognition by the mainstream audience, an interpretation readable in the new sculpture, with its giant size and large, muscular features. In this role, Sacajawea enacts for Native audiences a version of what William Bevis refers to as "homing in" in much contemporary Native American literature, the difficult process of returning to a locus of Native American community and identity after a time of wandering without cultural structure, precisely as a lost woman.[24] By claiming this person, the Eastern Shoshone people image their own "wandering" into the hands of the American nation in the encounter with the expedition and through the course of colonial history. Simultaneously "won" by Jefferson's successors and denied a share in their prosperity, the Shoshones have not assimilated to Euro-American society. The tribe has retained its status on the periphery of the United States and worked through the past several decades to revitalize ways of being and knowing that have been marginalized but not lost, even as much of their former homeland, relative economic stability, and political autonomy have been.

Sacajawea's historical afterlife is as vexed in some ways as her life itself: it is another story of captivity, servitude, and partial escape. The story of her long life among the Comanches and Shoshones gives us a solitary Sacajawea who guides no one but wanders somewhat haphazardly in the direction of Wind River. The Shoshones here are not quite her own people, and the place is not her home, any more than the expedition was something in which she chose to participate. Rather than returning to her country of origin and to her aboriginal self, she becomes Lost Woman, a somewhat worldly veteran of losses, gains, and strange experiences in a frontier of many cultures. Similarly, the possession of Sacajawea at present-day Wind River does not foster a classic Shoshone tribal identity but attempts to revitalize inherited endogenous knowledges and practices and to secure a place for the tribe, in economic as well as political terms, within the flows of U.S. society.

Sacajawea serves not only as the most effective means by which the

Shoshones are recognized in the society and economy of North America—systems from which the tribe has been excluded under the exigencies of colonialism—but as a memorial to the Native world in which she lived. Even as a captive and a sojourner among other tribes, Sacajawea stands for the Shoshone past, when the tribe roamed the Wind River, the Great Basin, and the western Plains, a flourishing collective with an integral endogenous knowledge system and effective material relation to their environment. The loss of access to land and of economic and political independence is recorded in her image, as in that of Washakie. Both figures serve to keep the memory of loss alive in the present time, not as loss that results in a cultural vacuum, but as loss that in itself acquires substance over time and marks off the differences of Shoshone styles of being and knowing that refuse to be forgotten and refuse as well the Euro-American invitation to an impossible assimilation—impossible because the colonial history has excluded the tribe from the economic bounty of the larger United States. Sacajawea and Washakie thus serve as bulwarks against assimilation, in spite of their historical actions as negotiators between Shoshone and Anglo interests.

MEMORIES OF WASHAKIE

Chief Washakie is honored in Riverton history as a friend of the government agents and Anglo missionaries who came to work at Wind River. In the Shoshone town named for him, a statue that once stood in the Rotunda in Washington looks out from the front of the tribal offices, a plaque beneath it bearing his words to his people, supposedly uttered not long before he died: "It has always been my fervent hope and policy through these long years to maintain peace and harmony. It is my earnest prayer that you will follow the footsteps which I have made for you."[25] The implied partner in this peace is the U.S. government, its agents, and citizens, a point made very clear in a speech Washakie delivered to the council of chiefs in 1868 shortly after signing the Treaty of Fort Bridger: "When the white man came into my country and cut the wood and made the roads, my heart was good, and I was satisfied."[26] These and other public reiterations of Washakie's sentiments have in common an emphatic call to cooperate, to negotiate, to participate in the projects of the United States government wholeheartedly. Of course, as a leader who retained his authority at Wind River for five decades, Washakie was

3-3. Statue of Washakie, Fort Washakie, Wind River Reservation

a much more complex person than this simple account would suggest. Indeed, his charisma and his political longevity were at least in part the effects of a canny sense of diplomacy and a gift for negotiating between multiple competing interests. Historical records suggest that the friendliness was only one of many dimensions of his relationships with the Anglo agents of Washington with whom he continuously had to deal through his years in power.

What we know of Washakie's life comes from few sources. A handful of Euro-American historians have narrated his career, and the Eastern Shoshone Tribal Cultural Center offers a collection of biographical materials, similar to those that tell the stories of Sacagawea's life. Washakie was born in Montana very early in the nineteenth century to a Selish (commonly but mistakenly known as "Flathead") father and a Shoshone mother.[27] In his teens, he began living with Shoshone bands, traveling the ample regions of Shoshone country that extended from the Bear River in southern Wyoming to the Yellowstone River in Montana and from what is now southern Idaho to the Big Horn Mountains.[28] As a young warrior, he took part in attacks on Blackfeet, Crows, Gros Ventres, and other Shoshone enemies, making a place for himself as leader of several bands and eventually as one of the principle chiefs of the Shoshone people. At the same time, as a novice hunter and trapper, Washakie befriended many white mountain men, among them the legendary Jim Bridger, with whom, according to Stamm, he became lasting friends.[29]

From early adulthood, then, Washakie found himself engaging in at least two very different cultural environments. Stamm describes him as one of several leaders "who sometimes fought with whites, but more often served as culture brokers and mediators of the needs of their people."[30] In a letter of 1867, the superintendent of Indian Affairs for Utah Territory, F. H. Head, described Washakie as "undoubtedly the most sagacious, honorable, and intelligent Indian" in the region. At the same time, however, Head became indignant when Washakie and other tribal leaders, deliberating with him about hostile relations that had developed between the U.S. military, on the one hand, and the Lakotas, Cheyennes, Arapahoes, and Crows, on the other, claimed that the government had been deceitful.[31] In addition, the military and political gifts that served Washakie well in his rise to authority among his own people also allowed him to manipulate relations between different groups of whites, including U.S. Indian agents, soldiers, Mormons, and trappers who vied for territorial control in and around Shoshone country in the middle of the nineteenth century. By accommodating their interests and by playing them off of one another, Washakie managed to situate himself in the eyes of the whites as key representative of the Shoshones in the Wind River Valley by the time of the Fort Bridger treaty negotiations.[32]

The territorial boundaries marked out by the Treaty of 1868 recognized Shoshone priority, and thus Washakie's leadership, but they left unaddressed the fact that the two white towns included in the reservation, the populations of which were supposed to be carefully controlled by U.S. authorities so as not to let the reservation be overrun by non-Natives, drew settlers and adventurers who, as historians make clear, were "unauthorized personnel" at Wind River Reservation.[33] From the beginning, Indian agents did little if anything to enforce the residency regulations stipulated by the treaty. Their efforts lay largely in exhorting the white population to live peacefully with the Indians, particularly since the Shoshones constituted a much-needed military defense against enemy tribes, including the Lakotas and to a lesser degree the Northern Arapahoes, for whom the Wind River Valley had been important hunting grounds. In continuing this traditional competition, the Eastern Shoshones became, not inadvertently, a bulwark between whites and other Indians.[34]

The central aims of the government agents were also to convince the Shoshones to settle down, so to speak: to stop traveling their customary, seasonal circuits through the region and to stay at Wind River to farm the land. Washakie was a key figure in effecting these shifts, even as he in many ways resisted them. He was instrumental in getting the agents to move their headquarters from Fort Bridger to the reservation and to establish a fort there so the Shoshones would not be solely responsible for defense against invaders. But he had a more difficult time convincing his people to take up permanent farming, since the tribe was powerfully attached to the spring and fall hunts that took them into the western mountains and south into the Great Basin and the eastern plains, far from the reservation. These journeys were important means of acquiring food supplies for the arduous winters at Wind River. By the early 1870s, Washakie was able to convince most of his people to stay on the reservation, but many continued the regular, lengthy rounds and refused to follow his lead. Stamm explains that "Washakie appealed to Irwin [the agent in the early 1870s] to bring in these recalcitrant groups, especially the Shoshones, ostensibly to keep them from getting into trouble." Although Stamm argues that this evidences Washakie's concern for his people and his willingness to act as an "intermediary" for them, it is also clear that he was willing to act on the agent's interests, in conflict with members of his own tribe. Stamm interprets the chief's request to Irwin as a complex statement with multiple meanings: "First, by asking Irwin to help him, Washakie kept in the agent's good graces. Second, the Shoshone leader had learned from extensive experience how to use whites to bolster his tribal control. Finally, he probably had a real fear that if the errant bands joined other Great Basin tribes in hostile actions against whites, his own reputation for peacekeeping would be sullied (which might result in a real loss of power or influence with whites and therefore within his own tribe)."[35]

In this description, Washakie might seem an embodiment of the privileged Native in a colonial environment described by Frantz Fanon in *The Wretched of the Earth,* one who uses his recognition by agents of empire to secure his authority among his people and to further his own interests.[36] Indeed, Washakie's position in the late nineteenth-century political environment of Wind River casts him as the sort of culturally and politically protean figure Fanon had in mind. But Washakie's efforts to get his people to stay and farm instead of roaming the traditional hunting regions were predicated on his assumption (or his hope) that Agent Irwin would be able to supply the tribe with all of its food needs through the winters, and thus his own role as leader would be secure. His centrality was challenged by smaller band leaders from time to time, few of whom would likely have been as effective as Washakie in representing tribal interests in negotiations with whites. In this sense, Washakie's continuous reassertions of his power were aimed at protecting his people's interests, although Irwin's report shows that the agent thought he had convinced Washakie to see nothing but the moral and material benefits of farming as ends in themselves.[37]

Similarly, while Washakie submitted himself to baptism by the Mormons at one point in his life and by the Episcopalian minister at Wind River at another, these baptisms, as Stamm strongly implies without having quite the evidence to overtly claim, were means by which Washakie undertook successfully to cure himself of disease.[38] The fact that several Shoshone baptisms followed Washakie's, like the fact that he had earlier enrolled some of his children in the Episcopal school, evidences the chief's diplomatic pragmatism as much as if not more than they do any substantial "conversion" on his part to Christianity.

In 1878, the Shoshones were taken by surprise when the government decided to locate the Northern Arapahoes on the Wind River

Reservation. For several years, Northern Arapahoe leaders had been lobbying the government to establish a reservation for them in Wyoming. In
1869 a meeting had been arranged by U.S. agents between Washakie and
a group of Arapahoe chiefs to initiate a dialogue that would help prepare
the way for an Arapahoe move to Wind River. The Shoshone leader
opted not to attend. The following year, however, a meeting did take
place, and an accord was reached between the two tribes for the Arapahoes to share the reservation on a temporary basis. Tensions and outright
hostility continued to vex the relationship, however, and arrangements
for the Arapahoes at Wind River were forestalled several times.[39] Eight
years later, Washakie still resisted the idea of the other tribe's move, but
he ultimately consented to the government's plans.[40] In the years that followed, he tried to keep the temporal limits of the agreement in view and
to urge officials to complete the Arapahoes' removal elsewhere, but by
this point, Washakie's primacy at Wind River had been compromised by
the presence of the Arapahoes, who attempted to conciliate the government and its agents to gain favor that rivaled that of the Shoshones.[41]
Stamm writes that as the years progressed, the Shoshones "continued to
follow Shoshonean traditions in combating pressures of increased white
populations and demands of 'civilization,' while Arapahoes emphasized
cooperation with whites in order to gain a homeland."[42] Eventually,
Washakie and his counterpart among the Northern Arapahoes, Black
Coal, came to share their contempt for representatives of Washington,
even as they remained ambivalent toward each other.[43]

    With the diminishment of the traditional economy, a result of life in
the enclosed spaces of the reservation, and the repeated failures of the
agents to secure sufficient food and other goods for all the Indians resid-
ing there, Washakie's power, attached to his ability to protect and provide
for his people, waned. His death in 1900 nevertheless left the Eastern
Shoshone's without organization and without a clear leader.

    Washakie's diplomatic skills secured his position of prominence among
white officials as well as his own people, but it is remarkable that he was
able to please both sets of interests, which were often conflicting, and to
elicit trust from both contingencies over a period of fifty years. What
Henry Stamm makes quite clear in his history of the Wind River Reservation is that Washakie was precisely a diplomat, a negotiator whose concerns were, indeed, to retain his own power, but that power resided in an

intense identification with the Eastern Shoshones, their history, their world views, and their needs.

In 1872, when Congress deputed Felix Brunot to proceed to Wind River in order to settle the ongoing disputes, between Shoshones and whites, that came with the disregarding of settlement regulations in the 1868 Treaty of Fort Bridger, Washakie was presented with the possibility of forgetting, of mourning the past in such a way as to let go of it. Brunot, who wanted the Shoshones to give up the southern portion of the reservation in exchange for land in Crow territory to the north, had several terse exchanges with Washakie in the process of negotiations, and these left both parties mindful of the difficulties they had had with one another since the treaty was struck. Brunot, in attempting to defuse the situation and proceed with the new treaty, advised the Shoshones in lyrical terms about the passage of time: "When the snow melts on the mountains, it is all gone, when the leaves are gone in the fall, you never see the same leaves anymore. So it is with these things that we have not done. They are all gone. They are away behind us. Let us leave them there and forget about them. But we want to begin again right here, and all that is before us, we can see and do."[44]

Rather than taking up Brunot's invitation to forget, Washakie and the Shoshones retained the memory of what they had lost in the past and a clear vision of the pain of what they were about to lose that day. Their refusal to mourn, or to let the anguish of those losses heal in the scar tissue of assimilation, generated an enabling melancholia, in the sense of this term that Eng and Kazanjian propose, which they bequeathed to their descendants at Wind River today.[45] The living memory of what had been, of the facts of loss, and of the pain that it has meant continues to furnish a living Shoshone difference, even as the tribe honors and reenacts Washakie's model of exchange and renegotiation with the forces of colonial authority that surround them.

The statue of Washakie that stands before the tribal offices at Fort Washakie today, with its message of peace and harmony between Shoshones and whites, meets the public as a sign of welcome. The complicating factors of his career with the U.S. government and its agents are not put forward, nor is the devastation that the government's measures wrought on Shoshone political economy. Recognizable reproductions of Washakie's face appear as well in other tribal public venues. He gazes out over the Wind River Range in the tribal logo that appears in stationery and on the Eastern Shoshone Web site. Photographs of Washakie, alone or positioned at the center of group shots, feature prominently in the pamphlets and histories available at the Eastern Shoshone Tribal Cultural Center. The ubiquity of Washakie's image and its over-seeing, benign authority invest him with the enduring role of tribal father for the modern or late colonial age. His statue, like Sacajawea's, looms large, but in contrast to her memorials, commemorations of Washakie emphasize his overt, unquestioned presence at the center of Eastern Shoshone history; and unlike the iconic woman, he speaks. Words from Washakie's speeches are reiterated in pamphlets and histories available at the Shoshone Cultural Center and the tribal offices, and his name is inscribed in the 1868 Treaty of Fort Bridger, on display at the center and posted on the tribal Web site.

Official and authoritative, Washakie presides over present-day Eastern Shoshone public self-representation as a patriarch who continues to frame his people's identity as a specific tribal collective descended from the buffalo hunters of the southern Rockies and the northwestern plains. While memorials to Sacajawea emphasize her roles as captive, explorer, wanderer, and the lost woman who finds her way to Wind River in old age, Washakie is in charge not only of his own life but of his peoples' well-being. In this sense, he figures as a stable presence among them. Sacajawea's silent emergence at the interstices of Shoshone history, in contrast to his visible and audible paternity, evokes a dimly outlined, disputed ancestor who embodies the loss and dispossession of the people who claim her. While stories of Sacajawea told at Wind River overtly dramatize her final separation and distance from white interests, Washakie's status as cautious diplomat images the disciplined negotiation with whites that he demanded of his progeny, a discipline that meant resisting as much as possible those gestures of the whites that threatened to weaken Shoshone political and cultural hegemony, as his actions demonstrated, in contrast to some of his most publicly remembered statements.

Washakie's grave, located in a small cemetery that is named and reserved for him and his family near the center of Fort Washakie, bespeaks the honor and importance of this man whose figure has had such a ubiquitous presence in contemporary tribal public self-representation. A large obelisk that rises some ten feet from the ground and is visible above the

Bureau of Indian Affairs' subsidized housing and the fences and cars that surround the cemetery marks the grave. Washakie lies among his people, his memorial in the sightline of the spaces of everyday life, his figure a crucial emblem of modern identity.

The homage to Sacajawea at the graveyard dedicated to her outside the boundaries of town and the odd mixture of cultural markers that decorate the grave itself, in contrast to Washakie's resting place, seem to evoke a complex identity, even if the name of the woman honored there is clearly given. To the extent that the combination of sacramental Shoshone objects and things of popular culture makes the grave difficult to read, the role of Sacajawea in Shoshone memory becomes rather evanescent. Her power as a representative figure of the Shoshone people today lies mostly in her place within the national culture of the United States, the society from which she may well have finally distanced herself in later life. Washakie, having less national notoriety, stands nevertheless more prominently in the local environment, distinctly a representative of his people. But in spite of the contrasts between their functions in tribal public rhetoric, Sacajawea and Washakie both focus the memories of earlier phases of the long colonial history and the compromises that frame the tribe's contemporary situation. In his sturdy imaging of tribal diplomatic intelligence and simultaneous resistance to U.S. interests, and in her allegorically peripatetic life and condition of being lost to her own past and people, both of these iconic Shoshone figures demonstrate the unsought effects of having to "deal" with the political, military, economic, and social forces of the United States. At the same time, they both tell the story of the tribe's marginalization from the material prosperity of European America. In these functions, Sacajawea and Washakie foster in their distinct ways the refusal to forget what has been lost, the continuousness of cultural difference that has attended marginalization, and the project of being properly recognized in public self-representations of a historic Eastern Shoshone identity.

THE POWWOW PRIMER AND THE EASTERN SHOSHONE INDIAN DAYS POWWOW

The practice of shaping public self-representations that elicit recognition and access to the larger economy while at the same time emphasizing cultural difference extends to the great public event of the Eastern

Shoshone calendar, the Shoshone Indian Days Powwow. Indian Days celebrates the signing of the 1868 Treaty of Fort Bridger.[46] Like the Navajo Treaty of 1868, the Shoshone treaty is an ambivalent document, simultaneously an official codification of U.S. policy in taking over Shoshone lands and a contract stipulating for the protection of Eastern Shoshone reservation boundaries as well as the people themselves from harm by whites and enemy tribes. The treaty is celebrated at Indian Days because it constitutes legal recognition of Eastern Shoshone territory, however diminished that territory was by 1868.[47] In addition, recognition of the homeland is implicitly recognition of the distinctiveness of Shoshone polity and culture. At the same time, though, the dancing and other features of the powwow can be read as commemorations of loss that lend a more weighty undercurrent to the events.

As the principle form of ostensibly secular, inter-tribal ceremonial gathering in which non-Natives are invited to participate, powwows have become an important means for tribal self-representation to off-reservation audiences. Robert DesJarlait describes the powwow as a "community-based" but nevertheless "inter-cultural event."[48] At most powwows, the hosting community invites members of other tribes and bands as well as non-Native dancers and observers to participate, whether the event at issue is a traditional powwow or a "contest" pow-wow, where material prizes are awarded for what judges deem the best dancing.

The genealogy of powwow in itself illustrates the form's heterogeneous outreach. Clyde Ellis summarizes powwow's generic origins as "part ceremony and part public show, with roots in Indian and non-Indian worlds."[49] Drawing on oral knowledge, Ojibwé writer Robert DesJarlait locates the origins of powwow's central event, dancing, in "the dawn of humankind when . . . Original Man, who could not walk or crawl, took his first two steps with his right foot, one harsh, one soft, on Mother Earth [which] became the dance step used . . . by today's male traditional dancers."[50] The powwow itself, however, derives its name from the Algonquian *powwaw*, which English colonists in New England translated as "priest." Ritualistic acts involving other members of the community often accompanied the *powwaw*'s practices, which included healing as well as divination and wisdom teaching.[51] The name for the religious practitioner eventually came to be used, among Anglo as well as Native speakers, as the term for the healing event and its ceremonial apparatus.

DesJarlait, like Clyde Ellis, describes the antecedents of powwow in the Hethuska dances of the Plains warrior societies. These dances and the songs and drumming that accompanied them were conducted to honor specific military actions and to rehearse spiritual knowledge that helped frame and interpret those events. Like other warrior societies elsewhere, those that conducted the Hethuska dance took responsibility for a variety of social needs in the community, from welfare to medicine to the supervising of rituals. Maintaining such broad roles, their acts as warriors were extensively contextualized within the tribe, and heroic martial events were repeated in the stylized forms of dance, songs, and drum. In this sense, the warrior dances exhibited what David Lopez and Talal Asad, among others, have described as the centrality of practice in religion, the element that binds and enables religion to reproduce itself.

As Ellis and DesJarlait describe them, these performance styles traveled up and down the Great Plains, to the north and east for hundreds of years, inspiring and supplementing other cultural performances and displays that helped to negotiate identity formations in pre-American indigenous history.[52] With the growth of U.S. power in the nineteenth century, the warrior societies and their dances came under suspicion by the Indian Office for their potential as sources of resistance to American occupation and even of revolutionary action. Like their forebears among the missionaries of New Spain, New England, and New France, Indian Bureau agents and their superintendents often understood dancing as an important and dangerous nutrient of Native psychology and a means for the warrior or medicine societies that hosted the dances to exert influence among the people at large.[53] Speaking in general terms, dance, as a means of religious practice and an embodied vehicle of belief for many non-Western faiths, has had a difficult career in the Christian West, where it has been abhorred at least since the Protestant Reformation as a licentious, demonically inspired form. Anglo-American distaste for dance on religious grounds clearly influenced political and social attitudes toward dance later in U.S. history. In order to eradicate the beliefs and practices they thought stood in the way of the introduction of their own social and cultural ideals, late nineteenth- and early twentieth-century U.S. government bureaucrats initiated a program of censoring

Native ceremonial dance on reservations throughout the trans-Mississippi region.[54] These efforts had mixed results, of course, suppressing certain dances for some years, particularly the Sun Dance and the Ghost Dance, but inadvertently prompting the establishment of secret dances and dance societies that wielded great influence beyond the agents' view.[55] In any case, the dances that survived the period of censorship returned to public community life as important means of performing oppressed identities.

In her memoirs of growing up as the daughter of a missionary on the Wind River Reservation in the late nineteenth century, Elinor Markley wrote, "At one time the Department of Indian Affairs prohibited the Sundance on the Reservation, but the dance was in abeyance for a few years only. Since then it has been held regularly every year."[56] In 1933, during the tenure of Indian Commissioner John Collier, the BIA policy of forbidding these dances was reversed, even though individual agents still frowned upon it and for many years continued to do what they could to discourage it. David Whitehorse writes about this period that "when the pow-wow tradition officially re-emerged in both the Northern and Southern Plains in the Collier days, it . . . possess[ed] a large repertoire drawn from the various participating tribes. Each regional tradition was fully developed and viable in its own right and there was little interaction between or sharing of one with the other."[57] Strengthened by the experience of being forced underground, warrior society dances reemerged as perhaps more powerful enactments of tribal identities than they had been before the colonizers suppressed them.

The fact that contemporary powwow dancing often derives from a common repertoire of Plains genres has been cited as evidence by some academics for a growing "pan-tribalism."[58] This term is, however, invoked with caution by most scholars of powwow, since it has come to be associated with the argument that the mixture of styles and general currency of certain dances are evidence that specific tribal knowledges and practices are dying. In this view, the sharing of forms and techniques is a step in an inevitable assimilation process and presages the dissolution of "Native American" as an ethnological category. The problem with this view is that it reduces the relationships and exchanges that events such as powwows afford to evidence for a single, synthetic identity. The argument repeats the problems of "melting pot" thinking in relation to U.S.

cultural processes generally, problems that were addressed in great degree by the turn to multiculturalism as a paradigm for the plurality of cultural legacies in the Untied States. Powwow's extension of the invitation to "mix it up" does not mean that the identification of certain dances or dance methods with specific tribes is erased simply because they are shared. The preferable term among powwow goers as well as among most scholars is "inter-tribalism," which suggests a mingling of different tribal forms instead of a melting of differences into a single, synthesized Indianism.[59] This is an important and somewhat tricky issue, since the prevailing ethos of powwow is openness and gregarious interchange, while tribal identities are put forward carefully as the foundation of collective self-representation. Perhaps a more plausible way to understand the issue is that, rather than fostering a syntheticism which broadens and threatens to weaken indigenous identity, powwows have helped to bolster specific tribal identities by providing means by which those identities are, in Clyde Ellis's words, "redefined, contested, and negotiated" in relation to the myriad ethnic, generational, and economic influences to which they are intentionally open.[60]

Historians of powwow point to the inheritances from Hethuska and other Native dance ceremonials as important to contemporary styles, but they also reference influences that might be rather surprising to those less familiar with these genealogies. Certain of the more common designs and featured programs of contemporary powwows derive, for example, from Buffalo Bill Cody's Wild West show of the late nineteenth and early twentieth centuries: the grand entry, led by veterans carrying the flag of the United States; the centrality of the master of ceremonies; and the reign of a tribal or powwow queen and her attendants throughout the event.[61] Daniel Gelo writes that the powwow MC inherits his styles not only from Wild West forebears but from Anglo carnival barkers, preachers, and even television game and talk show hosts.[62] The rodeo component of Wild West programs, highlighting feats of horseback riding and cattle roping of the Indians' nemeses, the heroic cowboys, are commonly featured as simultaneous events in contemporary powwow programs.[63]

Powwow's multicultural orientation is evident as well in its function as a medium of communication with the larger society. Displays of dance styles, costumes, and give-away ethics, for instance, can help instruct outsiders about tribal histories and ideologies.[64] Even non-Native "hobbyists" of Native American cultures, drawn to powwows for their aura of Indian authenticity, stand to gain different perspectives from the experience. Karl Eschbach and Kalman Applbaum note the irony in the idea that "powwows' resonance with non-Indian stereotypes about Native cultures makes them compelling displays of cultural authenticity."[65] The awareness of the presence of non-Native audiences and the address to them in powwows are part of what Victoria Sanchez calls "an effort to increase common understanding of Native America." Sanchez adds, however, that "powwow stresses American Indian commonalities in relation to mainstream American culture while also stressing tribal individuality within the American Indian community."[66]

If powwows exhibit such a mixed lineage, if they offer this "alternate form of communication" to make Anglos better understand Native histories and styles of self-representation, and if "the presence of members of the general public, as welcomed touristic spectators and potential participants, is actively encouraged," then they seem to function more overtly as means for the rehearsal of ceremonial actions and the renegotiation of tribal identities.[67]

The Eastern Shoshone Indian Days Powwow at Wind River Reservation is hosted every summer in the last week of June. The three-day celebration is a well-organized, carefully scheduled gathering to which members of this and other Shoshone and non-Shoshone tribal communities as well as non-Natives are invited. Indian Days is an opportunity for Anglo friends, Native and non-Native residents of the reservation, as well as complete strangers to mix it up with the people of Fort Washakie. Indeed, Indian Days is described by participants, by the master of ceremonies, and in promotional literature as an opportunity for Native friends and relatives, non-Shoshone as well as Shoshone, to encounter each other after long separations or to meet for the first time. In common with other powwows, Indian Days thus serves not only as an important annual social event, but as a means for members of different Shoshone groups—Eastern, Western, Bannock, Lemhi—to perform their collective identities as an articulated Shoshone cultural body.[68]

There is some irony in the fact that many of the descendants of warriors who sponsored the nineteenth-century dance ceremonies which Indian agents saw as provocative of rebellious activity are proud veterans of the modern wars of the United States: World War II, Korea, Vietnam, and Iraq. As the veterans enter the powwow grounds at the head of the Indian Days grand entry parade, the MC narrates the warrior biography of each flag bearer, not simply in a display of tribal patriotism to the United States, but of the veterans' memberships in the warrior societies revered in the local community.[69]

Behind the veterans in the grand entry parade, the powwow "royalty" appear, consisting of a tribal or powwow queen and attendants. At Indian Days in the summer of 2003, the Shoshone Indian Days Queen, who had been waiting for the event in the bleachers with a very European-looking, blonde, and fair-skinned young man, walked between two other pageant winners in a stately, subtle two-step. Her high, beaded crown bore the Shoshone rose on a white background. Her dress was draped with strands of shell and silver beads. Like Miss Navajo Nation and the royalty of Shiprock and other fairs, she was chosen for her ability to speak the tribal language, her knowledge of important dances, songs, practices, and the ideas associated with them. Rachel Buff, one of the few scholars who have written about Indian princesses, offers the following commentary on the institution: "The Indian Princess is a cultural myth that emanates from the myopia of cultural contact and the myriad oppressions of colonial control. The "princess comes from nowhere in precontact history, but becomes a standard feature at the powwow, a hybrid of postcolonial performances. Winning a Princess title represents fluency in various conceptions of tradition."[70]

Buff traces the figure of the powwow or tribal queen to the mythology of the Indian princess in colonialist literature and iconography, as well as to the rituals of U.S. beauty pageants.[71] Given these inheritances, the moniker of "hybrid postcolonial performances" is perfectly apt; but, as Buff herself notes, the institution of the powwow queen serves as a means for Indian women to draw recognition not only to themselves but to native styles of femininity inherited through Shoshonean more than through mainstream lines of influence and "circulating through an alternative media network: powwow circuits and their native-authored iconography."[72]

While the color guard leading the grand entry parade at Indian Days in 2003 included an Anglo veteran, and while the parade of dancers that followed included several Euro-American women in Native dress, not all outsiders at the powwow seemed to be openly "welcomed" by the

Shoshone hosts. Two young men in particular were treated with what was visibly polite forbearance. One had painted the upper part of his face a blaring white and the lower part a bright, shamrock green. His head was ringed with a mink band, and across his shoulder and around his waist he sported Balmoural plaids. His overweight friend wore a shirt with arrow designs that was too tight to completely button, and draped from his head to his shoulders was an elaborate and exotic array of white fox furs. As this pair lumbered around the perimeter of the dance grounds waiting for the grand entry to begin, an older woman watched them pass with a wary, sidelong glace and an expression that seemed to say, "What will they think of next?" A drum circle of young, serious-looking Shoshone musicians stopped what seemed to be a focused discussion of strategy as the colorful pair passed before them. When the two had gone by, the entire group of seven or eight drummers silently convulsed and slapped their thighs in muffled laughter.

David Whitehorse summarizes my own sense that the "welcome" extended to non-Native outsiders to Indian Days, as to many other tribal powwows, is more of a concept than a realized practice. Whitehorse writes that for many non-Indians, a powwow "is an event to be curiously viewed, but always from a safe distance."[73] Indeed, every summer the Wind River Heritage Association, a non-Indian organization located in the city of Riverton, hosts a weekly Powwow Primer at the town park during the summer to address a perceived discomfort among Riverton residents with the prospect of venturing onto the reservation, which surrounds the town, to attend tribal public events like Indian Days. Ernie Over, editor of the local newspaper and one of the Powwow Primer's organizers, explained to me that since the locals don't go to the powwows, "we bring the powwow to them."[74]

Over compares the multicultural mingling of powwow with that of the Anglo tradition of rendezvous. These multicultural gatherings between the various Native and non-Native constituencies in the Wind River Valley made possible the exchange of goods on a broad scale in the nineteenth century, particularly the products of Native market hunting and trapping, as well as gambling, drinking, and wife buying. In spite of the debauchery with which it is associated, not to mention the status of women it upheld, the rendezvous heritage appears to be the source of a good deal of pride among the contemporary European American population of Riverton. Referenced in any number of town logos and ceremonial themes, the trappers, mountain men, and the rendezvous are important metaphors in Riverton public identity. Every summer the 1838 Rendezvous Association organizes a reenactment at which participants dress, speak, and behave as if they were participants in the nineteenth-century originals. The four-day event, one of many of its kind held in the state of Wyoming each year, is largely a celebration of the Anglo-European American legacy, although a certain amount of playing Indian is part of the program.[75]

In many ways, the Powwow Primer appears to be an attempt to use the traditions of Anglo Wyoming rendezvous to frame and interpret powwow. Dressed in mountain man costume, with fox and coyote furs draped over his shoulders, Over introduces the program with a brief history of rendezvous and of Anglo-Native camaraderie at Wind River. He explains what historical research demonstrates, that before the establishment of the reservation and the systematic presence of the U.S. government in the region, European American trappers and traders frequented the Wind River Valley, often in large groups or bands. Social and marital relations between these mountain men and Shoshone band members, like the friendship between Jim Bridger and Washakie mentioned earlier, developed with the fur and hide trade.[76] From the early to mid-nineteenth century, rendezvous among the various groups, including other tribal bands, took place annually.

At the Powwow Primer in the summer of 2003, which took place just days before the Indian Days Powwow at Fort Washakie, Over introduced an Arapahoe scholar who described some of the dances common to real powwows. Following her introduction, dancers from the reservation, hired by the Wind River Heritage Association, took turns whirling across the stage in full regalia, demonstrating the grass dance, fancy dance, shawl dance, and jingle dance, while the scholar commented on the movements and on the skills and achievements of particular dancers. Finally, the "inter-tribal," the most gregarious of powwow dances, which everyone is urged to join, offered an ideal enactment of just the sort of friendliness the event was designed to orchestrate. A large group of high school volunteers, from a Wisconsin Christian organization, who were helping to build and repair homes on the reservation was seated in the grass, beaming up at the stage in rapt attention. With the announcement of the inter-tribal dance, the performers came down from the stage and drifted into the audience, choosing partners for the dance. A young man in elaborate fancy dance regalia who had been one of the stars of the show stepped up to a young blonde woman in jeans and a pony tail, extending his hand. The two leapt happily to the stage and led the curving line of paired Native and Anglo dancers. A genial elderly man asked me to join him, so I got up on the stage to play at powwowing along with everybody else.

As Ernie Over returned to the microphone, horns and sirens started to blare from the street adjacent to the park and threatened to drown his words. A troop of young Indian men suddenly emerged into view, parading down the main boulevard of Riverton on horseback, their fists in the air in what looked like a gesture of victory. At first it seemed as if they might have come to challenge the Powwow Primer for some reason or other, but Over quickly explained that an impromptu celebration had been organized to honor a Native woman who had just returned from a tour of duty in Iraq. She was being treated to what soldiers commonly come home to in Riverton: a ride down the main street in one of the city's fire engines, but in this case the soldier was accompanied by a troop of Shoshones on horseback.

The ironies were spinning. The riders were honoring the war itself by framing it in terms of their own warrior traditions, while in the same public space of the town the Anglos were offering a rendezvous interpretation of Native powwow dances. These dances in their origins had been ceremonials for warrior societies that directed their efforts against enemies, which included the United States. The mutual appropriations and revisions in these performances seemed in a certain sense to exemplify the cultural bounty and generous exchange typical of both powwow and rendezvous. But other meanings floated through the air as the two groups carried on in sight of each other, and the sound of hoofbeats, the sirens, and the cheering clashed with the words emanating from the band shell in a cacophony of incomprehensible noise. The dancers on the stage were gone in moments, and as I made my way to the car, I passed by a few of them who looked at me from beneath feathered headgear and bobbing roaches without the faintest shadow of a smile.

ALTHOUGH THE POWWOW DISPLAYS anything but the melancholic moods of statuary and funerary space at Wind River where Sacagawea and Washakie are honored, given its overt gregariousness and its celebration of the joys of collective self-identification, it does, in effect, repeat the histories of extended, repeated loss that was and is colonization by making plain the degree of hybridization in contemporary Native ceremonial forms. It also, however, shows how the presence of Native and non-Native styles of dance, music, and pageantry does not constitute blends or harmonious mixtures so much as tensions and contrasts which allow those histories to remain open, as living wounds and ironies out of which the present is built and in which Native American difference so often anchors itself. These open wounds, as it were, remember and repeat the pain of the loss of homelands and tribal political sovereignty. The memories and the wounds they bear, the wounds they are, carved and narrated in the memorials to Sacajawea and Washakie, get performed in powwow dancing. Ann Axtmann speculates about these memories as repeated communications to other dancers and to spectators in what she calls the "performative action" of powwow: "Resistance to oppression and great ingenuity and strength in the face of horror is part of the story [of Native American modern history]. As people live and remember through the flesh, blood, mind, and soul, moving bodies express and communicate the intensity of those experiences."[77]

In Axtmann's reading, the dances thus become the means of "positive embodiment of what it means 'to be Indian.'" She aptly cites Michel de Certeau's summary of the history of resistance to conquest "marked on the Indian's body as much as it is recorded in transmitted accounts." De Certeau's commentary on "this inscribing of an identity built upon pain" concludes that "the body is memory."[78] In the repetition of dance styles inherited through generations of practice and in the revisions of movement, gesture, and regalia that mark their transmission, "the collective memory of the social body"—not only the memory of the past but of the pains that mediate time and space between then and now—might be said to take the form of melancholia in Eng and Kazanjian's sense, as a productive attitude that engages with history as if it were open ended, a still painful, open wound that even now provokes resistance to the smooth closures of widely accepted narratives of history.[79] This refusal to let go of the past, a refusal to mourn properly, in Freud's sense of registering the pain of loss and allowing the wound to heal and to "get over" the loss, sponsors a paradoxically lively, celebratory event in which the participants' impacted, collective memories restore and reconfirm a Shoshone identity. The difference anchored by this melancholic resistance to getting over it is the point where the off-reservation audience is not invited, not shown, except to display the withholding of knowledges and practices that cannot be communicated across the sociocultural divide.

The non-Native streams of influence in powwow, the visible presence of mainstream popular culture, and the overtly welcoming gestures to non-Native visitors from on as well as off the reservation, taken together, mold what looks in many ways like a postmodern, mixed occasion. The Native history of powwow, the melancholic remembrance it performs, and the reconfirmation of identity the performance stimulates boldly project a coherent, specifically Shoshone style of being, even while Indian Days, like many other powwows, attributes its dance styles to a cannon of non-Shoshone, Plains traditions. These two perspectives invited by Eastern Shoshone tribal self-representations at the Indian Days Powwow—the continuousness of a specifically Shoshone style of being and a trans-tribal mode influenced by U.S. popular culture—flicker back and forth as the mind's eye moves, like the images in a hologram. These simultaneous but different visions stand side by side in complex, tense negotiations of postmodern Shoshone identity where traditional styles are prominent. Such tensions, visibly displayed in the community, are for various historical reasons treated as if they are accepted. This is not to say that they are not cause for amusement, or that the ironies go unrecognized. In fact, as self-representations, these accepted contradictions seem to work as effective means of pointing up difference: what are logically misplaced and laughably proximate reconfirm their respective proper spheres and repeat the pain of colonial cross-over in a performance of Native, Eastern Shoshone collective identity that promises to continue into future generations.

CHAPTER 4

Keeping History at Acoma Pueblo

THE MUSEUM AND INFORMATION CENTER at Acoma
Pueblo, like the Shoshone Tribal Cultural Center at Fort Washakie on the
Wind River Reservation, occupies a special place in relation to the village where it is located and whose culture it offers to public view. The
structure stands alone beneath the imposing mesa where the ancient
Acoma village of Sky City is situated. Visitors are allowed to enter the
village only in the company of native guides. Acoma Pueblo's museum
and village tour work to display a public face that teaches something
about Acoma aesthetic styles and the historical past to non–Native
visitors. At the same time, these public self-representations keep local
knowledge and spiritual traditions fairly well out of the picture. The
tribe's newer public enterprise, Sky City Casino, promises no lessons or
information about the tribe at all. The forty-foot-tall sign that blinks in
neon color from the exit ramp encourages tourists, truckers, and bored
drivers passing along Interstate 40 to stop in for a tryst with chance in an
Indian gaming environment. Some of the design motifs and advertisements for Sky City Casino project a certain "Indian" ambience, but
these are very attenuated gestures, deployed as they are at Foxwoods for
the sake of evoking an attractive recreational context for gambling. Unlike Foxwoods, though, Sky City Casino does not make much of an effort to authenticize the framework of Indian gaming. The interests of this
enterprise are simply and clearly to make money for a tribal nation
whose economy and sovereignty have been continuously challenged by
the many negative effects of colonialism. My interest in this chapter is
to show how the Acoma Pueblo has stepped outside the somber walls of
its ancient redoubt to make a strategic entry into the marketplace of
America for the sake of restoring tribal economic strength and political
sovereignty.

THE MUSEUM AND VILLAGE TOUR

Pottery has a prominent place in the museum's collection of historical and cultural artifacts. The cases are filled with pieces dating back as far
as the tenth century, many of which are placed beside recently made clay
pots that resemble them precisely in shape and design. This display of continued competence in the ancient craft certifies the traditionalism of
present-day potters; it also defines these works as copies, and as products
of an effort to duplicate earlier technologies and aesthetics as if to demonstrate an uninterrupted inheritance of them. Other display cases offer the
paraphernalia of nineteenth-century battles: bows and arrows, guns, war
bonnets, U.S. Army uniforms and charts, maps, texts that trace the course
of Acoma's history with the Europeans since the sixteenth century.[1]

The home of the objects in the museum and the subject of its historical narrative, the original Acoma Pueblo itself, is visible from the
doorway, approachable via a short, winding drive up the steep mesa wall.
It is a much visited site; tens of thousands of people come each year to
see the village.[2] After registering and paying an admission fee to visit Sky
City, tourists are shuttled to the venerable pueblo in small buses. Once
atop the mesa, a guide leads each group through a range of narrow streets
and narrates Acoma's history. Pottery is for sale from vendors who appear
along the tour route. Picture taking is permitted with the purchase of a
ticket at the information center, but no photographs are allowed of the
church interior, the grave yard, or the pueblo's residents without their
permission.

The guides' performative styles are crucial components of the tour
narratives. Pacing and intonation, gestures, body movements, and the
spaces maintained between themselves and the visitors work not only to
deliver information to the tourists, but to orchestrate relationships between the guests and Acoma, as represented by the guide. When I first
visited the pueblo, our guide was a young man who wore dark glasses
throughout the tour. He kept his distance during the bus ride, only in-
troducing himself as we arrived at the top of the mesa. After stating the
rules, he led us off the bus into a small square where he began narrating
Acoma's history from the thirteenth-century settlement to the present.
At one time inhabited by more than a thousand people, the pueblo now
has about thirty year-round occupants who take up some thirteen of the

4-1. Sky City Tour sign at the foot of old Acoma Pueblo mesa

roughly four hundred houses; the rest are used during the summer and holidays. Sky City is still important, however, as a site for ceremonial events to which most members of the tribe regularly return.

The invitation to view the village as an object of the spectator's interest was patently and visibly limited. The narrow channels of the tourist's Acoma, sealed off from the domestic interiors of sparsely occupied homes; the few residents, whose exchanges with the visitors have only to do with selling goods; and the rules of the tour, which control the visitor's visual experience as well as movements, work to wall off the unvisited quarters of the pueblo.

The tour does much more than point backward to the remote past, for the guides call attention to the tour itself, a practice which can have the curious effect of seeming to enlist visitors themselves in the demonstrations so that we become self-conscious strangers whose presence in the village is a heavily implied component of the conclusion to the historical narrative. As I will argue, visitors are given lectures that tell them not only about the pueblo itself, but about the role of Europe and European America in Acoma's development. In addition, for visitors the embodied experience of walking through the circumscribed spaces of the village, encountering its residents, and responding to the guide's information and performance mannerisms has the effect of including them as actors in an event that dramatizes the effects of colonial relations, in the present as well as the past. Our comments and questions echoed off the close walls as if they'd been asked many times before, and the confined spaces through which we walked seemed themselves to prescribe body move-ment and posture. With little other activity in which to contextualize our own, we seemed to be players on an otherwise nearly empty stage. We had paid to look at the pueblo itself and were given an opportunity to see ourselves in Acoma as part of the bargain.

The guide informed us that, like most contemporary people of Acoma, he lived off of the mesa, where schools and jobs were within eas-ier reach. Indeed, during our visit about twenty-five or thirty people turned out to sell goods, and a few others emerged here and there, going about their business without seeming to concern themselves with us. Aside from these, we only saw other tourists, who, like mirrors of our-selves, would appear now and then in groups at the end of a street or across a plaza.

Thus the pueblo appeared remarkably empty. Evidence of people going about their affairs behind screened doors, not participating in the business of the tours, did little to alter the appearance of the village as a staged display of itself, not as it might have looked in precolonial times when more people would have been visible in a more bustling daily life, but as precisely an emptied space where that life once pertained. The staged representation centered on the sparse and silent remnant of some style of being resonant in its absence, implicitly remembered in its overtly demonstrated lack. If, in its remoteness, the pueblo looks discon-nected from the evidence of historical and cultural change that surrounds it, the silent emptiness speaks to the losses which that history has meant as well as to a refusal to fill in the erosions with cultural forms and styles of the dominant society. The empty lanes and walls of Acoma Pueblo dis-play the very experience of loss as a continuous, lived consciousness and as an acted-out memory that counters the forces of assimilation. In addition, the palpable resonance of the empty cultural spaces simultaneously suggests and holds back from tourists any references to Acoma religion or to the contemporary cultural practices that belong to the pueblo exclusively.

Our guide's narrative worked in concert and counterpoint with this chiseled experience. His distantly ironic tone and the memorized sound of his material kept the fact of our being "on tour" continuously in focus. His basic rhetorical method was to string together different kinds of information: the measurements of a wall, a particular practice of contemporary life, an anecdote of local folklore. Often these lists concluded with a brief narrative of the many horrors committed by the Spaniards at Acoma during the sixteenth and seventeenth centuries. Finally, without a pause or change in pitch, he would ask in an uninviting and monotone voice, "Are there any questions?"

His discourse had the rather potent effect of bringing his listeners into the history he narrated by making European predecessors as much a part of the story as his own ancestors were. But perhaps more than the particular data, the tone of irony in his oration had this strangely effective way of implicating the listeners' culture in the account of his own.

As far as I could tell, this strategy seemed to have little effect on the majority of tourists in our group. Most of them seemed uninterested in questions of history or culture and chose instead to ask about the physical construction of the village. A gregarious older man, rotund and flushed from the walk and the heat, was particularly curious about the composition of the adobe, and his probing led to questions by others on the same topic, as well as to the matter of the shift in building trends from adobe to brick. Similar discussion arose around the issue of pottery: When did people begin using ceramic instead of simple clay, and what were the differences in firing techniques? A khaki-clad, tense-looking young man asked a few tentatively formulated questions about the density of walls, strength of beams, and so on. And there were others who, like this fellow's companion, covered in white cotton and veiled in gauze, never touched or questioned anything.

To answer such questions, the guide had ready at hand all sorts of information about heights, depths, and lengths of nearly every structure we encountered. Similar exchanges recurred several times during our visit, particularly after the guide had been describing some of the atrocities committed by the Spaniards. His "Are there any questions?" had the odd effect of eliciting queries of this sort about building materials. Its way of deflecting attention to the simple materiality of Acoma's construction left the unaddressed questions of history dangling in hollow air.

Spatial measurements and the construction of boundaries are regular fare of historical and archaeological tourism, and our guide performed his role in the expected, conventional manner, responding to these questions on their own terms and in comprehensive detail. Nevertheless, it was impossible to resist thinking there was something allegorically appropriate in the discourse about the composition of walls and ceilings. These data give the measure of the material dimensions of Acoma, and to that extent they can be said to provide real, rational knowledge of the place. At the same time, the list of figures helped reinforce in the mind's eye images of walls and boundaries that sealed Acoma from our sight. Boundaries are also very important in other Native American societies, where spiritual as well as geographical and political limits are crucial to the articulation of community and identity. But rather than eliciting transgressive desire, as boundaries commonly do in European American culture, they are respected and preserved as the marks that indicate home. All the talk about walls and what materials are used to construct them seemed to me like a walking trope for the barriers existing between our guide and his culture, on the one hand, and the traditions of the Anglo tourists, on the other, which include the desire to know about the Indians and Acoma.

The guide's presentation seemed rich enough to satisfy familiar touristic desires at the same time that it could be said to position the tourist as one who is also in a sense returning to Acoma, to a scene preserved from history where the determinations of European culture in the lives of indigenous people are massively evident. The role of guide allowed him to lecture his audience, in subtle terms, on the details of a limited number of horrors in a history that belongs to European American listeners as much as it does to the Indians. The stories of Spaniards enslaving Acoma Natives and throwing reluctant or recalcitrant workers over the rim of the mesa, of beatings, mutilations, and forced conversions, offered tourists the opportunity to recognize the European past in the conditions and situations that the guide narrated about the Acoma past.

Looked at in this way rather than as an inauthentic reproduction of Native American life, the tourist's Acoma would seem to be the product of a concerted and well-organized effort on the part of the people who claim the pueblo as their home to preserve a traditional lifestyle from the curiosity of strangers. But rather than speculate on the traditional content of what we don't see, it seems more plausible to consider what we do see and what we are not told unless we ask. The relation of touristic representation to actuality is difficult to trace, since the tourist market is certainly part of actuality and since it is continuously being renegotiated.[3] But to pursue the issue of traditionalism evinced by this particular tour through Acoma a bit further, a few more details of conversations with our guide might be useful.

My companion asked the guide at one point how extensively traditional religious practices are followed in present-day Acoma. He replied that they are still quite active, but added that this does not mean people have relinquished Catholicism. Neither does it suggest some sort of hybrid faith. Given the intensity of their ancestors' sacrifices in the long and bloody process of the establishment of the Spaniards' religion, he remarked, the contemporary Acoma people feel that they must honor their Catholic inheritance, or the ancestors will have suffered and died in vain. But the two sets of religious practices are kept largely separate. The guide was very clear on this point, as if he particularly wanted to disabuse people of the notion that Native American Catholicism, like the Native American Church, always mixes indigenous with Christian forms and practices.[4] But he gave no information about native religion, other than to explain what the kiva was and to point out a few other places in the village where festival events take place. He offered more information on the history of Christianity in the pueblo. Again, in this sense the tour and accompanying narrative concentrated attention on the European presence in Acoma's history and kept the data of the guide's own culture and ritualistic traditions to a minimum.

The two centers of religious practice at Acoma, the church and the kiva, seem to illustrate this point in their very different architectural forms. The disparity suggests the respectively announced and unannounced relations to spirituality that they represent. Between them, one sees a contrast something like that between the Vietnam and Lincoln Memorials in Washington, D.C.[5] These secular temples, located in close range of each other, differ markedly in their conceptualizations of the histories they recall. The Lincoln Memorial, projecting the transcendent authority of U.S. democracy in the figure of the hallowed president, rises nearly one hundred feet above the park where it is erected, visible from miles away, while the Vietnam Wall is almost hidden, designed to work with the landscape to evoke a different but equally "deep" range of emotions. St. Stephen's at Acoma, like many European Catholic Churches, rises well above the heights of all other structures in the village, and its two bell towers reach upward for another eight feet or so. The crosses planted above them fade at a distance, but there is no mistaking the Christian design of the highly visible building itself. The victory of the mission over indigenous spiritual and political powers is advertised across the land. The kiva, on the other hand, sits in a row of houses made from the same adobe stucco and brick, largely unnoticeable from the outside. Beyond our guide's identification of it, there was no evidence that this particular structure was other than one of the houses. We were not taken inside; and we were only told a few details about how one enters the kiva and how long one stays, who goes in and who doesn't.

I will not attempt to analyze the differences in conceptualization and practice of spirituality that the church and kiva suggest, since they have been extensively addressed elsewhere by scholars of comparative religion.[6] But it is interesting to note that the contrasting notions of power that the buildings themselves imply seem to have had curious effects in the guide's own sense of religious identity. Whatever powerful spiritualities are sponsored by the kiva, they do not demand overt expressions of belief, and they certainly do not fuel evangelical action outside the community. The Catholic Church, on the other hand, has been notorious for these very practices, and its political power through history has left its mark in contemporary life. The kiva's silent reverence for the spiritualities it hosts and the lack of attention it calls to itself seemed to be respected in our guide's spare references to the religion practiced there and in his insistence on its differences from Catholicism. My companion, whose own religious imagination is rather eclectic, asked the guide where he stood on these matters. He replied that he was "sort of stuck in between" things, but offered nothing more to explain what this meant. He candidly admitted that he did not know the old stories very well, since they had been passed along to him, as he claimed they often are, by grandparents who hadn't really listened very carefully. Nor, he said, does he speak Keresan, the language of Acoma Pueblo.

These self-descriptions could have been easily understood as evidence that the older Acoma cultural forms and practices in general have not survived the generations of competition with those of Europe and the United States. Before assuming such a conclusion, however, it should be noted that any number of Native commentaries on oral story-telling show that "tradition" often assumes the possibility of stories shifting somewhat from teller to teller and that, apart from sacred ritual contexts, it is not always expected that tellers recite exactly the same details or even story lines as have been used in the telling of such stories in the past.[7] Thus, the guides' grandparents would have had liberty to revise what they had heard, without the quality of their renditions being dependant on their having carefully listened to the details and narratives of the stories when they first heard them. In addition, it does not follow that because a person is unable to speak a tribal language they cannot know much about their tribe's culture. Considering these issues, it is plausible to conclude that the tour guide's comments did not necessarily demonstrate the "dying out" of Acoma ways of being and knowing. It seems to me more likely that they were intended to serve as the means for deflecting in advance further questions from his audience about religion or belief. This is not to suggest that the guide was perhaps disingenuous about what he knew, but that these particular comments might have been foregrounded in order to disrupt romantic visions of him as a teacher of tribal experience and perhaps to, in fact, protect that experience from exposure to the general public.

Such an instance of what I have been calling "displayed withholding" in this book does not preclude the idea that the inheritance of culture has become a somewhat kaleidoscopic process, with once-opposing terms shuffled into different and still-changing relations. On such a cultural terrain, once alien religious forms may become part of the tribal imaginary, but they are not necessarily absorbed in hegemonic terms. My friend asked if "the Protestants," meaning evangelicals, had become much of a presence in the pueblo. The guide answered that "some people are jumping the fence. You can see the missions along Route 40." Route 40, formerly Route 66, is the major interstate between Gallup and Tucumcari, but at points it diverges into a desolate-looking road that might be described as a belt of former strip culture. Abandoned gas stations, bars, and restaurants from the 1950s and '60s dot its borders, and the ghost cabins of defunct motels line up in shabby disrepair, among which one can find here and there a Baptist, Seventh Day Adventist, or Mormon mission.

The fence-jumping phenomenon, which, according to our guide, represents only about 10 percent of the population, occurs off the mesa. Protestantism is not gaining much of a foothold in Acoma itself, which accordingly represents it as a marginal movement. Catholicism, by contrast, stands on this side of the fence. Nevertheless, our guide's explanation that the people of Acoma would not give up their Catholicism because their ancestors had to sacrifice and suffer so much on its behalf suggests that it is not the institution in itself nor its theology that are primary to Acoma Catholicism but rather the association of the church with the pain of their ancestors. This ancestral suffering is kept in view, for visitors as well as for present-day citizens of the pueblo, as a way of remembering and continuing to mourn the wounds and losses of the past—losses that produced economic and political marginalization and that, together with this marginalization, mark the lack of assimilation to hegemonic ideology and forms of belief.

When I visited the mesa in the spring of 2003, a different guide accompanied the group in the bus, but his rhetorical strategies were very similar to the earlier one. The quickly paced monotone sounded like it had been memorized some time ago and repeated often. The information consisted at first of numbers—population and height of the mesa, number of cisterns, age of the church, and so on. This time, though, the guide at a certain point drew attention to that very speech style, telling us, in response to no prompt or question from anyone in the tour group, that visitors in the past had complained about the flatness and lack of dramatic effect in his manner of speaking. He answered this complaint, which I gathered he had correctly assumed we had been voicing to ourselves, by explaining that he had learned to recite his presentations by singing and chanting them, just as he had learned stories and prayers in childhood. According to this account, the delivery style that sounded as if it required little conscious presence on the part of the speaker was the effect of a religiously oriented practice he had inculcated long ago. The fact that it was used for the current performance suggests that this speech style has religious connotations—not that the dimensions of the buildings or the number of soldiers in Oñate's party in themselves have particularly sacred value, but that the recitation of the story of Oñate's attack on the village and the colonial history it references are parts of what Acoma poet Simon Ortiz describes as a necessary narrative for the sake of the social psychological health of the pueblo.[8] The example Ortiz offers is the Feast of Santiago celebrated at Acoma in early September, when Santiago, the conqueror saint of the Spaniards and inspirational figure for Moorish and American invasions alike, enters the pueblo in the company of Chapiyuh, a figure of a Franciscan priest wearing the familiar robes along with "thick-soled boots like a storm trooper" and "a hood over his face with slits cut in it for eyes."[9] The procession of the two elaborately disguised personae is accompanied by prayer and narrative that describe the movements of the actual historical figures as they arrived to wreak havoc and terror on the citizens of the mesa in 1598. Ortiz explains the value of this public performance: "It is the only way in which event and experience, such as the entry of the Spaniard to the Western Hemisphere, can become significant and realized in the people's own terms. . . . This perception and meaningfulness has to happen; otherwise, the hard experience of the Euroamerican colonization of the lands and people of the Western Hemisphere would be driven into the dark recesses of the indigenous mind and psyche. And this kind of repression is always a poison and detriment to creative growth and expression."[10]

Ortiz understands such processes of ceremonial repetition and performance of traumatic historical events as components in a centuries-long program of resistance on the part of American Indians to the assumptions held by colonizers and their successors in present-day America about the finality of conquest. The importance of resisting the closure of the historical narrative as the victors tell it is a matter not only of political positioning in a material world but of nurturing an Acoma cultural genealogy that includes religious practices. Chants, songs, and prayers derive their vitality in part from the ability to include references to experiences of otherness and to experiences of horror in the tribal religious imaginary. The tone our guide used to narrate Spanish oppression and violence was the same as the tone he used for religious performance, and that performance included reference to the historical pain. This ritualistic remembrance of the pain thus works to keep a political resistance alive; and the open, raw wound thus maintained allows the severe vision of difference—cultural and political—to nurture the inheritance of older Acoma styles of being and knowing.

The guide for the later visit evidenced this legacy of resistance not only in his speech style, but explicitly in the stories he related. Inside the

Church of Saint Stephen, he pointed to the vigas in the ceiling and explained their origins. During the seventeenth century when the church was built, the men of Acoma were required by the Spanish priests and monks, whose authority was upheld by nearby military garrisons, to travel by foot thirty miles to Mount Taylor to cut the extremely heavy tree trunks and carry them back to the mesa. Several died in the process of this forced labor, just as they did in the work of building the church and the rectory. According to the monks, these tasks were performed in payment for the work of converting the Natives: the church they built would save their souls. At the same time, though, the people of Acoma never relinquished their indigenous religion. The guide uttered the phrase "never quit" and used a particular gesture to signify this idea repeatedly during the course of his description of this history. He pointed out a series of construction designs in the interior that testify to the workers' subtle deployment of an Acoma symbology where Christian references were supposed to prevail. There are seven steps leading to the altar instead of the usual three in Christian churches: seven is a sacred number in Acoma cosmology. He knocked on the upper step, and the sound demonstrated that it was hollow beneath. As a way of burying the old religion, Father Juan Ramirez had had the church built over the very spot on the old plaza where the people of the pueblo had worshipped, and the altar is directly over the kiva. The people know this, and the kiva is thus present to them as they worship in the Christian church. In addition, the stations of the cross were arranged by the builders in a counterclockwise pattern, like the movement of Acoma cosmology, as the guide explained, in contrast to the arrangement of most churches, where the order is clockwise. The building of the church was done in such a way that it bears the dimensions of the traditions it was intended to muffle out of existence. The thickness of the walls, the length of the church, and the height of the ceiling take their measure from a series of sacred numbers. Oral legend says that many of those who died in the construction are buried in its walls. Father Ramirez, who was much hated for his role as architect of the project, was short tempered, particularly with the children who worked for him and assisted during the mass. As the story is remembered, he once hit a boy with a heavy silver chalice for making a mistake, and the boy was severely wounded. Ramirez was thus thrown off the cliff. Our guide added that in some versions his robes acted as a parachute, because when the men went down to get his body, they found no trace of it within miles of the mesa in any direction. The legend concludes with the monk sneaking down into Mexico, where he could be safe among his fellow Catholic clergy.[11]

These, then, were some of the ways in which the people who built the church were able to appropriate the alien structure for their own purposes. Their resistance to assimilation of Spanish systems of belief and ideology continued into the American era. Various nonconfrontational modes of resistance are practiced today, I would argue, as evidenced by the two guides' presentational styles and their disinclination to satisfy the visual consumerism and entertainment expectations of conventional tourism.

In conversation after the tour had concluded, I asked the guide what he most wanted non-Natives to take from his expositions. Without missing a beat, he responded simply, "Understand." He elaborated that he hoped people would listen seriously to what he said and that they would thus come to understand what happened at Acoma. He repeated the word several times. His hope that outsiders would "understand" implies that, in his experience, understanding—of the terrors of the past and of the political problems that have devolved from that past, including the constant challenges to sovereignty—is lacking in the present. His work, then, is to help address that lack, even if only by the histories he tells and by the manners and tones of his delivery.

Sky City Casino

The majestic and brooding, seventy-foot-high Sky City mesa rising from the flat valley floor and the aura of distant, unexposed styles of being and knowing in which it is embedded, together with the narratives of colonial history that make up such important parts of Acoma's contemporary self-representations, project a somber, contemplative portrait of tribal collective and public life. Fifteen minutes north of the Acoma Pueblo, just off of Interstate 40, another Acoma landmark, also labeled "Sky City," glitters in bright lights. It is Sky City Casino, the most profitable of the eight business ventures conducted by the Acoma Pueblo. Given its proximity to the highway, the casino caters to truckers and tourists from east to west, and its parking lot is almost always full. The twenty-foot-high neon sign flashes invitations to drivers to stop in for a

4-2. Sky City Casino sign, astride Interstate Route 40

game of blackjack, craps, roulette, poker, bingo, or keno or to play the slot machines. The thirty-foot-high road sign features a six-foot-square digital screen with a crawler advertising upcoming gaming events and prize giveaways.

Sky City Casino is a more modest affair than most of the Pueblo casinos that line the highway between Albuquerque and Santa Fe. Built in 2000, it consists of a bingo room, a restaurant, and an enormous gaming floor for blackjack, craps tables, and slot machines. In one corner of this floor a stage is erected for the country western and Native American musicians who perform on the weekends. A few references to the establishment's Native American ownership appear in the interior decorations, but they are so openly derivative of conventional motifs of Indianness in U.S. popular culture that it is hard to imagine that we are being asked to take them seriously. A glittering turquoise sign in the shape of a thunderbird announces a "megabucks game"; the carpeting has a southwestern Native geometric pattern; vigas set in the hallway ceilings that surround the gaming floor suggest the construction style of pueblo houses. In sections of the building, the floors and walls are set with reddish-brown tiles

4-3. Lobby of hotel at Sky City Casino

featuring animal designs, arrows, and thunderbirds drawn in the manner of petroglyphs. In the middle of the circular lobby, which is also the lobby to the adjacent 135-room hotel, sits a large, multileveled plaster rock over which water pours, as in the settings of Edward S. Curtis's photogravures of Acoma Pueblo from the late nineteenth century. An Acoma pot in the classical style is set in one of the rock's niches.

Pamphlets for the casino advertise experiences that blend "old and new" in "Acoma at the crossroads of nature, heritage and the spirit of fun." Old Acoma doesn't have a part in the casino, however. Its role in advertising is to identify the casino as a Native enterprise and, like the references to "Nature" and "Gaming in Its Natural State" in ads for Foxwoods, to give an indigenous gloss to an otherwise familiar form of popular entertainment. Just so, a slick Web site urges visitors to "See History, Make History, Where the Sky's the Limit, For Everyone."[12]

The deployment of terms like "history," "heritage," "nature," and "spirit" in order to attract potential players to Sky City seems like a violation of Acoma's cultural dignity in the name of what many Americans, Native and non-Native alike, perceive as rather undignified activities. But like the stereotypes of Indianness that appear at Foxwoods on the Mashantucket Pequot Reservation, these derive from an archive of familiar glitzy devices of American casino design. In this sense, Sky City Casino, like Foxwoods, exhibits itself as a business that operates within the dynamics of U.S. economic exchange, a recently and still tentatively achieved status which many Acoma residents welcome. In addition, however, these devices simultaneously display the ironies of a Native American community serving up romantic and reductive stereotypes of Indianness produced in and driving the colonial imagination of European America in order to draw a clientele of largely European American heritage and to secure the financial success that might help alleviate some of the agonies that still exist as part of the legacy of colonialism.

The differences in the visual rhetoric between the museum and mesa, on the one hand, and the casino, on the other, are remarkable and suggest very different, even contradictory, interests in the tribe's projects of self-representation. It goes without saying that the practices of display at the mesa are older by many years, and they have not changed with the casino's construction. Rather than tempering the aesthetic tones and cultural styles of the gambling house, the mesa village maintains the posture of silence and understatement that has characterized it for generations. Differences in architectural design between the museum and Sky City Casino cannot be cross-referenced like those between Foxwoods and the Mashantucket Museum and Research Center. Apart from the generic differences, these institutions inhabit separate worlds: the mesa, in its austerity and self-enclosure, and the museum project images of Acoma in terms of its ancient and colonial past, while the casino is seated solidly in a present that looks energetically toward the future. It promises cumulative economic success for the tribe in the future and a good time and good luck for guests in the coming hours. While the museum and the village finally seal off the interior sanctums of tribal life from the eyes and ears of visitors, the casino positions itself in the stream of cash and culture flows of postmodern American society, a posture nicely imaged by its location astride the highway. While the casino is part of the tribe's tourism complex described in the same brochures that invite tourists to the mesa, its relation to Acoma is to provide a reliable stream of much needed income for the once deeply impoverished pueblo without putting itself forward as an intentional representation of the tribe itself.

The contrasts between the tribal public self-representations at the mesa and in the casino are so striking that one wonders how the tribal members themselves make sense of it. In an effort to get some clarity on the question, I requested an appointment to speak with one of the tribal council members. The then governor of Acoma Pueblo, Fred S. Vallo Sr., was gracious enough to meet me himself, and when I asked how people in the pueblo thought of the casino, he responded with some resignation, "Well, you know, since day one, we've lived in two worlds." For the next hour, rather than directly defending gaming or venturing to describe the older practices or ideologies of the Acoma community, he spoke of economics. Thirty years ago, during the 1970s, the tribal government was so poor that it almost had to shut down. Perhaps in part due to the oil crisis of those years, few tourists came to visit the mesa, an important source of tribal income ever since the village was opened to the public in the 1960s. Unlike many other tribes whose members are in principle more eligible for bank loans because they own parcels of land, allotted to their families in the late nineteenth century, that can serve as collateral, and unlike those tribes that profit from the government's leasing of lands held in trust for grazing, mining, and ranching, the people of Acoma can neither rent nor sell nor borrow on the lots where they live, since all land within the pueblo is tribally owned and managed. Neither Acoma nor any of the other nineteen tribal communities known as the "Pueblos" was party to the 1887 Dawes Severalty Act, which carved reservations into 160-acre allotments and assigned them to individual Indian families, thus breaking up the old system of collective land ownership. These individual titles were in most cases held in trust by the government for twenty-five years, and land left over after allotment to Native families was at the government's disposition sold or leased, with the money going into trust accounts for the tribes.[13] While the Pueblo Indians were able to avoid the threat to the communal character of life on their reservation, a threat that came with the Dawes Act for other tribes, it has been very difficult for them to acquire bank loans or credit because no single family or individual owns land in the Pueblo of Acoma. By the 1970s, with a modern history of intense economic and political marginalization and with the tribal government itself on the edge of bankruptcy, little relief was in sight for the entrenched poverty of Acoma.

The bingo operation, which opened in the 1980s, relieved a great deal of economic stress in the Acoma community, beginning with the financing of the government. Profits began going toward the renewal of reservation infrastructure, and investments produced the capital that made the casino and hotel complex possible. Sky City is managed entirely by the tribe, with no outside corporate input, and, despite its modest scale, employs over a thousand people from Acoma and elsewhere, providing the largest payroll in Cibola County. With the income from the casino, reservation roads and the water and electrical systems have been greatly improved. The tribe has constructed new, quality housing, a nearly impossible achievement in the past. Four years ago, there was no fire department for the forty-eight-hundred-member tribal community. Now a handsome, well-furnished safety and security complex has been built for the fire, health, and tribal police departments, with new, reliable fire engines, ambulances, and police cars. While the museum described earlier in this chapter has since burned to the ground, funds from the casino have made possible the construction of a new building, which is scheduled to open in the fall of 2005.[14]

Casino profits have also made possible the purchasing of lands that Acoma people consider part of their homeland but which were sold to the government under great duress in 1958. Governor Vallo reported that the tribe was paid at the rate of 1902 land values. The repurchase price, however, has been at the current market rate. These are sacred lands, important for Acoma religious worship, and the governor seemed very pleased, indeed, to talk about them as being in tribal hands again. They are not, however, part of the reservation, and thus fall outside of tribal sovereignty jurisdiction. The tribe is currently attempting to buy back land they have claimed for centuries but which has been owned by the Bureau of Land Management since the late nineteenth century—a long, arduous process that has not yet been accomplished.

The Pueblo of Acoma owns several other businesses that have supported and been supported by casino gains, including Flower Mountain Travel Plaza, a fuel station and convenience store adjacent to Sky City Casino, and Acomita Lake, a fishing and water recreation enterprise located in the middle of the reservation between the casino and the mesa. These enterprises, together with the casino, the hotel and conference center, the restaurant, Sky City Cultural Center (which includes the museum and village tour), and Acoma Land and Cattle Company, are managed by the tribe's commercial department, established in 1996 as Acoma Business Enterprises. ABE is run by a board of directors and an executive staff which consists of tribal members and non-Native professionals, chosen by and answering to the Acoma Tribal Council.[15] ABE has been awarded for "significant progress in building sound and notable processes" in all its ventures. While the walking tour of Acoma Pueblo remains the centerpiece of the tribe's intentional self-representation to the general public,[16] the casino has become the star project of ABE, and it draws far more visitors than does the Sky City Cultural Center.

For all its popularity among outsiders, however, Acoma citizens themselves, the second tour guide assured me, are not among the casino's clients. I asked him the same question I asked Governor Vallo: "How do people at Acoma feel about the casino?" The guide's expression seemed to darken, and he answered simply that "Acoma people don't go there." In further discussion, he made it clear that from his perspective the casino is a compartmentalized institution, an entity sponsored by the tribal leadership because of its benefits to the tribal community, but not a business with which these same people identify. Given the tone of his lectures during the tour, it would make sense to conclude that the casino is embedded in the second of the "two worlds" in which Acoma people have had to live "since day one," as the governor put it, of European presence in the Western Hemisphere. While the bingo and casino business have in certain key ways made for an optimistic story of collaboration between the two worlds, the off-reservation world, the tour demonstrations imply, has been the source of the obstruction and oppression that necessitated the building of a gaming enterprise in the first place. Thus, engagement with it is both the cause and the solution of the problems that have beset Acoma since the sixteenth century.

But, of course, as Governor Vallo said, Acoma has been living in both worlds for several centuries now. The facility of tribal leaders in engaging with Western business practices and the familiarity of tribal cultural representatives with the expectations and assumptions of Western tourists are only the most obvious indicators of Acoma's extensive efforts to involve itself in U.S. financial and social circuits. By the early twenty-first century, it seems to make more sense to view Acoma Pueblo's decisions concerning the casino and other tourist businesses as the products of an activist, self-determining tribal leadership trying to achieve and sustain access for the tribe to the capital flows from which it has been traditionally excluded rather than as the effects of an oppressing master culture that enjoys genuine hegemony at Acoma. Certainly, political as well as legal, and therefore social as well as economic, forms of oppression are still very much alive and doing ill in Indian America; nevertheless, the fact that Acoma and other tribes have access to capital means that tribal subjects and collectivities can speak and act as participants in the dominant society that oppresses them and, *at the same time*, as participants in something else. Acoma Pueblo's desired distance from the dominant society, which is implied in the very idea of compartmentalization as well as in the narratives of the village tour, is supplemented and complicated by the desire to have access to the social and economic systems of the rest of U.S. society; but the latter desire does not cancel out the former one.

The tension between these interests appears to be very familiar and resignedly accepted at Acoma as on other reservations. To the extent that tribal businesses gain access to dominant economic circuits, that access derives from public recognition of tribes as distinct cultural and social entities. This means that federally recognized tribes can be articulated to the larger society's system of exchanges, if indeed they have gained access to it, even as their cultural boundary lines distinguish them from the general population. Like those at Wind River, these tensions help keep the historical losses that came with colonialism in view as open, unresolved features of contemporary self-representation. These are the living wounds and ironies out of which the present is built and tribal public identity is, in part, displayed. The narratives of the village lecture tours and exhibits in the museum ensure that the losses themselves will not be lost but re-membered and rehearsed, as in the Feast of Santiago, thus preventing their being, in Simon Ortiz's words, "driven into the dark recesses of the indigenous mind and psyche."

The first tour leader I encountered at Acoma Pueblo in effect revised what I had expected to find in the relationship between Native guide and non-Native travelers. More than presenting his visitors with special knowledge pertaining to Acoma in particular, he offered us some of our own European American history. This mirroring effect was evident from the start in his self-presentation. His Elvis haircut, sunglasses, and cloth-ing style suggested a familiarly "cool" persona that might be seen almost anywhere in the United States these days. Characteristically "American," in this sense, our guide conducted a tour through Acoma that implicitly critiqued the roles of the visitors as unimplicated strangers. Some of the tourists were more interested in the history of adobe walls than that of the European presence, and for all I know, they had their reasons. My companion and I went with the expectation of learning about the old culture, but our guide, like the women who run the Shoshone Cultural Center at Wind River, demonstrated that Native Americans clearly have their own ways of teaching history to the non-Native public.

Michel de Certeau, who studied the history and politics of indige-nous and European relations in the Western Hemisphere extensively, wrote in *The Practice of Everyday Life:*

> The ambiguity that subverted from within the Spanish colonizers' "success" in imposing their own culture on the indigenous Indians is well known. Submissive, and even consenting to their subjection, the Indians nevertheless often made of the rituals, representations, and laws imposed on them something quite different from what their conquerors had in mind; they subverted them not by rejecting or altering them, but by using them with respect to ends and refer-ences foreign to the system they had no choice but to accept. They were other within the very colonization that outwardly assimilated them; their use of the dominant social order deflected its power, which they lacked the means to challenge; they escaped it without leaving it. The strength of their difference lay in procedures of "con-sumption."[17]

De Certeau's words effectively describe what appeared to be happening in the Acoma village tours. In the guide's representations, the people of contemporary Acoma, like the people of Wind River, Navajo Nation, and Mashantucket, have appropriated familiar methods of mainstream tourism and historiography and, in the process, offered Euro-Americans information about their own culture and history. In this sense, the Indians have "consumed" some of the narrative mechanisms of late twentieth-century U.S. culture and have, in de Certeau's terms, made for themselves a place as "other within the very colonization that outwardly assimilated them." De Certeau emphasizes the term *outwardly* here. His reading demonstrates again what Ranajit Guha has termed "dominance without hegemony" in the context of the Spanish colonization of the indigenous people of America, including Acoma Pueblo.[18]

"SOVEREIGNTY, SOVEREIGNTY, SOVEREIGNTY"

The distinctiveness from the culture and society of the United States, as Governor Vallo put it, is most overtly and politically encoded in the concept of sovereignty. In response to my question ("What would you have outsiders know most about Acoma?") he reiterated, "Sovereignty, sovereignty, sovereignty," clearly indicating that this is the first line of difference that Acoma and other tribes located in the United States draw around themselves and their reservations. Sovereignty is probably the most important element of self-definition in contemporary tribal public displays in general, and it is also a central theme in legal, academic, and political discussions of Native America.

As much as tribal leaders and legal scholars assert the inherent nature of tribal sovereignty, however, they cannot but simultaneously recognize the need to defend it in the face of continuous challenges from local, state, and federal leaders, courts, and legislatures. Endless diplomacy, litigation, and other forms of political and legal exchange with non-Indian centers of power are necessary to elicit recognition of sovereignty in practice, and these efforts do not necessarily secure respect by off-reservation political entities of sovereignty as the legitimate status of Indian tribes.

Commentators generally agree on the meaning of sovereignty, but debates arise over the issue of its applicability to contemporary tribal status.

Native leaders and scholars tend to describe tribes as sovereign nations, properly subject to no laws or limitations other than those that govern international relations. Although this self-description posits a form of autonomy, it does not necessarily follow that most tribal spokespeople or their supporters assert independence in the final sense of secession. Rather, they tend to claim sovereignty as implied or articulated in treaties between tribes and the United States. By these treaties, which were struck between 1778 and 1870, Washington recognized indigenous homelands and self-governance. In exchange, the signatory tribe recognized the sovereignty of the United States, agreeing to cease hostilities against its soldiers and citizens and accepting the government's promised goods, services, and protections. Treaty relationships were, as Taiaiake Alfred writes, the means by which "European sovereignties in North America first legitimated themselves . . . as legal entities." This legitimacy came "only by the expressed consent through treaty of the original occupiers and governors of North America."[19] Thus, the treaties documented original, government-to-government relationships between the United States and the tribes.

The form of sovereignty expressed in the treaties is commonly understood to imply, if not to overtly stipulate, that tribal polities and territories are, with the signing of the treaties, to be honored by the United States and to remain as they are described there, no more and no less. It is also commonly known, however, both in and outside of Indian Country, that virtually all the treaties that the United States signed with Native nations have been violated to one degree or another, and that neither the territorial boundaries nor the political authorities stipulated in them have been honored.

The chief means by which Washington has justified the systematic diminishment of tribal sovereignty since the earliest years of the republic has been to create laws that extend power over the tribes to the United States, in contradiction of many treaty provisions. Article I, Section 8 of the Constitution stipulates that Congress has the power to regulate commerce with Indian tribes, a clause that is often rightly interpreted as a vehicle for shielding tribes from commercial intervention by states and unethical individual traders, but which has also served from the beginning as a means of securing congressional exclusivity, in the regulation not only of Native commercial activities but of criminal and political matters.[20] In 1802, Congress passed the Trade and Intercourse Act, which consolidated three previous, temporary acts confirming the exclusive authority of Congress to regulate trade with Native tribes and individuals. The 1802 act, however, extended the breadth of the previous acts by empowering Congress to regulate criminal activity between whites and Indians on reservations; to position government agents on Indian lands in order to distribute and give instruction in the use of tools and other materials for agricultural development; and to send troops onto reservations when deemed necessary to apprehend violators of the act's provisions.[21] While they do not constitute a particularly coherent code of federal Indian law, these and a host of subsequent Congressional legislation as well as Supreme Court cases have sponsored the intensification of federal authority over tribes.[22]

Beginning with the "Marshall trilogy"—the set of decisions articulated by Chief Justice John Marshall in the early nineteenth century, referred to in chapter 2—terms and principles were articulated that have come to define federal relations with the tribes as if the treaties themselves formed a distinct literature having little bearing on actual conditions. The plaintiffs Joshua Johnson and Thomas Graham in *Johnson and Graham's Lessee v. William McIntosh* had purchased land from the Illinois and Piankeshaw tribes a few years before the Revolution, in 1773 and 1775, while the defendant William McIntosh had purchased his parcel from the United States in 1818.[23] Recent research has shown that the contesting parties' properties did not, in fact, overlap and that the plaintiffs and the defendant actually colluded in the case in order to make it appear that they had an interstate conflict, such that they could get the case before the Supreme Court. Whichever way the decision went, then, the parties would win.[24] In any event, Johnson and Graham claimed their prior title overrode that of McIntosh, but the court ruled in 1823 in favor of McIntosh, on the argument that Indians did not hold fee-simple, or full, titles to their aboriginal lands. Their titles, Marshall asserted, were thus limited to occupancy and could not be sold or otherwise alienated. Marshall justified this assertion by claiming "discovery gave an exclusive right to extinguish the Indian title of occupancy, either by purchase or conquest." This superseding right vested absolute title in the United States, as the successor to the original "discoverer" of the region, Britain.[25] While the tribes, who had acted on the assumption that they had the prerogative to transfer the lands at issue, were not party to the suit, their actions in selling to Johnson and Graham resulted in this decision which has structured subsequent Court decisions and congressional legislation concerning Native American tribal rights to the present time.[26]

In the infamous commentary he wrote in 1831 on *Cherokee Nation v. Georgia*, Marshall articulated the idea that Indian tribes are not foreign nations but "domestic dependent nations" and that, therefore, their suit against the state of Georgia could not be heard by the Supreme Court. Marshall explained in his commentary on the case that although the Cherokee Nation had an unquestionable right to the territory where they lived "until that right shall be extinguished by a voluntary cession to our Government," the United States nevertheless claimed title to that territory "independent of their will." This superior title, he wrote, meant that the Cherokees lived "in a state of pupilage." The United States government was guardian to its indigenous wards, and all that might be expected in such a relationship pertained to this one, including the paternalistic authority over tribal affairs by the "Great Father," the president.[27] With this commentary, Marshall portrayed the Cherokees—and by implication other Native populations in North America—as a people with a weak form of sovereignty that left them, in effect, a colonized people beholden to and protected by their colonial masters in quite literal terms. The vocabulary and imagery of wardship and domestic dependency gave literary shape to political attitudes, prevailing in Marshall's generation, that have been perpetuated by courts and legislatures with sporadic exceptions ever since.

Marshall's majority opinion for *Worcester v. Georgia* in 1832 took a different course vis-à-vis the relationship between the Cherokees and the state of Georgia. In this situation, a non-Native named Samuel Worcester, a protestant missionary who lived and worked on the Cherokee Reservation, had been arrested, tried, and sentenced to two years of hard labor for failing to obtain the requisite permit from the state of Georgia to live on the reservation and for failing to swear an oath of allegiance to Georgia's laws. Worcester contested the decision, and when the case ended up in Marshall's hands, the chief justice this time found opportunity to assert federal as opposed to states' rights in regard to Indian affairs. This time he stipulated that the Cherokee tribe "occup[ied] its own territory" and that the laws of Georgia did not apply within the boundaries of the Cherokee Reservation because legal relations with the Indians were reserved to the federal government. Nevertheless, while the Cherokees won the case against the state along with Worcester, the decision did not recognize tribal sovereignty in any comprehensive sense, but rather reconfirmed the status of wardship to Washington. In spite of its seemingly pro-tribal stance, *Worcester* not only reiterated the federal government's view of the tribes as in need of its protection but reinvigorated this classically colonialist position for future court decisions.[28]

From the federal point of view, as articulated in *Johnson, Cherokee Nation*, and *Worcester*, Indian tribes, as the original inhabitants of North America, have "aboriginal title," or "Indian title," to their homelands, but those decisions also demonstrated how federal law tended to treat Indian title as an abstract, in fact, limited concept. This ambivalence has remained palpable in subsequent Court rulings that concern Native collective rights. The 1978 decision in *United States v. Wheeler* summarized the terms of the Marshall trilogy in stark language: "The sovereignty that the Indian tribes retain is of a unique and limited character. It exists only at the sufferance of Congress and is subject to complete defeasance. . . . Until Congress acts, the tribes retain their existing sovereign powers. In sum, Indian tribes still possess those aspects of sovereignty not withdrawn by treaty or statute, or by implication as a necessary result of their dependent status."[29]

As Bruce Duthu explains, in rulings like *Wheeler* the Supreme Court honors tribal sovereignty "within the matrix of American democratic structure through language that alternately affirms tribal political existence into perpetuity and consigns such political existence to the whims of a superior power."[30] The "contingencies" on which Duthu sees sovereignty depending, linked as they are to national political interests and "institutional imperatives," clearly pull the rug out from under the very meaning of sovereignty as a stable, recognized status centering on political self-determination.[31] This "legal shell game—'now you see it, now you don't,' " as Peter d'Errico puts it, has sustained a compromised form of American Indian sovereignty within a larger structure of federal authority that grants Congress plenary power over affairs in Indian country.[32] Chief Justice Thurgood Marshall summarized this point precisely in his ruling in *McClanahan v. Arizona Tax Commission* of 1973, where he referred to the "platonic notion" of sovereignty as a thing of the past and argued that "the Indian sovereignty doctrine is relevant . . . not because it provides a definitive resolution of the issues in this suit, but because it provides a backdrop against which the applicable treaties and federal statutes must be read."[33]

While Governor Vallo's assertion at Acoma Pueblo that sovereignty is the key feature of contemporary Native identity of which non-Natives should be aware, and while many other tribal leaders, activists, and intellectuals share his views, other scholars supportive of Native interests have taken a critical look at the concept of sovereignty itself. The Osage historian Robert Allen Warrior complains that the term itself is problematic since it derives from "European theological and political discourse" and "does little to describe the visions and goals of American Indian communities that seek to retain a discrete identity." Nevertheless, Warrior notes that "to simply abandon such terms risks abandoning their abiding force and utility."[34] Addressing the intensely centrist principles that inform conventional notions of sovereignty as a model of state structure, Taiaiake Alfred writes that "sovereignty is certainly not Sioux, Salish, or Iroquoian in origin."[35] Citing the substantial differences, between Native and Western principals of governance, that make sovereignty an inappropriate concept for tribes, not to mention the lack of institutional power in Native communities to compete for the same kind of state sovereignty claimed by the United States and Canada, Alfred urges tribes to embrace indigenous perspectives in efforts toward self-determination by observing the central relationship between humans and the earth, by managing environmental sustainability in economic projects, and by empowering individuals in governance. These indigenous methods toward achieving and maintaining a different kind of sovereignty would result, he envisions, in "respectful coexistence" between neighboring tribes and other polities: "True indigenous formulations are non-intrusive and build frameworks . . . by acknowledging the integrity and autonomy of the various constituent elements of the relationship[s]" with others, unlike Western statist models that envision sovereignty as a means of acquiring dominance.[36] In a similar argument, Peter d'Errico envisions a "post-sovereign future" for indigenous-state relationships in Canada and the United States and a post-colonial status for indigenous peoples. D'Errico emphasizes the limitations of the concept of sovereignty in the hopes that tribes will not simply repeat that structure in their own communities.[37] Instead, he applauds the directions Native American politicians and intellectuals are taking at the present moment along the lines Alfred describes in "working toward a terminology and perspective that will link postmodern world politics and premodern indigenous roots."[38]

Whether these ideals differ substantially *as ideals* from those expressed in iconic Western documents of political philosophy is a question that from my point of view remains unanswered. Tribal leaders like Fred S. Vallo Sr. assert what is perhaps a familiar, Western notion of sovereignty in reconfirming political boundaries to match the cultural and identity boundaries that separate their communities from the dominant society at the same time that they seek recognition as viable participants in economic and social systems of the larger national scene. Perhaps, given the ways that wealth has been distributed, the environment sustained, and individuals empowered at Acoma Pueblo and other indigenous communities where a degree of sovereignty has been achieved with the help of economic success, it makes sense to say that it is in the *practice* of the ideals Alfred describes—more than in the rhetorical identification with them—that indigenous polities appear more often and more visibly different from those of the West.

The fact that the U.S. government maintains its trust obligations to federally recognized tribes implies Washington's recognition of the distinct origins and sovereign political characteristics of tribal entities at the present time. But these forms of recognition are far more theoretical and conceptual than practical or materially real, given the actions taken by Congress and the Supreme Court in violation of treaties and, therefore, of trust. The most recent, well-publicized challenge to tribal treaty rights and, by implication, sovereignty occurred in 1997, when a comprehensive attempt was made in the Senate to erase any recognition by the federal government of Native sovereignty. This attempt would have repeated congressional action of the 1950s, when the Termination Acts eliminated federal recognition of sovereignty and of its treaty obligations to many tribes in the West. After much lobbying on the part of Native leaders and supporters, the 1997 bill was defeated, but the incident demonstrated that tribal sovereignty is indeed still threatened.

As the next chapter demonstrates, since the early 1970s Native leaders and activists have responded to this long history of disempowerment within the governmental framework of the United States by attempting to take control of their destinies and turning the tide on colonialism. These movements emerged with the organizing of inter-tribal political demonstrations that culminated in the occupation of the Bureau of Indian Affairs offices in Washington in 1972 and the 1973 siege of Wounded Knee. At the same time, on the legal front, a few tribes in the Northeast began gaining federal recognition by invoking the 1790 Trade and Intercourse Act and through new congressional legislation.[39] In addition, the 1970s saw the beginnings of Native American participation in rights activism and claims of sovereignty on the international level. Currently, these movements are coalescing around the United Nations Human Rights Commission and the newly created Permanent Forum on Indigenous Issues. Whether participation in global indigenous activism will result in recognition of the sovereignty of Native American tribes is a question undertaken in the last chapter as well.

CHAPTER 5

Indigenous Internationalism

NATIVE RIGHTS AND THE
UNITED NATIONS

WHEN JOHN MARSHALL WROTE HIS DECISIONS regarding American Indian sovereignty, he was working in the unstable legal environment of the early United States, some of the most conflicting issues of which pertained to the political status of indigenous peoples and the disposition of their lands. Several writers who were involved in expeditionary, missionary, and even military actions in the Western Hemisphere in Marshall's time and before attempted to keep the authority of the indigenous populations, as prior inhabitants of the New World, in view in the execution of colonial enterprises. Antonio de Montessinos and Bartholomé de las Casas in early Spanish America and Thomas Morton and Roger Williams in seventeenth-century New England were a few among many characters of empire who lobbied their respective colonial and metropolitan governments to honor the cultural differences as well as political sovereignty of the Indians. In Marshall's own time, Thomas Jefferson defended tribal sovereignty in his 1784 *Notes on the State of Virginia;* and Daniel Webster, arguing for the plaintiffs in *Johnson and Graham's Lessee v. William McIntosh* before the Supreme Court in 1823, asserted that the laws of all "civilized states" gave precedent to the idea that Native ownership of tribal lands was to be respected in the United States.[1] These discourses of natural rights and privileges, however, as history plainly shows, were most often articulated in eloquent and politically persuasive but nevertheless theoretical terms more than they determined actual practices. In effect, they were weak counter-voices to the assertions of superiority and extensions of material and political power that characterized most European and European American interests in excursions into other peoples' worlds. Debates in Spain, in England, and later in the United States over the proper legal conceptualization of the people and land of the Americas indeed showed that nagging pressures of morality and ethics continuously disturbed the material powers and pleasures of conquest. To soothe these irritations, partial arguments for the natural rights of the original inhabitants were often appropriated for positions taken by agents of empire, which made such arguments, in the end, only serve to dress bald claims to power in the finery of moral consideration.

In his efforts to articulate the relationships between colonizer and colonized, Marshall not only was conscious of his role in a Supreme Court that was still claiming its authority in the early United States, but looked to international law and to the court of world opinion as precedent and audience for his decisions.[2] As "domestic dependent nations," the indigenous peoples of America figured in his writings as actors on the world stage along with European powers, even if he ultimately used that term to claim that European culture and authority superseded Native rights and powers.

This chapter considers the extent to which the legacy of international law that Marshall perpetuated and that legitimized the colonization of indigenous populations since the sixteenth century is in our own time being critiqued, in practice, by indigenous peoples themselves as they participate in the U.N. bodies that address indigenous issues: the Commission on Human Rights, the Working Group on Indigenous Populations, the Working Group on the Draft Declaration of Indigenous Rights, and, most importantly, the Permanent Forum on Indigenous Issues. Human rights, as a field of international law institutionalized within the United Nations system, has elicited a great deal of global attention and acquired a privileged moral authority in international relations ever since the adoption of the Universal Declaration of Human Rights by the United Nations in 1948. The Universal Declaration made no references to the world's indigenous peoples. Nevertheless, representatives of indigenous populations have come to the international level via the Commission on Human Rights to make their claims of sovereignty, self-determination, land and other rights with increasing regularity since the early 1980s, when the commission's renowned Working Group on Indigenous Populations was founded.

As a new component of the "United Nations family," the Permanent Forum on Indigenous Issues represents the institutionalization of the United Nation's long engagement with indigenous peoples and the most elaborate commitment in its fifty-five-year history to the advancement of indigenous interests.[3] In anticipation of this moment, indigenous lawyers and activists from the United States and elsewhere had collaborated in the formation of numerous committees, in the writing of statements that circulated throughout the United Nations and human rights communities around the world, and in organizing conferences aimed at calling attention to and changing the status of indigenous peoples in individual countries and at the United Nations itself. They participated substantially as well in the debates concerning the structure and mandates of the Permanent Forum.

The mandate that emerged from those deliberations is to provide expert advice and recommendations concerning economic and social development, culture, the environment, education, health, and human rights to the Economic and Social Council and other bodies within the UN system, based on information presented by indigenous representatives from around the globe. Staffed by indigenous activists and sponsored by member governments that make up the United Nations, the Permanent Forum is an attempt to bridge what Richard Falk has described as a historic tension in international relations between government sovereignty and collective human rights.[4] Native observers and their supporters around the globe are waiting to see if this novel, transnational indigenous council will be able to influence the powerful intergovernmental entity that houses it, an entity that many of these observers believe has traditionally acted on an inherited ambivalence among Western authorities toward indigenous populations.

My question, in a nutshell, is whether the United Nations promises to make a dent in the legacy of colonialism on indigenous life, or whether it continues that legacy in revised form, as some analysts of First World indigenous international relations, and of the United Nations in particular, have claimed. My contention is that although the United Nations has overtly and inadvertently helped to sustain the inherited order of neglect of indigenous rights, it has also created openings in the dense fabric of international state politics, such that indigenous peoples have been able to assert their claims to human rights with increasing effectiveness. These openings are widening, it seems, with each session of the Human Rights Commission and its sub-bodies, and with the emergence of the Permanent Forum. I do not want to claim a continuous story of progress on the United Nations' part in these matters, since the openings also contract with regularity. But, so far, they do not appear to be closing either.

Progress, of course, is a relative term, and some indigenous groups will likely position themselves against the rights developments at issue insofar as these imply not only advancement toward sovereignty and land rights, if governments should extend them. Human rights as described by the United Nations also tend to assume that modernization, democratization, and the enshrinement of individualism within tribal nations are valuable processes. Given the tensions that can arise between such processes and alternative systems that go by the name of traditionalism, it is risky to claim that the recognition of human rights is progress for everybody. But I think it fair to say that representatives of the Native nations and nongovernmental organizations working with the UN system do for the most part speak unequivocally on the desirability of realizing the promises of a human rights agenda, with adjustments made in these norms as proposed in the draft Declaration of Indigenous Rights, which I discuss below.

VITORIA, MARSHALL, AND THE LEGAL RHETORIC OF INDIGENOUS RIGHTS

Before addressing the UN's responses to indigenous demands on its attentions, I want to take a brief look backwards into the history of Western legal thought concerning the international rights of indigenous peoples. Of the many thinkers responsible for this legacy, two of the perhaps most influential are Francisco de Vitoria and John Marshall, whose ideas in many ways provided the legal imprimatur for the colonial situations in which most indigenous people still live, and which the UN human rights agencies are expected by their Native constituencies to challenge.

Vitoria, a Dominican legal advisor to the Spanish crown, was professor of theology at the University of Salamanca from 1526 to 1546, a period of great intellectual debate in Spain centering on the legal and ethical grounds of conquest and colonization in the Indies. Concerned specifically to codify the natural rights of Indians and European responsibilities for honoring them, Vitoria's lectures, in the words of legal historian

Robert Williams, "are widely recognized as a primary source of the basic principles of post-sixteenth-century Spanish colonial legal theory as well as of the treatment of indigenous colonized peoples under modern international and United States law."[5]

Vitoria's thinking drew extensively on Thomas Aquinas's concepts of natural law, particularly Aquinas's idea that all human beings are blessed with a component of reason and that this gift, divine in its origins, extends to persons outside Christian society. The gift of human reason not only demands a fundamental respect but also implies "the natural law right and duty [of people] to rationally order their political and social lives."[6]

The Thomistic idea articulated "a universally binding Law of Nations," founded on the good, or reason which is an essential component of human character and relationships and that preexisted human history and social institutions.[7] This disinterested priority determines natural law's privileged status. Such an understanding of natural law was, for many late medieval thinkers, a version of the divine law that preexisted and unified all human social organizations, but this more secular good constituted for Renaissance and early modern thinkers a "rule of life and society discoverable by human reason apart from any special revelation or the decision of any particular authority."[8]

Invoking Thomistic humanism and natural law in the context of Spanish America, Vitoria rejected the doctrine, established by Pope Alexander VI's fifteenth-century donations of territory to Spain, on which the Spanish monarchs based the legality of their rights of conquest and title to Indian lands, that the act of coming upon a place hitherto unvisited—or "discovered"—in the Indies by Spanish agents vested title to that place in the Crown.[9] As Williams explains in *The American Indian in Western Legal Thought,* Alexander's thinking in *Intercaetera divina* derived from that of thirteenth-century Innocent IV, who, in commenting on moral and legal issues pertaining to the Crusades, raised the resonant question, "Is it licit to invade a land that infidels possess or which belongs to them?"[10] His answer anticipated the logic of many Western writers on empire in generations to come: first acknowledging the natural law rights of "infidels," he then argued that violations of these laws by infidels against other people (in particular, against Christian Crusaders who represented the natural law rights of Christendom to dominate the Holy

Land, the birthplace of Christ) constituted cause for papal intervention, including military action. The norms assumed in Innocent IV's notions of natural law were, of course, entirely European, so that papal intervention and jurisdiction were virtually automatically justified.[11]

Because he dismissed such Crusader-era logic, Vitoria is often assumed to have been a sympathizer with the indigenous people of the Western Hemisphere.[12] As Williams demonstrates with painstaking care, however, Vitoria's arguments not only helped confirm the rectitude of Spanish colonizing practices in the Indies but gave them formal legal status. As evidenced by his influential lecture of 1532, "Of the Indians Lately Discovered," published by one of his students in 1557, Vitoria, like many of his contemporaries, supported the legitimate, natural rights of the Indians to their sovereignty, their governments, and their property.[13] These rights came with certain responsibilities, particularly the responsibility to recognize the natural rights of others, including, of course, the Spaniards. Spanish rights included travel, trade, and, most of all, the teaching of Christianity, "because the natives would otherwise be outside the pale of salvation, if Christians were not allowed to go to them carrying the Gospel message. . . . Because brotherly correction is required by the law of nature just as brotherly love is."[14]

In summarizing the duties to which the indigenous peoples are bound, Vitoria writes "If the Indian natives wish to prevent the Spaniards from enjoying any of their . . . rights under the law of nations, . . . the Spaniards can defend themselves and do all that consists with their own safety, it being lawful to repel force by force." He concludes that if "after recourse to all other measures, the Spaniards are unable to obtain safety as regards the native Indians, save by seizing their cities and reducing them to subjection, they may lawfully proceed to these extremities."[15]

As is obvious in these arguments, and as many legal historians have argued, Vitoria articulates a distinctly ambivalent point of view. He rejects the doctrine of discovery in what first appears as a defense of native rights but follows this with a set of demands that would be difficult at best for the Indians to fulfill, particularly the injunction to "love the Spaniards," given what we know of Spanish practices in the Indies from their first arrival. Nevertheless, and particularly because he maintains such a conceptual, theoretical distance from his object of study, it is important to note that Victoria does recognize in his codification of the

Law of Nations the inherent rights of Indians as men among men in the Thomistic tradition, that their duties are appended to these rights, and if the duties go unfulfilled, so go the rights. "In order to make his rights effective," as Robert Williams summarizes Victoria's position, "the Indian . . . had to recognize the reciprocal duty of accepting the universalized cultural, political, and ethical norms contained within the Christian European tradition."[16] I want to emphasize this last point in particular, that in order to "make his rights effective"—to realize those rights, to dissent from the dominant society's negation of them—indigenous people must accept the norms of their oppressors. As oxymoronic as this position may appear, it becomes quite an ordinary problem in debates of our own time, particularly concerning the rights of indigenous and Third World populations in the United Nations and other legal forums of the world's ruling societies. I will take up this matter in more detail later.

Vitoria's arguments were in many ways symptomatic of the hegemonic ideology of conquest and colonization in his day, but his particular style of honoring the rights of natives only to ultimately justify dishonoring them became a pattern in Western legal rhetoric concerning indigenous peoples in the Americas and elsewhere. The seeds of a secular ethos in Vitoria's Renaissance humanism, relocating the sources of universal rectitude from the divinely inspired knowledge of the pope to the rationalism common to all humankind, flourished in the nationalist discourses of England throughout the seventeenth century and of the United States in the eighteenth and early nineteenth centuries.

John Marshall looked to Vitoria's ideas and methods in writing the decisions (discussed in the previous chapter) which brought the much-disputed issues of indigenous natural law, land, and sovereignty in the early republic to a head. In *Johnson v. McIntosh*, Marshall wrote, "All our institutions recognize the [former] absolute title of the Crown, subject only to the Indian right of occupancy."[17] Right by occupancy was, in fact, the basis of Daniel Webster's argument for the defense, Johnson and Graham's lessee. Webster cited Grotius in claiming that the Indians were "proprietors of the soil, and could not be divested of their rights of property . . . by a mere act of executive government."[18] Indeed, Marshall's first cousin Thomas Jefferson had shown in his *Notes on the State of Virginia* that numerous acts of purchase of Indian lands by European American individuals and governments presupposed that the Indians had had clear title to them.[19] Nevertheless, Marshall's ruling stipulated that since discovery leant a superior title to the governing nation, that government could revoke the right of occupancy as it saw fit.[20] Marshall maintained Vitoria's notion that, in theory, the indigenous peoples have natural law rights and that the appropriation of their conquered lands "may be opposed to natural right." "Most usually . . . the rights of the conquered to property should remain unimpaired," he wrote, as they learn to live and "mingle with" the new inhabitants. Since the Indians of America, however, were "fierce savages" who drew their living from the forest and lived in entirely different ways from the Europeans, they could not speak to or engage with the dominant society in order to claim those rights. Natives were so entirely different from the Europeans and their reactions to colonization so systematically hostile that they were "a people with whom it was impossible to mix."[21]

Thus Marshall allows for the possibility that, were the Indians to relinquish their hostilities and adapt sufficiently to European ways, they might be recognized as deserving title to their own lands. As if to override even this very ambiguous opening to the recognition of indigenous rights, however, he puts forward the larger principle that "discovery gave title to the government by whose subjects, or by whose authority, it was made, against all other European governments, which title might be consummated by possession." In contemporary times, tribes in the United States have interpreted the term pragmatically in order to make it work for the development of casinos and tourism generally. In this sense, they are joining the global marketplace on their own terms, as a means of keeping or regaining land, recognition, and material security that make possible the reproduction of tribal knowledges into the future. The irony in this lays in the way it manifests Marshall's notion, expressed in *Johnson v. McIntosh,* that if Indians were to adapt to European ways, their titles to homelands might be recognized by the European powers.

Unlike Vitoria, Marshall embraced the doctrine of discovery: "The rights of the original inhabitants were, in no instance, entirely disregarded . . . but their rights to complete sovereignty, as independent nations, were necessarily diminished, and their power to dispose of the soil at their own will, to whomsoever they pleased, was denied by the original fundamental principle, that discovery gave exclusive title to those who made it."[22] The opinion in *Johnson v. McIntosh* established the legal framework for U.S. official attitudes toward Indian rights to land and sovereignty; but, as Williams amply demonstrates, the thinking derived from medieval sources. Marshall's decision, Williams writes, "is regarded as the textual source of the basic principle of modern federal Indian law, but its acceptance of the Doctrine of Discovery and its denial of territorial sovereignty to American Indian nations actually represents a point of closure, not a point of origin, in U.S. colonizing discourse."[23]

Marshall's commentary in *Cherokee Nation v. Georgia,* where he coined the term "domestic dependent nations," condemned indigenous peoples around the globe for centuries to come to a legal identity that denied their existence as independent collectives.[24] The complaint that the Cherokees brought to the Supreme Court concerned Georgia's efforts to seize Native lands for immigrant settlement. Marshall considered the matter and drew from it a very different problem concerning jurisdiction. He introduced his commentary on the case (not an opinion, since the Court had declined to rule on it) by asking, "May the plaintiff [the Cherokee] sue in [the Supreme Court]? Is the Cherokee nation a foreign state in the sense in which that term is used in the Constitution?"[25] Marshall argued that, even though in numerous treaties the U.S. government had acted as if the Cherokee nation were a state, "they acknowledge themselves in their treaties to be under the protection of the United States."[26] Since they, like the other tribes, also live "within the acknowledged boundaries" of that country, he argued, "it may well be doubted whether [t]hey . . . can, with strict accuracy, be denominated foreign nations. They may, more correctly, perhaps, be denominated domestic dependent nations. They occupy a territory to which we assert a title independent of their will, which must take effect in point of possession when their right of possession ceases. Meanwhile, they are in a state of pupilage. Their relation to the United States resembles that of a ward to his guardian."[27]

The concept of "domestic dependent nations" was, as Vine Deloria explains, a compromise term, in which Marshall pasted together his own emphasis on the tribes' dependency and location within the borders of the dominant entity and the dissenting justices' desire to recognize them as legitimate nations.[28] The term efficiently identified the prevailing attitude of the U.S. government concerning Native sovereignty and made the guardian-ward model of the conquering state's relationship to indigenous peoples, observed in theory and practice since the medieval crusades, official U.S. policy.[29] As Deloria puts it, Marshall's domestic dependent nation definition "has plagued *everyone* ever since."[30] Indigenous peoples in colonized territories around the globe came to be treated according to Justice Marshall's model, as wards of the state; and "trusteeship" came to be the common term for the state-indigenous relationship.

CONTEMPORARY HUMAN RIGHTS
DISCOURSES AND THE UNITED NATIONS

Marshall's nineteenth-century deliberations bestowed legal honor on the medieval logic of the doctrine of discovery and the concept of domestic dependent nations. They became models for colonial relations not only in the United States but also in the other European-derived settler states of Canada, Latin America, New Zealand, and Australia. In James Anaya's words, these "decisions figur[e] prominently in the fabric of international jurisprudence concerning indigenous peoples" to this day.[31]

Since the later twentieth century, however, the colonized nations of the "Fourth World" have reemerged on the international scene to dispute the entrenched marginalization this Western legal history has sustained. They have done so in increasing numbers by invoking human rights. As a term in international political and diplomatic discourse, "human rights" has acquired a privileged edge since the end of the Cold War. Its deployment raises the possibility of profoundly abusive acts or forms of negligence that deny human dignity. The normative implications of the term hark back to the concept of natural law and natural rights, irrefutable and agreed to among all nations, as Vitoria had described them in the sixteenth century, and Aquinas before him.

"Historically," Anaya writes, "international law developed to facilitate empire building and colonization, but today it promotes a very different model of human encounter and provides grounds for remedying the contemporary manifestations of the oppressive past."[32] And Richard Falk notes, "To some extent, the growth of an international human rights law in recent decades has challenged the deference [in classical international law] to governmental supremacy."[33] Over the past fifty years, the United Nations has represented itself as the primary overseer of international law concerning human rights. Has it succeeded in overcoming the ambiguities in legal rhetoric that sponsored the "oppressive past"?

Although the 1948 Universal Declaration of Human Rights had mentioned nothing about the rights of indigenous peoples specifically, as early as 1957 a UN agency, the International Labor Organization, adopted its Convention 107, which took a sympathetic but assimilation-ist approach to indigenous rights in the demands it made on signatories. A 1989 revision, ILO Convention 169, improved on the more problem-atic assumptions but still left much authority for indigenous labor and other matters to signing governments.[34] With the adoption in 1966 of the International Covenant on Economic, Social, and Cultural Rights and the International Covenant on Civil and Political Rights, "self-determination of peoples" was declared a universal right, secured by in-ternational law, that indigenous peoples could claim.[35]

As Elsa Stamatopoulou has argued, indigenous leaders engaging with the United Nations deployed the language of rights quite con-sciously when they began approaching the world body in the early 1970s since many of them were familiar with it from their experiences as ac-tivists in the civil rights movement in the United States, Australia, Canada, and elsewhere.[36] In this "school," North American Native ac-tivists had adopted the concept of rights alongside African Americans, Latinos, and Latinas, as well as other ethnic groups that were lobbying local and national governments and demonstrating for the recognition of their struggles.[37]

"Red Power" became a rallying cry in the United States, alongside other minority ethnic power movements; and indigenous involvement in the movement helped stimulate a renewed consciousness of the histori-cal violation of Indian cultural and political as well as civil rights in the late 1960s. With the 1969 American Indian occupation of Alcatraz Island in San Francisco, the 1972 Trail of Broken Treaties caravan and occupa-tion of the Bureau of Indian Affairs, and the resistance to government forces at Wounded Knee, South Dakota, in 1973, indigenous peoples in the United States took what they had learned about the effectiveness of a rights discourse to the streets.

By the early 1970s, many international indigenous political-action groups had emerged in the United States, Canada, and Central America, prominent among them the International Indian Treaty Council, the World Council of Indigenous Peoples, and the National Indian Brother-hood of Canada.[38] Frustrated by the repeated failure to gain recognition of political or cultural rights, even those promised by treaties, from na-tional governments, representatives of indigenous groups around the globe now began turning to the world arena of the United Nations.

The 1977 UN-sponsored International Nongovernmental Organization Conference on Discrimination against Indigenous Populations in the Americas in Geneva was a landmark event for indigenous groups. In the words of Robert Coulter, one of the conference organizers, it was "the formal beginning of Indian participation in international forums."[39] James Anaya has written that the conference "contributed to forging a transnational indigenous identity that subsequently expanded to embrace indigenous peoples from other parts of the world."[40]

Out of this conference, two resolutions emerged that have shaped UN-indigenous relations ever since: to establish a Working Group on Indigenous Populations, to create a Declaration of the Rights of Indigenous Peoples, and to initiate a Permanent Forum for Indigenous Issues.[41] Since its inception in 1982, the Working Group on Indigenous Populations (WGIP) has acquired a reputation for inclusiveness, vigorous debate, and organizational rigor in the charting of a global indigenous rights agenda.[42] The five-member WGIP was formally established in 1982 under the auspices of the Sub-commission on the Promotion and Protection of Human Rights with a two-fold mandate: to annually review recent events concerning the protection or violation of rights of indigenous peoples and to set international standards for the promotion of these rights.[43] WGIP has initiated many projects and sent countless proposals to the Commission on Human Rights on behalf of indigenous peoples, and it has hosted numerous expert analyses of indigenous situations as well as sponsored extensive studies of discrimination against indigenous peoples and of treaties and agreements between indigenous peoples and governments. Throughout these activities, representatives of indigenous peoples and organizations with and without nongovernmental organization (NGO) consultative status in the United Nations have been able to participate.

As part of its mission to set standards for international rights for indigenous peoples, the WGIP worked for many years to fulfill the second of the three major resolutions to emerge from the 1977 Geneva conference, the creation of a Declaration of the Rights of Indigenous Peoples. As a declaration, it was not intended to be a legally binding instrument; but if and when completed, the declaration would carry "considerable moral force," according to the Office of the High Commissioner for Human Rights' "Guide for Indigenous People."[44] In 1993, the WGIP forwarded a draft, compiled with the input of thousands of indigenous participants, to the Human Rights Commission for its approval.

One of the most crucial features of the draft declaration is its systematic deployment of the term "indigenous peoples," the "s" constituting an important political signifier in international discourse since "peoples" is the term used in the United Nations Charter to refer to independent, sovereign nations. Among the draft declaration's many substantial and controversial provisions are Article 3, which declares the right of self-determination; Article 12, which declares the right "to maintain, protect, and have access in privacy to their religious and cultural sites"; Article 19, which grants the opportunity "to participate . . . if they so choose" in any decisions that affect their "rights, lives and destinies"; Article 26, which ensures the ability to "own, develop, control and use the lands and territories, including the total environment of the lands, air, waters, coastal seas, sea-ice, flora and fauna and other resources which they have traditionally owned or otherwise occupied or used"; Article 27, which describes rights to the "restitution of the lands, territories and resources which they have traditionally owned or otherwise occupied or used, and which have been confiscated, occupied, used or damaged without their free and informed consent," or, where this is impossible, to "just and fair compensation"; and Article 30, which grants authority to "require that States obtain their free and informed consent prior to the approval of any project affecting their lands, territories and other resources."[45]

After the World Conference on Human Rights in Vienna in 1993, the WGIP was charged with helping establish the Permanent Forum on Indigenous Issues, the first meeting of which was held in May 2002 in New York. With its broad mandate, the Permanent Forum serves as a high-level expert body that hears complaints from indigenous national representatives and NGOs and advises and makes recommendations on issues concerning indigenous people, including economic and social development, health, education, environment, culture, *and* human rights.[46] It is composed of sixteen independent experts on indigenous issues, half of whom were nominated by indigenous organizations and half by governments and whose selection was based on "the diversity and geographical distribution of indigenous peoples, transparency, and equal opportunity for all indigenous peoples."[47] As part of the Economic and Social Council, the parent body of the Commission on Human Rights, the Permanent Forum on Indigenous Issues occupies the same level within the UN institutional hierarchy as the Human Rights Commission itself, a placement that gives it tremendous prestige within the world body as well as among member governments. Given its broad mandate, its privileged status, and membership of experts, the hope of the WGIP and the Human Rights Commission is that the Permanent Forum will be effective in permeating the intergovernmental machinery of the United Nations and that indigenous peoples will thus acquire a higher profile and a more palpable presence on the international scene than they have had in the past.

PROBLEMS IN IMPLEMENTING THE PLANS

These recent advances in the status of international indigenous rights reflect serious efforts within the UN system to continue reversing the structures of colonialism and its legacy among the indigenous populations of the planet. There have been problems, however, in the execution of these plans and projects.

In 1995, work on the draft Declaration of the Rights of Indigenous Peoples was turned over to the new Working Group of the Commission on Human Rights on the Draft Declaration. This working group consists of representatives of state governments, although indigenous representatives may participate in deliberations.[48] However, as Russell Barsh of the Four Directions Council of Alberta has reported, in order to do so, indigenous representatives must submit to an application process thick with bureaucratic requirements, delays, and limitations.[49] By the time of the first meeting in November 1995, only forty-five applications by indigenous NGOs to participate had been approved; according to Barsh, this amounted to half of the total applications received. Thirty-one indigenous NGOs ended up attending the first meeting through the mechanism of the special application procedure, and only "six of the sixty-one governments attending the session had included an indigenous person in their official delegations."[50] What Barsh describes is a good example of Richard Falk's claim that the "statist character of [such] international arenas means that those who are being challenged exert comprehensive control over such matters as agenda and budget, thereby impairing even the claiming process."[51]

Barsh was an observer at the first meeting, and his report suggests that most governments represented on the Working Group of the Commission on the Draft Declaration will not be eager to approve the draft declaration submitted to them, even though they have agreed to accept it as their working text. Objections have been raised to many of its articles. Just to cite one of the several more controversial ones, Article 26 has elicited controversy for its granting of rights to "own, develop, control and use" traditional homelands. The governments of Australia, Canada, and the United States have indicated a preference to use the formula of the International Labor Organization Convention 107 from 1957, which, as Barsh summarizes it, "only secures rights to lands and resources that remain in use," adhering to the principles of John Marshall's 1823 ruling in *Johnson v. McIntosh*. Other states have taken the position that the disposition of land resources for indigenous populations needs to be "compatible with national land tenure systems, state ownership of minerals, and state power to expropriate land."[52]

The government-dominated Working Group of the Commission on the Draft Declaration has "expressed serious technical and philosophical criticism of [the draft's] construction . . . [and] complained of ambiguities, internal inconsistencies, redundancy, and failure to define or explain key concepts."[53] Foremost among the latter is the term "indigenous," which, according to the draft declaration's Article 8, should be left to indigenous peoples themselves to define. But several governments have pressed for an internationally applicable definition to distinguish indigenous from minorities groups.[54] Many of these same governments have asserted that they do not have indigenous populations, and the establishment of a definition would allow them to demonstrate as much. Such assertions would, unless successfully contested, exempt the governments at issue from compliance with UN-mandated obligations concerning human rights for indigenous peoples, current or to come under the provisions of the declaration.[55]

As I mentioned earlier, the term "peoples" in reference to indigenous collectivities has also drawn fire. In the eyes of many governmental representatives, the term speaks directly to self-determination, often a threatening concept for governments since they commonly take it as an opening to demands for self-government and land as well as to threats of secession, even though many indigenous leaders and participants in the

WGIP have made it quite clear that indigenous nations for the most part are not interested in secession.[56] Their interests are rather to achieve political autonomy within the states where they are located. Nevertheless, governmental resistance to this and other features has been so strong that to date the Working Group of the Commission on the Draft Declaration has adopted only two of the forty-five articles of the draft submitted by the WGIP in 1993.[57]

Resistance on the part of UN member governments to the draft declaration in general can be attributed at least in part to First World inclinations to privilege individual over collective rights. In addition, it is not difficult to see how, in general, these and governments in the developing world might interpret native claims to land proprietorship and political self-determination as direct challenges to their own sovereignty; and these are primarily matters of power more than of international legal or political philosophy, however much the latter may be brought to bear in order to confirm that power.

Russell Barsh wrote in 1983 that the matter of international human rights is quite simple: "States acquire nothing by force. Every people has a right to exist, to be left alone, to be a state. The complex fictions and endless exceptions of [particularly U.S.] Indian law are, by comparison, a cruel parody of reasoning and justice."[58] In part because it has not been able to solve the problems besetting its efforts in recent decades to advance indigenous rights, the United Nations has suffered a seemingly inerasable reputation for being too diplomatically fastidious to do much more than uphold governments' interests in their relations with the world's indigenous peoples. Insofar as this reputation locates the United Nations largely in the camp of world governments, its human rights policies privilege states and individuals and do not address the more collectivist concerns poignant for indigenous peoples.[59]

"PRIESTS" AND NOBLE PRIMITIVISTS?

At this point, I would like to consider whether, given the delays, compromises and other problems in the execution of the UN's plans toward remedying indigenous issues, it is fair to argue, as some have, that the United Nations, as a body dominated by the world's governments, is motivated by the signature ambivalence, inherited through Vitoria, Marshall, and others, of Western powers toward indigenous populations.

I want to look at two such arguments that offer representative views and that have been particularly persuasive since the United Nations has actively opened its doors to indigenous speakers. These are Ashis Nandy's often-cited essay of 1986, "Shamans, Savages, and the Wilderness: On the Audibility of Dissent and the Future of Civilizations," published in 1989 in *Alternatives,* and Chris Tennant's "Indigenous Peoples, International Institutions, and the International Legal Literature from 1945–1993," which appeared in *Human Rights Quarterly* in 1994.

Nandy writes that the United Nations "represents only an edited version of the present global nation-state system. For the United Nations itself has acquired many of the trappings of a modern state. Its building blocks are nation-states and its unit of analysis is the nation-state."[60] As a replicant nation-state itself, the United Nations, according to Nandy, refuses "to abdicate [its] status as the ultimate unit of political analysis." Moreover, "those exposed to the mass culture of global politics"—not just the states that govern them—are unable "to think in terms of categories even partly independent of the idea of nation-state."[61]

Recalling Vitoria's and Marshall's positions, Nandy asserts that "ahistorical societies" cannot "transcend or dismantle" the systems of the global civilization that sustains their colonization unless they follow that civilization's own "ground rules" for dissent, which means using the language of liberation and the "institutional instrumentalities" of the dominant societies.[62] Unlike Vitoria and Marshall, however, he does not end the discussion with the assumption that they will not be capable of doing so. As an alternative to ascent, Nandy points to the resistance of "the shaman," his metaphor for traditionalists who have not become "captive to the historical mode" and whose resistance is expressed in words and gestures deployed from indigenous lexicons as well as in "criticism of human violence and oppression which are implicit in the ways of life, myths, legends, and above all, in the spontaneous defiance and rebellions of the oppressed."[63]

If the shaman wants to be heard in the modern, global civilization with which she or he resists identifying, however, the shaman must speak that civilization's particular language of liberation, with all its enlightenment apparatus, including individualism, statism, the alienation of territory, and a prevailing subject-object relation between persons and nature. Nandy claims that as soon as the shaman begins to speak this language, the shaman "becomes a part of the everyday world [of that civilization it sought to resist], a priest."[64] "The priest helps consolidate" whichever culture it attends, and in that role translates the knowledge of the shaman into the language of the oppressor; and "once you explain a shaman properly, you turn him or her into a guru, or worse, a priest."[65]

While he imagines a resistant discourse that would permit the shaman to function as shaman instead of as priest, Nandy does not believe this discourse can be deployed in Western institutions under the prevailing knowledge regimes operating in even the most humanitarian, liberal states and organizations. His effort is to convince Western powers that they need to recognize the alterity of indigenous, colonized peoples and their distinct ways of representing themselves, including their collective human rights, in international legal forums that the West supports. He harbors little hope, however, that world governments or the United Nations will listen. He finds instead that UN efforts to recognize indigenous rights are circular and ultimately serve to reinforce First World statism, which habitually ignores or denies indigenous political and cultural priorities.

But do the United Nations programs I have just described, even with their limitations and other problems, have this effect? Do they necessarily change the "shaman" into a "priest," as Nandy claims? Perhaps; but perhaps this is too purist of a position. Indeed, Nandy himself argues that "the old classification between the historical and ahistorical societies may not have broken down, but all large ahistorical societies now have sizeable sections of population which have become . . . entirely captive to the historical mode."[66] Those who remain shamans are, in effect, consciously resisting "mainstreaming" themselves. This means, then, that they are not unaware of the "historical" parts of the world or untouched by their massive influence.

In taking this position concerning indigenous consciousness in the performance of indigenous identity in the international public sphere, Nandy raises a question that hovers in Ranajit Guha's theory of "dominance without hegemony" that I have born in mind throughout this book.[67] If an indigenous person has, under the conditions of dominance without hegemony, not assimilated to the dominant culture, then, if she or he does begin to be embraced by it, or at least begins to have access to its institutions and opportunity to act within them, does she or he suddenly become assimilated by taking those steps? If they should find themselves speaking the liberal lingua franca of the exogenous forums of the United Nations, must we assume a shift in "being" occurs, as Nandy suggests when he writes, "The moment the shaman uses the available institutional instrumentalities, he or she becomes a part of the everyday world, a priest"?[68] It may be awkward or uncomfortable to approach the United Nations; it may be satisfying for the wrong reasons; but I would argue, along with Guha, that the situation does not, by its own weight, introduce such a dramatic shift in being or necessarily initiate such a hopeless form of cultural schizophrenia.[69]

Chris Tennant makes a similar argument when he claims that the "primitivization" of indigenous peoples in the literature of the United Nations and other international legal forums since the 1950s, even in the more "noble" interpretation of the term he finds in UN documents since about 1971, is characterized by a general uninvestigated effort on the part of writers in these venues to construct "different narratives of the modern Western self."[70] Indigenous peoples are enlisted in these efforts, according to Tennant, to represent alternatives to modernity. "They are defined in part by a spiritual relationship to land and resources: indigenous peoples are stewards of nature, at one with their natural environment . . . [and] indigenous peoples are the victims of progress, their culture threatened always by development."[71] "The image of indigenous peoples in the recent literature," he concludes, "follows the contours of the noble primitive."[72] The thrust of Tennant's argument is to show how Western workers in international law seek to represent something about themselves rather than to claim anything about indigenous styles of being or knowing. Nevertheless, his framing of the terms and images of UN and international law discourse about indigenous people implies that indigenous speakers, as indigenous, are not really heard in UN forums but only enact Western notions of indigenousness, that is, as voices of a romantic Western critique of progress and modernity.[73]

Tennant's argument calls to mind Gayatry Spivak's haunting argument, "Can the Subaltern Speak?" in which Spivak wonders whether it is ever possible for an indigenous agent to speak in an indigenous voice and subject position as such in the public spaces and institutions of the dominant societies, given hegemonic representational codes and strategies as well as the demand that speakers use these strategies in representing themselves.[74] In this sense, Tennant shares Nandy's notion that there is something that troubles indigenous subjectivity as such when it attempts to speak in Western public, political forums.

Tennant's argument, however, takes another step that challenges Nandy's. He shows that indigenous peoples themselves, as participants in international legal fora like those hosted by the United Nations, resist representation as primitives and noble victims in the legal literature by taking political action in the Permanent Forum on Indigenous Issues, the Working Group on Indigenous Peoples, and other bodies. Rather than becoming co-opted by Western ontologies and ideologies simply by stepping into the ring, "indigenous peoples have made both substantive and procedural claims in opposition to their primitivization. Substantively, indigenous peoples have asserted their right to self-determination. Procedurally, they have repeatedly demanded greater participation for indigenous peoples in these same fora."[75] By demonstrating that in venues like the Permanent Forum indigenous peoples create stages for a form of self-representation that has potential for political efficacy, Tennant shows how, in spite of the problems of the legal literature, the United Nations and other institutions that describe themselves as seeking to strengthen international indigenous law have some claim on reality.

Nevertheless, Tennant writes that the UN's way of taking action, when it does attempt to do something in the name of indigenous rights, is limited to creating new institutional bodies and issuing formal statements. He finds in these moves a great deal of what Anthony Giddens has called "institutional reflexivity," in other words, action that is about the institution more than about indigenous rights: "If a study uncovers a problem (or if it confirms the problem it was created to study . . .), the solution is a committee, a working group, or a convention."[76]

Indeed, the United Nations does seem to operate much on this level of rhetorical and bureaucratic formulation. The WGIP, for instance, was created to address a need perceived by the Sub-Commission on Prevention of Discrimination and Protection of Minorities, which itself was founded early by the Commission on Human Rights to manage problems the commission had found within its mandate; and the recent, new offspring of the Working Group for the Draft Declaration has emerged to fulfill a project of the WGIP, and so on. By taking part in such a maze of an institution, Tennant argues, "indigenous people risk having their political aspirations captured and diffused through their struggle to participate," precisely as Nandy puts the case in declaring that indigenous representatives must speak "in the narrow forms dissent has to take to be audible or politically non-cooptable."[77]

One could look at a map of the UN organizational system and find in it a reflection of what Tennant calls "increasingly meaningless bureaucratic rhetoric."[78] But it seems useful to recall that the various committees, sub-committees, etc. divide up the work of oversight and reporting in ways that are necessary to the dialogic, diplomatic ways in which, I think, most of us want the United Nations to operate most of the time. All the offices of the United Nations responsible for some measure of monitoring human rights receive periodic reports from governments on rights matters in their countries, as well as responses and counter reports by the indigenous peoples themselves. These documents, including the responses of the UN bodies to the reports of government and indigenous organizations, are published and distributed among all member governments and other parties at issue; and this practice of publishing the affairs of individual governments, while it may not produce dramatic or even openly legible effects, has some bearing on the reputations and public relations of those governments; and, thus, the bureaucrat business of endless reporting can, I believe, have some influence, however incremental, on the ways those governments behave.

Tennant's charges that the language of the United Nations sustains a primitivist perspective, like Nandy's claim that the shaman cannot speak as such in the United Nations, have more than a little persuasive power, insofar as they recognize that agents of the United Nations, indigenous as well as non-indigenous, are wrong when they assume that, because the institution wishes to cease operating from the ideologies and desires of the West's colonial past in its dealings with indigenous peoples, it will therefore cease deploying the discourses that helped sustain colonialism. But if the officials and representatives that make up UN bodies are not, in fact, operating on such idealistic bases, it does not follow that they are necessarily reconfirming the old discourses of empire in their efforts to address worldwide indigenous issues. And if power relations in the world are to be changed to any degree at all in favor of indigenous peoples, native agents will need to deal with institutions like the United Nations that attempt to operate as brokers of that power.

In responding to these critical views, we might consider as well the extent to which the United Nations offers the space that Nandy prophesies will be necessary in the near future to accommodate an alternative, indigenous voice. The Office of the High Commissioner for Human Rights in Geneva has posted on its Web site a set of guidelines for indigenous people interested in approaching the United Nations to claim their rights.[79] There is nothing subtle or coercive in the language of this "Guide for Indigenous People." The instructions, written in clear, practical terms, explain to readers how to speak, organize, write speeches, and lobby UN members and consultative NGOs in Geneva and New York to get what they want. Are such instructions means by which the United Nations co-opts native resistance, killing it with kindness? To assume so would be to assume a very reductive model of education in which the students are only listeners and consumers of the discourses of the teachers. The United Nations, through UNESCO, supports an indigenous initiative, the International Training Center of Indigenous Peoples, in Nuuk, Greenland. The ITCIP was established in the early 1990s for representatives of indigenous nations and NGOs to give instruction in political activism to native students from around the globe. The core curriculum centers on human rights and rehearses participants in issues ranging from the debates on collective versus individual rights to the politics of environmental rights and to the ratio of pitfalls to benefits of the relatively recent field of "developmental rights." In this and other rights seminars for indigenous activists, as in most effective academic situations, the purpose is not to dispense information or model practices that the learners will precisely imitate, but to stimulate debate, dialogue, and the continuous shaping of positions. Thus, indigenous participants can be as instrumental as they wish in formulating the proposals for UN policies and practices that emerge from these seminars and training sessions.

In the late twentieth and early twenty-first centuries, the number of indigenous persons approaching the Working Group on Indigenous Populations has increased dramatically,[80] and it has become a complex, dynamic site for the airing of impassioned accounts of Fourth World suffering and for the "mobilization of shame" in offending governments. Andrea Muehlebach writes that "no other global forum has ever enabled such a large and diverse group of activists and their organizations to fully articulate their problems."[81] Muehlebach also describes it as "a site of particular discursive density where indigenous identities and cultures are generated and articulated, . . . a vital nodal point in the global 'indigeno-scape,'" and "a transnational locality where notions of indigenous identity and cultural difference are discursively 'spatialized,' . . . an 'Indigenous place.'"[82]

Although many of the proposals they have made through the WGIP have been described as overly optimistic or utopian, it is important to note that the practice of overreaching with claims few governments would be quick to honor has nevertheless worked to call attention to indigenous issues and has had some important results. Among these is the Permanent Forum on Indigenous Issues. In his remarks to the forum, Kofi Annan emphasized perhaps the most politically significant implication of its mandate. "You will have to convince governments," he declared, "that they must join these efforts and increase the attention they pay to indigenous issues."[83] Although governments have a good deal of say in nominations of members to the Permanent Forum, the members they have selected so far have not functioned as mere guardians of government interests in indigenous matters. At the May 2002 session, 207 groups representing indigenous interests, including NGOs and native nations, presented their cases concerning human rights violations by governments and a host of other issues needing attention, from health to the environment to education. Indigenous participants, it appears, can be as instrumental as they wish in formulating the proposals for UN policy and practice that emerge from Permanent Forum sessions. Proposals may be disputed by governments when they reach the Human Rights Commission or the General Assembly, but indigenous voices will have an established role in debates over policies that concern them. In a more just world, they would have more determining power in these matters; but important openings have been made.

An important point to keep in mind in considering the efficaciousness of the Permanent Forum and other UN initiatives concerning indigenous peoples is that "the United Nations" is not a univocal entity, and its work vis-à-vis indigenous peoples does not tell a story of univocal progress, but of continuous debate. Indigenous people can hope for incremental gains within these debates as long as they remain on the stage. So in response to Nandy and Tennant, I would prefer, cautiously, to conclude that indigenous people can find a place at the UN bargaining table without surrendering their differences and redress the daunting legacies of colonialism by showing what they have lost and by claiming their human rights. Indeed, in a recent edition of *Indian Country Today*, the editors wrote an opinion focused on the Permanent Forum on Indigenous Issues: "While the U.N. covenants come slowly and lack teeth, the way leading to them is filled with potentials and possibilities for networking tribes and communities to more prominence and more clout in the media and among institutions of concern. . . . [This is a] hard-gained opportunity for peoples to share the spotlight at the U.N."[84]

Notes

Introduction

1. For accounts of the episode at Wounded Knee that comment on the role of the press as well as make use of print media information, see Peter Matthiessen, *In the Spirit of Crazy Horse* (New York: Penguin, 1991), 59–82; and Ward Churchill, "The Bloody Wake of Alcatraz: Political Repression of the American Indian Movement during the 1970s," in *American Nations: Encounters in Indian Country, 1850 to the Present*, ed. Frederick Hoxie et al. (New York: Routledge, 2001), 378–382.

2. I use the terms "peoples" and "North America" here to emphasize, respectively, the sovereign self-determinism of indigenous nations, keyed by the term "peoples" in the language of the United Nations' Universal Declaration of Human Rights, and the resonance of the Native renaissance in Canada as well as the United States in the wake of Wounded Knee.

3. I use the terms "performance" and "display" in the broader senses assumed in Performance Studies, where performance refers not simply to theatrical fiction or to daily-life versions of the same but to the shaping of selfhood, culture, and identity, in embodied practices and material designs. Performance thus has the sense not of covering up or hiding such phenomena but of exploring their meanings in physical, symbolic display, of, in a sense, shaping them in display. In many cases tribal public self-representations provide information about culture and identity that is partial, limited to what the tribe agrees to share with the public, as the last of the animating questions in the text suggest. Where this occurs, the performance simultaneously offers accurate information and occludes a larger story of which it is only a part. In such cases, the term "performance" retains some of the sense of covering or screening another reality, without functioning overtly as fiction.

4. The Census Bureau's text explains that the figure of 4.3 million includes "the number of people estimated to be American Indian and Alaska native or American Indian and Alaska native in combination with one or more other races, as of July 1, 2002. They made up 1.5 percent of the total population." According to the Census Bureau, of the total self-identified American Indian and Alaska Native population, 538,300 live on reservations or other trust lands. Http://www.census.gov/Press-Release/www/releases/archives/facts. For statistics on Native Americans living on reservations, see http://factfinder.census.gov/servlet/BasicFactsServlet.

5. Anna Lee Walters, *Talking Indian: Reflections on Survival and Writing* (Ithaca, N.Y.: Firebrand Books, 1992), 134.

6. Anna Lee Walters, "The Buffalo Road," in *Here First: Autobiographical Essays by Native American Writers*, ed. Arnold Krupat and Brian Swann (New York: Modern Library, 2000), 372.

7. Mary Louise Pratt, *Imperial Eyes: Transculturation and Travel Writing* (New York: Routledge, 1994), 6–7.

8. David Eng and David Kazanjian, "Introduction: Mourning Remains," in *Loss: The Politics of Mourning*, ed. Eng and Kazanjian (Berkeley: University of California Press, 2002), 5.

9. For the implications of the term "peoples" in this context, see note 2 above.

10. See, for example, James Clifford, *The Predicament of Culture: Twentieth-Century Ethnography, Literature, and Art* (Cambridge, Mass.: Harvard University Press, 1988); James Clifford and George Marcus, eds., *Writing Culture: The Poetics and Politics of Ethnography* (Berkeley: University of California Press, 1986); Michel Foucault, *Language, Counter-Memory, Practice: Selected Essays and Interviews* (Ithaca, N.Y.: Cornell University Press, 1977) and *Power/Knowledge: Selected Interviews and Other Writings, 1972–1977* (New York: Pantheon, 1981); Clifford Geertz, *Local Knowledge: Further Essays in Interpretive Anthropology* (New York: Basic Books, 1983) and *The Interpretation of Cultures* (New York: Basic Books, 1973); and Victor Turner, *The Anthropology of Performance* (New York: PAJ Publications, 1986).

11. Frantz Fanon, *The Wretched of the Earth* (New York: Grove Press, 1968), 209–210.

12. Ibid., 210.

13. Ibid., 223–224.

14. Ibid., 258.

15. Achille Mbembe, "On the Power of the False," *Public Culture* 14, no. 3 (2002): 629.

16. Achille Mbembe, "African Modes of Self-Writing," *Public Culture* 14, no. 1 (2002): 257.

17. Stuart Hall, "The Local and the Global: Globalization and Ethnicity," in *Culture, Globalization, and the World System: Contemporary Conditions for the Representation of Identity*, ed. Anthony King (Minneapolis: University of Minnesota Press, 1997), 22.

18. Ibid., 34.

19. Ibid., 35.

20. Ibid., 36; Hall, "What Is This 'Black' in Black Popular Culture?" in *Stuart Hall: Critical Dialogues in Cultural Studies*, ed. David Morley and Kuan-Hsing Chen (New York: Routledge, 1996), 472.

21. Hall, "The Local and the Global," 36.

22. Hall, "What Is This 'Black' in Black Popular Culture," 472.

23. Fredric Jameson, *Postmodernism, or the Cultural Logic of Late Capitalism* (London: Verso, 1991), 51.

24. Stuart Hall, "On Postmodernism and Articulation: An Interview with Stuart Hall," ed. Lawrence Grossberg, in *Stuart Hall*, ed. Morley and Chen, 142.

25. Arjun Appadurai, *Modernity at Large* (Minneapolis: University of Minnesota Press, 1996), 32, 90; Mbembe, "On the Power of the False," 637.

26. James Clifford, "Identity in Mashpee," in his *The Predicament of Culture: Twentieth-Century Ethnography, Literature, and Art* (Cambridge, Mass.: Harvard University Press, 1988), 277–346.

27. James Clifford, "Indigenous Articulations," *The Contemporary Pacific* 13, no. 2 (2001): 482.

28. Ibid., 483.
29. For another example of the effectiveness of Hall's articulation theory in relation to African diaspora, see Brent Edwards's *The Practice of Diaspora: Translating Black Internationalism in Harlem and Paris* (Cambridge, Mass.: Harvard University Press, 2002).
30. Steve Maxwell, "Native Places, Native Stories," *American Indian* (summer 2005): 16.
31. Robert Allen Warrior, *Tribal Secrets: Recovering American Indian Intellectual Traditions* (Minneapolis: University of Minnesota Press, 1995), 24.
32. Maxwell, 16, 26.
33. Laurie D. Webster, "Woven by the Grandmothers" (Review Essay), *American Anthropologist* 100, no. 4 (1999): 999.
34. Richard West, foreword to *All Roads Are Good: Native Voices on Life and Culture*, ed. Terence Winch (Washington, D.C.: Smithsonian Institution), 9.
35. Robert DesJarlait, "The Contest Powwow versus the Traditional Powwow and the Role of the Native American Community," *Wiscazo Sa Review* 12, no. 1 (spring 1997): 116.
36. David Whitehorse, *Pow-wow: The Contemporary Pan-Indian Celebration* (San Diego: San Diego State University Publications in American Indian Studies, no. 5, 1989), 1.
37. For the text of the Indian Gaming Regulatory Act, see http://www.nigc.gov/nigc/laws/igra/overview.js.
38. Http://www.nigc.gov/nigc/nigcControl?option=TRIBAL_REVENUE.
39. For information about the National Indian Gaming Association and for the Indian gaming statistics that the NIGA provides, see http://indiangaming.org/library/index.html. Exceptions to the argument that gaming is materially beneficial need to be recognized, particularly in situations where internal strife on reservations over the propriety of gaming has resulted in intense divisiveness or violence, as, for example, in the case of the Mohawks at Akwesasne in New York State. For a discussion of the history of gaming at Akwesasne, see Paul Pasquaretta, "On the 'Indianness' of Gambling and the Native American Community," *Critical Inquiry* 20, no. 4 (summer 1994).
40. For one of the lengthiest and most critical examples of this kind of reporting, see Donald L. Barlett and James B. Steele, "Wheel of Misfortune," *Time*, December 16, 2002, 44–58.
41. John M. Findlay, *People of Chance: Gambling in American Society from Jamestown to Las Vegas* (New York: Oxford University Press, 1986), 79–109.
42. Reuven Brenner and Gabrielle Brenner, *Gambling and Speculation: A Theory, a History, and a Future of Some Human Decisions* (Cambridge: Cambridge University Press, 1990), vii.
43. Ibid.
44. Http://www.indiangaming.org/library/index/html.
45. I use the term "flows" here to suggest the back-and-forth movement of influence between reservation and metropolitan sources rather than to assume influence moves in only one direction. I hope to avoid the naturalizing effects of Arjun Appadurai's use of the term, as described by David Graeber in "The Anthropology of Globalization (with Notes on Neomedievalism and the End of the Chinese Model of the Nation-State)," *American Anthropologist* 104, no. 4 (December 2002): 1222–1223.
46. Mbembe, "African Modes of Self-Writing," 266. Mbembe writes specifically about processes of self-making in contemporary Africa, but much of what he

has to offer makes sense in the context of Native America as well. His critique of African nativism and "the politics of heritage" (266), wherein African indigenous groups seek to recover lost cultural coherencies, is aimed at redirecting critical attention to deeper, disturbing issues of African implication in the great problems of modern African history: slavery, colonization, and apartheid. Thus, Mbembe's hostility for essentialist traditionalism common to contemporary nativist projects, "each [with] its own historicity, its own way of being . . . its own certificate of origin" ("On the Power of the False," 635) might be brought to bear in a critical analysis of contemporary Native American tribal recuperations. The histories are very different, though, and in the latter case we do not find the extent of violence imposed by indigenous Americans upon each other in connection with the history of colonization as we might, on Mbembe's urging, in Africa. See Mbembe's follow-up piece, "On the Power of the False." As I will argue in the chapter on the Mashantucket Pequots, tribal essentialism has its strategic uses that should not be dismissed out of hand by academics whose inclination is to suspect cultural properties and assertions that found themselves on a concept of essence.

47. Ranajit Guha, *Dominance without Hegemony: History and Power in Colonial India* (Cambridge, Mass: Harvard University Press, 1997), xii.

48. Susan Power, "First Fruits," in her *Roofwalker* (Minneapolis: Milkweed, 2002), 120.

49. Some of the more recent studies in this vein include Thomas Biolsi and Larry Zimmerman, eds., *Indians and Anthropologists: Vine Deloria Jr. and the Critique of Anthropology* (Tucson: University of Arizona Press, 1997); James Collins, *Understanding Tolowa Histories: Western Hegemonies and Native American Responses* (New York: Routledge, 1998); Devon Mihesuah, ed., *Indians and Academics: Research and Writing about American Indians* (Lincoln: University of Nebraska Press, 1998); Ruth Phillips and Christopher Steiner, eds., *Unpacking Culture: Art and Commodity in Colonial and Postcolonial Worlds* (Berkeley: University of California Press, 1999); and Russell Thornton, ed., *Studying Native America: Problems and Prospects* (Madison: University of Wisconsin Press, 1998).

50. See, for example, Winch, ed., *All Roads Are Good*; Tom Hill and Richard W. Hill Sr., eds., *Creation's Journey: Native American Identity and Belief* (Washington: Smithsonian Institution and the National Museum of the American Indian, 1994); David Murray, *Forked Tongues: Speech Writing and Representations in North American Indian Texts* (Bloomington: Indiana University Press, 1991); and Greg Sarris, *Keeping Slug Woman Alive: A Holistic Approach to American Indian Texts* (Berkeley: University of California Press, 1993).

51. Gayatry Spivak, "Can the Subaltern Speak?" in *Marxism and the Interpretation of Culture,* ed. Cathy Nelson and Lawrence Grossberg (Urbana: University of Illinois Press, 1988), 271–314.

52. Dipesh Chakrabarty, *Provincializing Europe: Postcolonial Thought and Historical Difference* (Princeton, N.J.: Princeton University Press, 2000), 111.

CHAPTER I   IDENTITY IN MASHANTUCKET

1. In its first full year of operation, the two-thousand-seat bingo hall netted the Mashantuckets $2.6 million. In just over one year, it drew more than four hundred thousand players. See James D. Wherry, afterword to *The Pequots in Southern New England: The Fall and Rise of an American Indian Nation,* ed. Laurence

Hauptman and James D. Wherry (Norman: University of Oklahoma Press, 1990), 219; Sioux Harvey, "Two Models to Sovereignty: A Comparative History of the Mashantucket Pequot Tribal Nation and the Navajo Nation," *American Indian Culture and Research Journal* 20, no.1 (1996): 181; Kim Eisler, *Revenge of the Pequots: How a Small Native American Tribe Created the World's Most Profitable Casino* (Lincoln: University of Nebraska Press, 2001), 107. Kim Eisler reports that when the casino opened in February 1992 the parking lot, which at that time accommodated 1,730 cars, was filled by noon and that by six o'clock that evening there were ten thousand people in the casino (164). Almost two years later, Christopher Rowlands wrote that "although the tribe's total wealth is a secret, some estimates put gross annual revenues at more than $400 million since the casino opened in February 1992." Christopher Rowlands, *Geographical Magazine* 65, no. 12 (December 1994): 24. Its earnings have outrun those of its neighboring corporate institutions, Electric Boat and Pfizer Pharmaceuticals. National business journals have featured articles analyzing the financial success, and the gambling industry has kept a keen, competitive eye on the casino's good fortune. See David Collins, "Casino Profits Soaring," *New London Day*, July 15, 1993, A1, and "Foxwoods' Earnings Go beyond 'Incredible,'" *New London Day*, July 16, 1993, A1; Hilary Waldman, "Casino's Start Exceeds Expectations," *Hartford Courant*, February 22, 1992, B1; and Francis X. Clines, "The Pequots: It's One Thing for Tribal Casinos to Strike It Rich, But When a Tiny Band of Nearly Extinct Indians Beats the Industry at Its Own Game, They Strike a Nerve," *New York Times Sunday Magazine*, February 27, 1994, 51.

2. The casino has also had a significant influence on the economy of southeastern Connecticut. Since Foxwoods, the tribe has provided a significant stimulus to the local and state economies. The Pequots have been credited with making possible as many as forty-one thousand jobs between their own enterprises and non-tribal companies with which they do business. In late 2000, the Pequots were publicly acknowledged by the state government for their crucial role in the recuperation of Connecticut's economy in the wake of the demise of military contracting and insurance industries. Paul Zielbauer, "Study Finds Pequot Businesses Lift Economy," *New York Times*, November 29, 2000, B5.

3. National Indian Gaming Commission Annual Report 2004, 4, http://www.nigc.gov/nigc/documents/biennial_reports/nigc_2004_annual_report.pdf.

4. William R. Eadington, introduction to *Indian Gaming and the Law*, ed. William R. Eadington (Reno, Nev.: Institute for the Study of Gambling and Commercial Gaming, 1998), v–ix and 3; W. Dale Mason, *Indian Gaming: Tribal Sovereignty and American Politics* (Norman: University of Oklahoma Press, 2000), 43–69; and Eisler, *Revenge of the Pequots*, 100–101, 111–116, 118. *California et al. v. Cabazon Band of Mission Indians et al.*, No. 85-1708, U.S. Supreme Court, February 25, 1987; *Seminole Tribe of Florida v. Butterworth*, 658 F.2d, U.S. Court of Appeals for the Fifth Circuit, 1979.

5. Suzette Brewer, "'State of the Indian Gaming Industry' Delivered by National Indian Gaming Association Chairman Ernie Stevens, Jr. on First Day of NIGA Tradeshow in San Diego," http://www.indiangaming.org/info/pr/press-release-2005/4-11b-state-of-indian-gaming.pdf (April 11, 2004); Tom Wanamaker, "Gaming Is Healthy and Growing," *Indian Country Today*, September 10, 2003, A1. Over two hundred of these casinos are engaged in either

Class II or Class III gaming (see below, note 6). Jacob Coin speaks directly to the continuing poverty among tribes in spite of the much-publicized casino wealth in "Fighting the Myth of the Rich Indian," *Indian Country Today*, March 3, 2004, A1.

6. The National Indian Gaming Association explains in its Web site that "it is a myth that Tribes who entered into gaming are 'rolling in dough.' Only the top 20 tribal gaming operations, because of their proximity to major population center, in the country make up 55.5% of the total portion of Indian gaming revenue," (http://www.indiangaming.org/info/pr/presskit/PROCEEDS.pdf). For an analysis of the continuing poverty on reservations, see the U.S. Commission on Civil Rights, "A Quiet Crisis: Federal Funding and Unmet Needs in Indian Country," July 2003, http//www.usccr.gov/pubs/na0703/na0731.pdf.

7. The Indian Gaming Regulatory Act describes Class I gaming as "traditional Indian gaming and social gaming for minimal prizes"; tribes maintain regulatory authority over these games. Class II games are the various forms of bingo, including electronic bingo and pull tabs. These are also regulated by the tribes, but in conjunction with the federal government's National Indian Gaming Commission. Class III gambling includes the common forms of casino gaming: slot machines, black jack, craps, roulette, and electronic games. Class III games can only be conducted under compacts negotiated between tribes and states. See 25 U.S.C. § 2701, 1. The text of the act is available on the Web at http://www.nigc.gov/nigc/laws/igra. For histories of the Indian Gaming Regulatory Act and analyses of its effects, see Mason, *Indian Gaming*; Angela Mullis and David Kamper, eds., *Indian Gaming: Who Wins?* (Los Angeles: UCLA American Indian Studies Center, 2000); Francis Paul Prucha, ed., *Documents of United States Indian Policy* (Lincoln: University of Nebraska Press, 1990); Eisler, *Revenge of the Pequots*; and Eadington, *Indian Gaming and the Law*.

8. On some reservations, the issue of gambling has had mixed responses. At Navajo Nation, for example, the matter was voted down in two referenda in 1994 and 1998. While local tribal authorities at the Navajo satellite reservation of To'Hajilee have legalized gaming, it remains a contentious issue for the rest of the Navajo population. The question may come up again in the near future, however, given Arizona's passing of Proposition 202 two years ago, which allows for a set number of slot machines and other forms of gaming to each Native American tribe located within state borders. According to the Navajo public information officer, "One group of individuals says that if a casino comes, we'll have x problems; another says x benefits will come with it. So it's a very questionable issue right now" (author interview notes with Christopher Morris, February 2002). On the Oneida and Mohawk reservations in upstate New York, tribal populations have for years been sharply divided over the very idea of gaming as well as the distribution of profits for existing casinos. See David Chen and Charlie LeDuff, "Bad Blood in Battle over Casinos," *New York Times*, October 28, 2001, B1; and Paul Pasquaretta, "On the 'Indianness' of Bingo: Gambling and the Native American Community," *Critical Inquiry* 20, no.4 (summer 1994): 703–707.

9. Felix Cohen, *Handbook of Federal Indian Law* (Washington, D.C.: U.S. Government Printing Office, 1948), 122; Charles F. Wilkinson, *American Indians, Time, and the Law* (New Haven: Yale University Press, 1987), 57–58; David E.

Wilkins, *American Indian Sovereignty and the U.S. Supreme Court: The Masking of Justice* (Austin: University of Texas Press, 1997), 21; Prucha, *Documents of United States Indian Policy*, 282–283, 285–286, and 287.

10. See above, note 7 for definitions of the different classes of gaming as articulated in IGRA.

11. On the recognition process, see below, note 30.

12. See David Chen, "Begrudging the Neighbors Their Good Luck: Suit by Newly Rich Oneida Stirs up Other Resentments," *New York Times*, January 22, 1999, B1.

13. In 2003, the Delaware Tribe of Oklahoma began negotiating with the state of Pennsylvania to recover 315 acres in the town of Easton, which was once part of the Delaware, or Lenape, homeland. The tribe has federal recognition, and its agents hoped to reclaim land they argued was taken by the state in the nineteenth century, in violation of the several Indian Trade and Intercourse Acts passed between 1790 and 1834. See Prucha, *Documents of United States Indian Policy*, 14, 17, 64; Cohen, *Handbook of Federal Indian Law*, 92, 348–349. A federal court rejected the tribe's claim, but an appeal is still in process. If the Delaware had been successful, and the land they claimed in Easton returned to them, tribal spokespeople had made it known that they intended to open a casino. The state went so far as to look for an alternative location to offer the tribe in exchange for the Easton site in case it became necessary. The Delaware indicated that they would accept such an exchange. See Paul D. Davies, "Indians Want Casinos in PA," *Philly.Com*, May 15, 2003; Brett Marcy, "Mellow May Have Ally in Indian Tribe Eying Casino," *Times Leader.Com*, August 22, 2003; Frank Whelan, "Centuries-Old Records Gap Clouds Indian Land Claim," *Allentown Morning Call*, February 8, 2004, A1; and Elliott Grossman, "Federal Court Rejects Tribe's Claim To Land," *Allentown Morning Call*, December 3, 2004, A1.

14. Negotiations with Buffalo failed because the parties were not able to settle on where the casino should be situated; and several Erie County towns declined to pursue negotiations, since officials there are opposed to gaming.

15. Jim Adams, "Senate Crushes Dodd's Call for Tribal Recognition Freeze," *Indian Country Today*, September 30, 2002, A1.

16. See 2004 Term Opinions of the Court at www.supremecourtus.gov/opinions/ 04slipopinion.html. *City of Sherill v. Oneida Indian Nation of New York*, No. 03-855, U.S. Supreme Court, March 29, 2005.

17. Alvin Josephy Jr., "New England Indians: Then and Now," in *The Pequots in Southern New England*, ed. Hauptman and Wherry, 13–16; Laurence Hauptman and James Wherry, editorial commentary in *The Pequots in Southern New England*, ed. Hauptman and Wherry, 177; James Clifford, *The Predicament of Culture* (Cambridge, Mass.: Harvard University Press, 1988), 277–278.

18. In the early days of Foxwoods, much indignation appeared in local public discourse about the Pequots, based on the assumption that they had simply made up a tribe for themselves and fooled Congress as well as the Bureau of Indian Affairs into supporting them. Samples of such commentary are summarized in Penelope Overton's "Tribe's Non-Indian Neighbors Feel Threatened: Residents Have Little Knowledge of Indian Culture," *New London Day*, December 15, 1993, B4. The argument resurfaces periodically. Jeff Benedict, for example, a law student at the time, published *Without Reservation: The Making of America's Most Powerful Indian Tribe and Foxwoods, the World's Largest Casino*

(New York: Harper Collins, 2000), in which he argued that the tribe had gained recognition illegally and that Richard Hayward, who was tribal council chair at the time of recognition, "had never represented himself as an Indian until it became expedient for filing a lawsuit" (145). Benedict went so far as to charge that the Pequots under Hayward's leadership "had distinguished themselves as the only American Indian tribe without a single member whose professed racial origin is Native American" (145). His book was roundly refuted by Native commentators; for an example, see Kevin Gover, "How the Eastern Pequots Overcame the Big Lie," *Indian Country Today*, July 12, 2002, A3. A similarly fierce critical account of the Pequots and other tribes with successful casinos appeared in Donald L. Barlett and James B. Steele, "Special Report on Indian Casinos: Wheel of Misfortune," *Time Magazine*, December 16, 2002, 48–58. Barlett and Steele assume that all Native American gambling casino profits ought to be pooled and the proceeds shared among the general Native population. In fact, the Pequots share a good deal of their wealth with other Native tribes. More to the point, though, while the systematic distribution of corporate wealth might be a worthy idea in principle, it is not a common practice in the United States, nor is such a concept held in great esteem in most popular, public discourse. Corporations in the United States aren't generally expected to share their profits with like institutions or distribute their proceeds among ethnic groups with which personnel might be associated. Jim Adams's "For Time Magazine, Sovereignty 101" (*Indian Country Today*, December 23, 2002, A1) is one of many Native responses to Barlett and Steele and offers a learned, detailed refutation of their arguments.

19. Applications are vetted by a committee of elders who meticulously scrutinize the documents to determine whether they evidence the required relationship. By late 2002, the tribal population stood at 680, an increase of almost six times the 1983 level. Until recently, applicants also had to demonstrate that they had at least one-sixteenth Mashantucket Pequot "blood," but this criteria was eliminated since it meant children born to mixed parents would not be tribal members. Stan Decoster, "Mashantuckets Solidify Children's Place in Tribe: Tribal Members OK Revisions in Bloodline Requirements," *New London Day*, December 17, 1996, A1; Sam Libby, "Who Is an Indian and Who Decides?" *New York Times*, January 14, 1996, 7; and Mashantucket Pequot Public Relations Director Suzanne Viafora, interview with author, June 20, 1996.

20. Suzanne Viafora, interview with author; Kirk Johnson, "Tribe's Promised Land Is Rich but Uneasy," *New York Times*, February 20, 1995, A1; Ellen Lieberman, "Tensions in the Family: Some Members Fear Business Success Will Erode Tribal Values," *New London Day*, December 15, 1993, B1; Leslie Goffe, "Hitting the Genetic Jackpot: How Native Blood Paid Out for Some African Americans," *Utne Reader*, May–June 1999, 76–78. An article in the *Pequot Times* issue for July 2003 focused on the Miss Mashantucket pageant held during Pequot Days and included a photograph of the finalists that images the spectrum of skin tones among members of the Mashantucket population. Some of the contestants look African American, while one is a very pale Anglo-looking blonde, and another tiny girl might be described as "Native" looking.

21. Johnson, "Tribe's Promised Land Is Rich but Uneasy"; Goffe, "Hitting the Genetic Jackpot"; Maria Hileman, "Mashantuckets Ready to Build Two New

Schools: Concern about Youth Prompts Tribe's Move," *New London Day*, December 10, 1995, A1; Penelope Overton and Maria Hileman, "Pequot Teens Struggle for Identity," *New London Day*, December 11, 1995, A1; Suzanne Viafora, interview with author.

22. In addition to the social, economic, and cultural work of restructuring a Mashantucket Pequot community, the tribe's leaders have been engaged for many years in efforts to recuperate the Pequot language. To date, approximately one thousand words have been identified, and the Pequot Language Project has been initiated, which will involve three phases over ten years. The first will involve hiring researchers and enlisting a set of interested tribal members to form a "language nest," that is, a group that will "develop a foundation for understanding and learning the language" and use what they take from this experience in the course of daily life on the reservation. The second phase will consist of the construction of a dictionary and a grammar, as well as an instructional curriculum. The final phase, then, will be to use these materials to teach tribal members how to speak and understand the Pequot language. Karen Hatcher, "Jones Leads Tribe's Language Revitalization," *Pequot Times*, May 2003; and Maria Hileman, "Lost Civilization Being Reconstructed," *New London Day*, December 14, 1993.

23. Neil Asher Silberman, "Pequot Country," *Archaeology* 44, no. 4 (July/August 1991): 37–38; Maria Hileman, "Lost Civilization Being Reconstructed," *New London Day*, December 14, 1993, E3; and Kevin McBride, "The Historical Archaeology of the Mashantucket Pequots, 1637–1900," in *The Pequots in Southern New England*, ed. Hauptman and Wherry, 98.

24. Laurence Hauptman, "The Pequot War and Its Legacies," in *The Pequots in Southern New England*, ed. Hauptman and Wherry, 73.

25. McBride, "Historical Archaeology of the Mashantucket Pequots," 104.

26. This designation distinguishes the Mashantuckets from the Eastern or Pawcatuck Pequots, who had been under the control of the Narragansetts in Rhode Island since the war and were given a five-hundred-acre reservation in 1650 near the town of North Stonington. McBride, "Historical Archaeology of the Mashantucket Pequots," 105. The Eastern Pequots gained recognition from the Bureau of Indian Affairs in the summer of 2002.

27. McBride "Historical Archaeology of the Mashantucket Pequots," 106.

28. Many Pequots fought for the British in the French and Indian Wars and later for the rebels in the American Revolution. See Jack Campisi, "The Emergence of the Mashantucket Pequot Tribe, 1637–1975," in *The Pequots in Southern New England*, ed. Hauptman and Wherry, 124; and Maria Hileman, "Special Report on Mashantucket Pequots, the Rebirth of a Nation: Tribe Endured Long Period of Poverty, Injustice," *New London Day*, December 14, 1993, E6. Later, many men left for Oneida, New York, to join the Brothertown Indians, a trans-tribal Christian communitarian movement, initiated by the Mohegan preacher Samson Occum, that attempted to distance itself from white controls and influences. According to McBride, the flight to Brothertown "was the single biggest blow to the Pequots since the Pequot War" (quoted in Ellen Lieberman, "Special Report on Mashantucket Pequots, the Rebirth of a Nation: Disease, War, Migration, Emptied Indian Land," *New London Day*, December 13, 1993, B4). Still others left the reservation to indenture themselves in nearby white households, and to work as laborers on white-owned farms. In addition, much of the Mashantucket male population

joined the whaling and fishing fleets that dominated the New England economy of the first half of the nineteenth century. See Campisi, "The Emergence of the Mashantucket Pequot Tribe," 125.

29. Campisi, "The Emergence of the Mashantucket Pequot Tribe, 132.

30. Jack Campisi writes that "trespassers were driven off the Mashantucket Reservation at gunpoint" by Plouffe and Ellal, who even treated state and local officials "with extreme belligerency" when they approached the reservation. J. R. Williams, the state agent responsible for overseeing the reservation during this time, maintained an attitude "most accurately defined as racist and hostile. The agent's notebook for the period is filled with derogatory comments concerning the Pequots' presumed racial origins, their supposed lack of morality, and their alleged tendencies toward criminal behavior. None of the statements recorded by the agent bore a shred of truth." Campisi, "Emergence of the Mashantucket Pequot Tribe," 137, 243.

31. Recognition is, in principle, a simple concept: tribes are recognized as sovereign entities by the United States government, and a government-to-government relationship should ensue. In practice, however, it has become a complex legal status, having different implications for different tribes. For tribes that were defeated by or allied themselves with the United States government during the eighteenth, nineteenth, and early twentieth centuries, recognition was assumed as a feature of their treaties. Others never had treaty relations with the U.S. government, particularly tribes that were conquered by settler armies before 1776, and thus they, like the tribes that were "terminated" under the Termination Act of 1953, have had to go through arduous and costly processes to reacquire recognition by the federal government. Most often, tribes gain recognition by application through the Interior Department's Bureau of Indian Affairs. This is a notoriously difficult process that requires demonstrating the continuous existence of a population in a specific place over time and a continuous system of governance. It is also possible to attain recognition through the court system and, as the Pequots did, through congressional legislation. These methods are only possible, however, where very specific conditions and histories apply. For some good discussions of the problems at issue, see Cynthia Brown, "Unrecognized Tribes: The Vanished Native Americans," *The Nation*, October 11, 1993; and Jack Campisi, "The New England Tribes and Their Quest for Justice," in *The Pequots in Southern New England*, ed. Hauptman and Wherry, 79–193. For detailed discussions of treaty relations and the forms of sovereignty recognized in specific treaties, see Francis Paul Prucha, ed., *American Indian Treaties: The History of a Political Anomaly* (Berkeley: University of California Press, 1994) and *Documents of United States Indian Policy*, 2nd ed. (Lincoln: University of Nebraska Press, 1990).

32. Eisler, *Revenge of the Pequots,* 123–126.

33. According to Virginia Groark, "Ten Years After," *New York Times*, February 17, 2002, the state earned $190.7 million from Foxwoods' slot machines in the fiscal year ending June 30, 2001; and as of February 2002, the state had received about $1.4 billion from Pequot slot machines since the casino opened (3). Tom Wanamaker notes that during the final six months of 2003, the Mashantuckets contributed $100 million to the Connecticut treasury ("Victims of Success? Recognition and Gaming Tied Tightly in Connecticut," *Indian Country Today*, February 11, 2004, A1).

34. Suzanne Viafora, interview with author.

35. Noelle Crombie, "Pequots Give \$5 Million to Aquarium," *New London Day*, June 22, 1996, A8.

36. See Clifford, *The Predicament of Culture*, 277–346. There is an explanation of Clifford's argument in the introduction to this book.

37. Clifford, *The Predicament of Culture*, 344.

38. Gayatry Spivak's term "strategic essentialism," described in "Subaltern Studies: Deconstructing Historiography," *Subaltern Studies* 4 (1985): 193–221, as a way of describing the work of the Subaltern Studies Group, obviously comes to mind as a potentially useful concept for understanding this tendency. Reading Spivak's analysis, however, gives rise to the question, Is a strategic essentialism really a form of essentialism?

39. Clifford, "Indigenous Articulations," *The Contemporary Pacific* 13, no. 2 (2001) 468–490: 482. Also see Clifford, *The Predicament of Culture*, 277–346. There is an explanation of Clifford's argument in the introduction to this book.

40. Robert Allen Warrior, *Tribal Secrets: Recovering American Indian Intellectual Traditions* (Minneapolis: University of Minnesota Press, 1995), xvii and xix.

41. See, for example, George E. Marcus, "Contemporary Problems of Ethnography in the Modern World System," in *Writing Culture: The Poetics and Politics of Ethnography*, ed. James Clifford and George E. Marcus (Berkeley: University of California Press, 1986), 122–140; Talal Asad, "The Concept of Cultural Translation in British Social Anthropology," in *Writing Culture*, ed. Clifford and Marcus, 141–164; and Clifford Geertz, *Local Knowledge: Further Essays in Interpretive Anthropology* (New York: Basic Books, 1983). More recent studies of postcolonial cultural identity, studies that expand Clifford's work in terms of global politics, are exemplified in Arjun Appadurai's "Grass Roots Globalization and the Research Imagination," *Public Culture* 12, no. 1 (2000): 1–19. Appadurai argues that traditional anthropological methods map cultural "areas" by drawing boundaries too statically conceived. These conceptions depend upon what Appadurai refers to as "some sort of trait list—of values, languages, material practices, ecological adaptations, marriage patterns and the like"—which assumes more immobility and enduring unity than is realistic to suppose of human cultural activity. Instead, he proposes an anthropology "based on process geographies [that] sees significant areas of human organization as precipitates of various kinds of action, interaction, and motion—trade, travel, pilgrimage, warfare, proselytization, colonization, exile, and the like" (6). In *Modernity at Large* (Minneapolis: University of Minnesota Press, 1996), however, Appadurai notes that tribal and ethnic claims to ancientness, to what I refer to here as "essentialist" identities, have been crucial to processes of modernization in a global as well as postcolonial context.

42. Stuart Hall, "The Local and the Global: Globalization and Ethnicity," in *Culture, Globalization, and the World System: Contemporary Conditions for the Representation of Identity*, ed. Anthony King (Minneapolis: University of Minnesota Press, 1997), 22.

43. Ibid., 34.

44. Ibid., 35.

45. As Andreas Huyssen wrote in "Present Pasts: Media, Politics, Amnesia," in *Globalization*, ed. Arjun Appadurai (Durham, N.C.: Duke University Press, 2001), 63, "the fault line between mythic past and real past is not always that easy to draw—one of the conundrums of any politics of memory anywhere."

46. Hall, "The Local and the Global," 36; Stuart Hall, "What Is This 'Black' in Black Popular Culture?" in *Stuart Hall: Critical Dialogues in Cultural Studies*, ed. David Morley and Kuan-Hsing Chen (New York: Routledge, 1996), 472.
47. Ella Shohat, "Notes on the Post-Colonial," *Social Text* 31/32 (1992): 109.
48. Hall, "The Local and the Global," 36.
49. N. Scott Momaday, *House Made of Dawn* (New York: Harper Collins, 1999). I thank an anonymous reader at *American Quarterly* for the suggestion to view the Pequots' centuries-long experience of loss and recuperation of tribal identity as a form of "outwaiting" and as an experience in which they learned much about the society where they were located, such that they became "casino owners who know their audience and that there is a role reversal going on here (at least from the Pequot point of view) in which all that long outwaiting pays off."
50. Frederic Jameson, *Postmodernism, or the Cultural Logic of Late Capitalism* (London: Verso, 1991), 51.
51. For the idea of culture as defined by a list of traits, see Appadurai, "Grass Roots Globalization," 6.
52. Gayatry Spivak, *In Other Worlds: Essays in Cultural Politics* (London: Methuen, 1987), 204; Satya P. Mohanty, *Literary Theory and the Claims of History: Postmodernism, Objectivity, Multicultural Politics* (Ithaca, N.Y.: Cornell University Press, 1997), 10–24. For a theory of postpositivist realism that attempts to make room for identity formation which does not get caught in the binary between postmodernism and essentialism but instead charts the connections between "social location, experience, cultural identity, and knowledge" and at the same time acknowledges "the cognitive component" of cultural identity, see Paula M. L. Moya, "Postmodernism, 'Realism,' and the Politics of Identity: Cherrie Moraga and Chicana Feminism," in *Feminist Genealogies, Colonial Legacies, Democratic Futures*, ed. M. Jacqui Alexander and Chandra Mohanty (New York: Routledge, 2000).
53. Foxwoods compares in particularly striking ways with the Bonaventure Hotel in Los Angeles, part of the Westin system, which Jameson uses in *Postmodernism*, 39–45, as an exemplary space for demonstrating some of the key psychological and social effects of daily life set by postmodern, late capitalist forces.
54. Iver Peterson writes in "And They're Off, as States Race to Add Gambling Sites" (*New York Times*, November 18, 2002, B1) that the gambling industry has now become part of many state investment profiles, particularly in the Northeast, where "states are rushing to complete their plans [for building casinos] ahead of their neighbors," and that Indian gaming is a significant part of the picture, given the substantial contributions to state coffers that often come from gaming compacts with tribes. Peterson explains that "gambling revenues are an easy way to close the budget deficits that nearly all the states in the region are facing" and cites potential earnings of from $300 to $400 million per year for state and local governments from the windfalls that gambling operations are now conventionally thought to bring.
55. Mashantucket Pequot Tribal Nation, pamphlet for Foxwoods Resort Casino, issued August 2003.
56. These outfits have been the topic of much debate and have in a sense become the reference point for claims that the casino does nothing but rehearse Anglo stereotypes of Indian lifestyles, or that, therefore, so does the tribe in

its self-constructions. For an analysis of this issue, see Celeste Lacroix, "Wealth, Power, and Identity: A Critical Reading of Competing Discourses about the Mashantucket Pequots and Foxwoods" (PhD diss., Ohio University, 1999), 138–139.

57. Jameson, *Postmodernism*, 17–20.

58. Ibid., 17–20. The readability of the mechanics of global capital in public architecture like Foxwoods is addressed in other works that might be cited here, e.g., David Harvey's *The Condition of Postmodernity* (Oxford, England: Blackwell, 1989), especially chapter 3, "Postmodernism," and chapter 4, "Postmodernism in the City: Architecture and Urban Design"; and Michael Sorkin's introductory essay to his collection *Variations on a Theme Park: The New American City and the End of Public Space* (New York: Hill and Wang, 1992).

59. "Inside the Museum," Mashantucket Pequot Museum and Research Center brochure.

60. Lisa Stillman comments on the relatively minor role in the museum of conflicts that led to colonial occupation and on the rather "balanced and scholarly—maybe even a bit dry [presentation] for such an emotionally charged event," in "Mashantucket Pequot Museum," *Curator* 41, no. 4 (December 1998): 276.

61. In issues of December 13 and 14, 1993, and March 10, 1996, for example, *The Day* published detailed chronicles of Mashantucket history and laudatory accounts of the museum and the Mashantucket Pequot Ethnohistory Project.

62. Virginia Groark, "Learning to Live in the Shadow of a Giant," *New London Day*, September 6, 1993, A1.

63. Steven Slosberg, "What Is Our Destiny as a Destination?" *New London Day*, July 14, 1996, F1.

64. Kirk Johnson, "Town's Anger at Rich Tribe Is Measured by the Acre," *New York Times*, May 4, 1995, B5.

65. The Court declined to hear the case. Nevertheless, in a gesture of appeasement toward the towns, and because other claims contesting annexation are outstanding, the tribe has set aside efforts to take the acreage into trust. Adams, "For Time Magazine, Sovereignty 101"; Paul Zielbauer, "Pequot Tribe Withdraws Annexation Plan Opposed by Neighboring Towns," *New York Times*, February 26, 2002, B5.

66. Johnson, "Town's Anger at Rich Tribe Is Measured by the Acre."

67. Quoted in Adams, "For Time Magazine, Sovereignty 101."

68. Quoted in Meg Richards, *New London Day*, July 10, 1996.

69. Michael Stoll, "Tribes Use New Riches to Recast History," *Christian Science Monitor*, August 11, 1998, 3. A sampling of articles on the museum in the local and regional press includes, for example, David Collins, "Pequots Planning $100M Museum," *New London Day*, October 21, 1993, A1; Joseph Albano, "Breaking Ground—Mashantucket Pequot Museum a Wonder to Behold," *The Resident* (Stonington, Conn.), November 3–16, 1993, 5; Marrecca Delicato, "Museum Chronicles History of Eastern American Indians," *Mystic River Press*, May 7, 1998, 13; Virginia Groark, "Respecting the Land: Mashantucket's New Museum Sits on Ground That Is a Reminder of the Past," *New London Day*, May 23, 1998; M. R. Montgomery, "Connecticut's Pequots Build Largest Center of American Indian Culture on Mashantucket Reservation," *Boston Globe*, August 9, 1998, D15; Bill Van Siclen, "The Pequots' First Class New

Museum Chronicles the Tribe's History," *Providence Journal-Bulletin,* August 9, 1998, D1; Mary Jo Palumbo, "The Art of Gambling: New Pequot Museum Is Dealer's Choice at Foxwoods," *Boston Herald,* August 10, 1998, 32; editorial, "Mighty Museum in the Woods," *Providence Journal-Bulletin,* November 23, 1998, B6; Charles Bakst, "Casino Offspring: Pequot Museum Makes You Think," *Providence Journal-Bulletin,* February 16, 1999, B1; Darlene Arden, "Mashantucket Pequot Museum Celebrates Heritage in Grand Style," *Boston Herald,* November 15, 1999, 67; and many reviews of the museum in the *New York Times* from August 1998 through the present. In "Imagining the Nation with House Odds: Representing American Indian Identity at Mashantucket" (Ethnohistory 50, no. 3 [2003]: 549–565), John J. Bodinger de Uriarte writes about the contrasts between the museum and the casino and draws on Benedict Anderson's theory of "imagined communities" to argue that both sponsor an emergent Pequot identity. For a sampling of the many academic commentaries praising the museum's mission, see Neil Ascher Silberman, "Invisible No More," *Archaeology* 51, no. 6 (November–December 1998): 68–73; Stillman, "Mashantucket Pequot Museum"; Ben Winton "Reclaiming History," *Native Peoples* 11, no. 3 (May/July 1998): 60–61; Raul Barreneche, "A New Museum and Research Center by Polshek and Partners," *Architecture* 88, no. 7 (July 1999): 84–92; Jill Knight Weinberger, "The Mashantucket Pequot Museum and Research Center," *American History* 36, no. 4: 16; and William Morgan, "The Light in the Forest: The Mashantucket Pequot Museum," *Art in New England* 22, no. 2 (February/March 2001): 9.

70. Suzanne Viafora, interview with author; Penelope Overton, "Tribe Separates Business, Culture," *New London Day,* September 4, 1993, A1; Joanne Nagel, *American Indian Ethnic Renewal: Red Power and the Resurgence of Identity and Culture* (New York: Oxford University Press, 1996), 53.

71. Silberman, "Pequot Country," 36. At a press conference on the museum plans held in New York in 1997, Hayward declared, "All the Tribe's activities over the past decades have been conducted with the goal of preserving Pequot history and culture. We have worked hard to re-establish our community on tribal land, and opening our museum will be the culmination of that effort and determination" (quoted in David Holahan, "Tribe's Museum Plans Detailed at New York Press Conference," *Pequot Times,* March 1997).

72. Bethe Dufresne, *New London Day,* March 20, 1996, A8.

73. Stoll, "Tribes Use New Riches to Recast History," 1.

74. Richard Hayward, "Introduction of Keynote Speaker, John Echohawk," presented at the Mashantucket Pequot History Conference, Mashantucket Pequot Museum and Research Center, September 20, 2002.

75. Foxwoods Resort Casino brochure.

76. Roy Harvey Pearce, *Savagism and Civilization: A Study of the Indian and the American Mind* (Berkeley: University of California Press, 1967), 169–195; Robert Berkhofer Jr., *The White Man's Indian: Images of the American Indian from Columbus to the Present* (New York: Random House, 1978), 38–44. More recently, Fergus Bordewich, *Killing the White Man's Indian: Reinventing Native Americans at the End of the Twentieth Century* (New York: Doubleday, 1996); and Shepard Krech, *The Ecological Indian: Myth and History* (New York: Norton, 1999), have focused attention on Western vocabularies and iconographies of Native spirituality and environmentalism that continue to have influence at the end of the twentieth century. Philip J. Deloria, in *Playing Indian* (New Haven: Yale University Press, 1998), addresses similar ideas as performed or

acted out by European Americans in a variety of ways in their interpretations and "imitations" of what they thought Native life and identity meant in the early twentieth century.

77. James Fenelon, "Traditional and Modern Perspectives on Indian Gaming: The Struggle for Sovereignty," in *Indian Gaming: Who Wins?* ed. Mullis and Kamper, 108.

78. Paul Pasquaretta,"On the 'Indianness' of Bingo: Gambling and the Native American Community," *Critical Inquiry* 20, no. 4 (summer 1994): 698.

79. Reuven Brenner and Gabrielle Brenner, *Gambling and Speculation: A Theory, a History, and a Future of Some Human Decisions* (Cambridge: Cambridge University Press, 1990), 3, 210.

80. Gary Snyder, conversation with author, September 8, 2003.

81. It should be noted that this argument has a great deal of power among many Native representatives as well. Among the Mohawk community at Akwesasne in upstate New York, the passions run so strong between those who find such practices to be profanations of older, culturally contextualized forms of gaming and those who support casinos that violence has erupted several times. See Pasquaretta, "On the 'Indianness' of Bingo," 697–698, 703–707, and *Gambling and Survival in Native North America* (Tuscon: University of Arizona Press, 2003), chapter 5.

82. In "Casino's Start Exceeds Expectations" (*Hartford Courant*, February 22, 1992, B1), published shortly after the casino opened, Hilary Waldman reported that in response to criticism of the cocktail waitress's outfits, "tribal leaders countered that the . . . tunics . . . were chosen because they are comfortable and conform to the casino's Indian motif." At about the same time, Kenneth Reels, tribal council vice chairman, commented, "The Pequots, not the hired . . . managers, selected the uniforms because they make a statement. This is not just any casino. The uniforms say, it's an Indian casino." See also Waldman, "New Casino a Sure Bet for a Good Story," *Hartford Courant*, February 12, 1992.

83. Laurence Hauptman, "The Pequot War and Its Legacies," in *The Pequots in Southern New England*, ed. Hauptman and Wherry, 78.

84. Sioux Harvey, "Two Models to Sovereignty: A Comparative History of the Mashantucket Pequot Tribal Nation and the Navajo Nation," *American Indian Culture and Research Journal* 20, no.1 (1996): 174–175.

85. Bell quoted in Kirk Johnson, "Seeking Lost Culture at a Powwow," *New York Times*, September 19, 1993, 45.

86. Hayward quoted in David Holahan, "Tribe's Museum Plans Detailed," *Pequot Times*, March 1997.

CHAPTER 2   DISPLAYING LOSS AT NAVAJOLAND

1. Gladys Reichard, *Navajo Religion: A Study of Symbolism* (Princeton: Princeton University Press, 1977), 20; John Farella, *The Main Stalk: A Synthesis of Navajo Philosophy* (Tucson: University of Arizona Press, 1984), 104; Klara Bonsack Kelley and Harris Francis, *Navajo Sacred Places* (Bloomington: Indiana University Press, 1994), 114.

2. See, for example, Harry Walters, "The Navajo Concept of Art," in *Woven by the Grandmothers: Nineteenth Century Navajo Textiles from the National Museum of the American Indian*, ed. Eulalie Bonar (Washington, D.C.: Smithsonian Institution Press, 1996), 30; and Vine Deloria, *God Is Red: A Native View of Religion*

(Golden, Colo.: Fulcrum Publishing, 1994), 81–82, 93–94. Reichard writes, "Mountains, though places, are so personalized that I have classified them as deities" (*Navajo Religion*, 452). Reichard references the religious values of Navajo places and place names throughout her book, but for extended discussions of the meanings associated with particular landmarks, see chapter 2, "World View," chapter 9, "The Nature of Symbolism," concordance A, "Supernatural Beings," and concordance B, "Ritualistic Rites." Farella offers a compelling synopsis of the human place in this world view: "By means of *ní ch'i* [air or breath, which is sacred since inhabited by divinities] we are connected to all beings around us, and by this means our feelings and thoughts are aspects of connectedness, rather than attributes of an illusory self" (*The Main Stalk*, 181). To help explain this concept in more specific terms, Farella cites the Navajo idea that "skin is a very permeable interface, especially at the whorls of our feet, our hands, our fingertips, and the top of our head" (*The Main Stalk*, 181). At these points of porousness, exchange with the world of which humans are a part is particularly active.

3. Kelley and Francis, *Navajo Sacred Places*, 20.

4. These narratives are for the most part available to outsiders only in texts compiled by ethnologists. Based as they are on the accounts of oral informants, ethnographic texts which include creation narratives generally reveal that different recitations of creation will differ in important details, including sequences and locations of events and the priorities and powers of the first, or holy, people. English oral recitations are often prefaced with disclaimers concerning the inadequacy of English to convey key passages, the older meanings of which are thus understood to be available only to speakers of the Navajo language. At a Diné College seminar held in the fall of 1997, the curator of the Ned Hathatl'i Museum, the director of the Navajo Studies Program, and the director of Development each introduced accounts of creation in precisely this way. They also commented on the difficulty of translating the Navajo language generally, a difficulty that they felt goes beyond the usual troubles attendant on translation of any kind (author notes, October 10–12, 1997, 5–6). The summaries of Navajo creation stories presented here are derived from published translations compiled by well-regarded scholars, each of whom studied Navajo language and narrative over a period of many years. Nevertheless, if a reader were to heed the warnings of the Diné College seminar leaders, my summaries as well as the translations on which they are based would be taken only as rough equivalents of Navajo oral version. This presents another example of the phenomenon of public self-representation that I refer to as "displayed withholding."

5. Reichard notes that when the mountains were created, they became the first homes of the deities. Once they had been properly blessed, they themselves became hogans (*Navajo Religion*, 565).

6. Reichard, *Navajo Religion*, 22.

7. Further events in the making of the world might be worth knowing here. Again, I render these stories in rather broad strokes from the sources listed. Creation emits not from a single, particular author. In a dark, or black, first world, First Man and First Woman appear, as well as the elements for the development of earth—air, soil, moisture, light. First Man and Woman are responsible for subsequent materialization of beings and conditions, including the sacred directional mountains that would mark the boundaries of the

Navajo homeland. Strife emerges, fire ensues, and the people migrate upward, through a reed, to the second world. Clans and kinship terms begin to organize the people socially. Again, disputes occur that result this time in a flood, from which the people escape through a reed into the third world. Agriculture appears in this world, centered on corn. Marriage occurs here too, as well as one of the central events in the creation sequence, known as the separation of the sexes. An argument breaks out between First Man and First Woman, which results in the women leaving the men to live on the opposite side of a river that runs through their home. The women have sex with various plants and animals and give birth to monsters. The men and women are reunited when a flood develops, and First Man makes it possible for all to escape to the fourth and present world, again through a reed. The monsters, however, continue to thrive, and the people are plagued by their evil deeds. At this point, known as emergence, one of the most significant figures in Navajo spirituality, Changing Woman, is born. She is found by First Man and First Woman, who raise her to become the most beautiful woman in the world, synonymous with Earth itself, transforming from youth to old age to youth again through the course of the year. She meets Sun and makes love with him, giving birth to the two hero twins, Monster Slayer and Born for Water. The twins go about killing off the monsters, attempting to make the world safer for human society. Evil does not leave in a categorical way, however. From this time on, other holy people begin to emerge, but the greater import of the emergence phase of creation is that the entities created in the lower world acquire full embodiment and a certain "inner form," quick with spiritual power, what John Farella calls "animation" (*The Main Stalk*, 71–72). For other comprehensive studies of Navajo creation, see Reichard, *Navaho Religion*; Berard Haile, "Navajo Chantways and Ceremonials," *American Anthropologist* 40, no. 4 (October–December 1938): 639–652, *Origin Legend of Navaho Enemyway* (New Haven: Yale University Press, 1938), and *Women versus Men: A Conflict of Navajo Emergence: The Curly To Aheedliinii Version* (Lincoln: University of Nebraska Press, 1933); Washington Matthews, *Navaho Legends* (Salt Lake City: University of Utah Press, 1994, reprint of Boston: Houghton Mifflin, 1897); and Kelley and Francis, *Navajo Sacred Places.*

8. Reichard, *Navaho Religion*, 309, 572.
9. Kelley and Francis write, "These places of special power are the most alive, and stories usually go with them. People visit the places to connect with their power. They use ceremonies to establish proper social relations with the Holy People who are, or have been, evident there. These places are sacred in the broadest sense . . . they anchor the ways of Navajo life, the stories about the origins, and correct pursuit of those ways. . . . [W]hen Navajos pass down their chronicles . . . the landscape provides a material anchor for those stories and thereby stores them. . . . [T]he landscape is part of the 'text' " (*Navajo Sacred Places*, 2). Jean Beaudrillard, *America*, trans. Chris Turner (London: Verso, 1989), 1–12.
10. The Navajos have no casino, since the matter was voted down in two referenda in 1994 and 1998, held to decide whether the tribe would establish casino gaming on the reservation. While local tribal authorities at the satellite Navajo community of To'Hajilee, New Mexico, have legalized gaming, it remains a contentious issue for the rest of the Navajo population. Legalized gaming has been voted down twice in referenda; nevertheless, the possibility

is still in the air. Given Arizona's passing of Proposition 202 in 2002, the question may come up again in the near future. The Navajo reservation is located partly in New Mexico and partly in Arizona, where Proposition 202 allows each Native American tribe a specific number of slot machines as well as other forms of gaming. If the Navajos wanted to, then, they could establish casino gaming or lease their slot machine rights to other tribes. According to the Navajo public information officer, however, "one group of individuals says that if a casino comes, we'll have *x* problems; another says *x* benefits will come with it. So it's a very questionable issue right now" (Lawlor, interview notes). The official title of Proposition 202 is "An Initiative Measure Proposing Amendments to Title 5, Chapter 6, Article 1, Arizona Revised Statues . . ." The text of the legislation can be found at the Web site for the Arizona secretary of state: www.sosaz.com/election/2002/info/pubpamphlet/english/prop202.html. On the Oneida reservation in upstate New York, the tribal membership has for years been sharply divided over the distribution of profits and the very existence of Turning Stone Casino. See David Chen and Charlie LeDuff, "Bad Blood in Battle over Casinos," *New York Times*, October 28, 2001, B1.

11. Saba Mahmood, "Feminist Theory, Embodiment, and the Docile Agent: Some Reflections on the Egyptian Islamic Revival," *Cultural Anthropology* 16, no. 2 (May 2001), 209–210. Although Mahmood writes about an entirely different cultural context—that of the Mosque movement in contemporary Cairo—her approach emphasizes the non-hegemonic forms of agency that dominated peoples, in this case Islamic women, often take in relation to cultural inheritance and modernity, both of which might otherwise limit and restrict the terms of individual and collective subjectivity. Her work thus offers useful analyses for studying Navajo self-representations.

12. James Clifford introduces himself at the outset of his essay "Four Northwest Coast Museums" (in *Exhibiting Cultures: The Poetics and Politics of Museum Display*, ed. Ivan Karp and Steven Lavine (Washington, D.C.: Smithsonian Institution Press, 1991), 212–254] as "an outsider, a white American visitor" who "linger[s]" in the museums he studies, compiling his written account from "conversations with curators and local people and . . . printed information (213–214). While this self-description at first glance appears in several ways like my own, I want to distinguish between Clifford's need, as one of the most well known ethnographers in the United States today, to identify his essay as a series of personal reflections "closer to travel writing than to ethnography" (214) and my own efforts. Not trained in the methodologies of ethnography, I make no claim whatsoever to be operating within the codes or knowledges of that discipline. Here I repeat the point I make in my introduction: I would prefer this book, a critical reading of indigenous self-representations, to be understood as an interdisciplinary work which draws on the methods of literary criticism and cultural studies in its efforts to interpret contemporary Native American public rhetoric.

13. As I argue in the introduction to this book, some of the most revered writers on theories of native and national character have taken positions of this sort. See, for example, Frantz Fanon's "The Pitfalls of National Consciousness" and "On National Culture" in his *The Wretched of the Earth* (New York: Grove Press, 1968); and, more recently, Achille Mbembe's "African Modes of Self-Writing," *Public Culture* 14, no. 1: 239–273 and "On the Power of the False," *Public Culture* 14, no. 3: 629–641.

14. This position has been taken recently by Arjun Appadurai in a more broadly theoretical context in *Modernity at Large* (Minneapolis: University of Minnesota Press, 1996) and more specifically in relation to Native American negotiations of ethnicity and identity by James Clifford in *The Predicament of Culture* and "Four Northwest Coast Museums" and Joanne Nagel in *American Indian Ethnic Renewal: Red Power and the Resurgence of Identity and Culture* (New York: Oxford, 1996).

15. Doris Sommer, "Rigoberta's Secrets," *Latin American Perspectives* 18, no. 3 (summer 1991): 37.

16. Aamir R. Mufti, "The Aura of Authenticity," *Social Text* 64 (fall 2000): 88.

17. N. Scott Momaday, *The Way to Rainy Mountain* (Albuquerque: University of New Mexico Press, 1966), 4. Subsequent references to this book appear in parentheses in the text.

18. Although the building was completed in 1995, financial problems kept it from opening for more than a year. Marley Shebala, "B[udget] & F[inance] Committee voices concerns, support for N[avajo] F[orestry] P[roducts] I[ndustry], museum-library," *Navajo Times*, February 22, 1996, A1; George Hardeen, "Commentary: Navajo museum, library will outlast politicians," *Navajo Times*, March 7, 1996, A5; Bernardine Martin, "Navajo A[bandoned] M[ine] L[eases?] program monies not for museum," *Navajo Times*, March 7, 1996, A5; Bill Donovan, "N[avajo] A[rts and] C[rafts] E[nterprises] wants museum out, clothing in," *Navajo Times*, June 6, 1996, A11; Leslie Linthicum, "Museum Houses Doubts," *Albuquerque Journal*, November 9, 1996, A1.

19. For discussions of the attributes and powers of the cardinal directions, see, for example, Farella, *The Main Stalk*, 109–110; and Reichard, *Navajo Religion*, 20–21, 188–197.

20. Rex Lee Jim, "A Moment in My Life," in *Here First: Autobiographical Essays by Native American Writers*, ed. Arnold Krupat and Brian Swann (New York: Modern Library, 2000), 232.

21. Ibid., 231.

22. Farella, *The Main Stalk*, 153, 171.

23. For discussions of sa'ah naagháí bik'eh hózhóón that take into account the complexities of reformatting it for English readers, see Farella, *The Main Stalk*, especially 153–187; Reichard, *Navajo Religion*, 43–48; William Overstreet, "The Navajo Nightway and the Western Gaze," *boundary 2* 19, no. 3 (fall 1992): 60 n2.

24. See www.missnavajo.org/history/pageant.html.

25. Harry Walters, "The Navajo Conception of Art," in *Woven by the Grandmothers*, ed. Bonar, 27.

26. See www.missnavajo.org/currentmissnn/biography.html.

27. See www.missnavajo.org/generalinfo/mission.html.

28. Ibid.

29. David Eng and David Kazanjian, "Introduction: Mourning Remains," in *Loss: The Politics of Mourning*, ed. Eng and Kazanjian (Berkeley: University of California Press, 2002), 5.

30. Eng and Kazanjian, "Introduction: Mourning Remains," 4; Sigmund Freud, "Mourning and Melancholia," in *The Standard Edition of the Complete Psychological Works of Sigmund Freud*, trans. and ed. James Strachey (London: Hogarth Press, 1957), 256.

31. Peter Iverson writes in *Diné: A History of the Navajos* (Albuquerque: University of New Mexico Press, 2002) that "the Long Walk was not a single event."

Dating from 1863 to 1866, it meant that "in some instances just a handful of people made the trip; in other cases, hundreds of Diné were herded along to Fort Sumner. The trip took several different routes. . . . The time of the year, the inclinations of the army personnel in charge, and the general well-being of those making the trek all affected the experience" (51).

32. Robert M. Utley, *The Indian Frontier of the American West, 1846–1890* (Albuquerque: University of New Mexico Press, 1984), 84–85; Iverson, *Diné*, 48–49; Carl Waldman, *Atlas of the North American Indian* (New York: Checkmark Books, 2000), 166–167.

33. Utley, *The Indian Frontier of the American West*, 85–86, 120. An excellent series of oral accounts of the Long Walk and the Bosque Redondo experience appears in Broderick H. Johnson, ed., *Navajo Stories of the Long Walk Period* (Tsaile, Ariz.: Dine College Press, 1973). On Comanche and Apache hostilities, see the narrative by Howard W. Gorman in Johnson's book, 34–37.

34. Utley, *The Indian Frontier of the American West*, 85.

35. Eulalia H. Bonar, introduction to *Woven by the Grandmothers*, ed. Bonar, 5–7.

36. Ann Lane Hedlund, "'More of Survival Than an Art': Comparing Late Nineteenth- and Late Twentieth-Century Lifeways and Weaving," in *Woven by the Grandmothers*, ed. Bonar, 54–56; Joe Ben Wheat, "Navajo Blankets," in *Woven by the Grandmothers*, ed. Bonar, 77–78; Iverson, *Diné*, 64; Kent McManis and Robert Jeffries, *A Guide to Navajo Weaving* (Tucson, Arizona: Treasure Chest Books, 1997), 12–13.

37. Author notes from conversations with museum staff during visits in October 1997 and February 2003.

38. Wheat, "Navajo Blankets," 70; Iverson, *Diné*, 24; McManis and Jeffries, *A Guide to Navajo Weaving*, 8.

39. Laura Jane Moore, "Elle Meets the President: Weaving Navajo Culture and Commerce in the Southwestern Tourist Industry," *Frontiers: A Journal of Women Studies* 22, no. 1 (2001): 26.

40. Ibid.

41. Eulalia H. Bonar, "Notes on Selected Collectors," in *Woven by the Grandmothers*, ed. Bonar, 173.

42. 104 STAT. 3048: Public Law 101-601, November 16, 1990. The Native American Graves Protection and Repatriation Act, commonly known as NAGPRA, provides for the repatriation of human remains, funerary objects, sacred objects, and objects of cultural patrimony to federally recognized tribes that can demonstrate former ownership or control of such objects from federally funded museums or federal agencies, with the exception of the Smithsonian (Section 2, paragraphs 4 and 8). Even if this exception did not exist, NAGPRA can be read as preventing the repatriation of the materials in the Smithsonian's Navajo textile collection by its stipulation that objects at issue "shall have been considered inalienable by such Native American group at the time the object was separated from such group." It can be argued that, although weavings are produced in a sacred context and thus have sacred value, as I explain below, they have always been treated as objects for trade or sale. Thus, individual pieces may not have been "inalienable" because they had "ongoing historical, traditional, or cultural importance to the Native American group or culture itself, rather than the property owned by an individual Native American" (Section 2, paragraph 3 D). In addition, the legislation requires evidence that those requesting repatriation be "the direct lineal descendant of an individual who owned the sacred object [or object of cultural

patrimony]" (Section 7 a, subsection 5 A). Since the textiles in the Smithsonian collection are not attributed, this requirement cannot be fulfilled. Patricia Penn Hilden notes in "Race for Sale" that "with the merger of the Smithsonian with the old Museum of the American Indian, bones and other remains were to be returned for reburial. Other items were not mentioned, however, although the Museum's many discussions of this issue insist that it will comply with demands for objects covered by NAGPRA" (*TDR: The Drama Review* 44, no. 3 [fall 2000]: 34 n13). As might be imagined, NAGPRA has been a central cite of exchange, including litigation and other disputes, between tribes, non-Native museums, and the federal government since it was passed on November 16, 1990. For the text of NAGPRA, see www.cast.uark.edu/other/nps/nagpra/DOCS/lgm003.html.

43. Eulalia H. Bonar, introduction to *Woven by the Grandmothers*, ed. Bonar, 5–7.
44. See www.nmai.si.edu/exhibits/index.html, n1.
45. Rita Reif, "Blankets That Tell the Tales of Their People," *New York Times*, October 27, 1996, 47.
46. Leslie Linthicum, "Work of Ancestors Comes Home," *Albuquerque Journal*, September 21, 1997, B5.
47. Hilden, "Race for Sale," 12.
48. Mbembe, "On the Power of the False," 636; Appadurai, *Modernity at Large*, 32, 90.
49. Appadurai, *Modernity at Large*, 115.
50. Author notes, October 1997.
51. In addition to the exhibition catalog, *Woven by the Grandmothers*, see Kathy M'Closkey, *Swept under the Rug: A Hidden History of Navajo Weaving* (Albuquerque: University of New Mexico Press, 2002); Roseann Sandoval Willink and Paul Zolbrod, *Weaving a World: Textiles and the Navajo Way of Seeing* (Santa Fe: Museum of New Mexico Press, 1996); and Kathleen Whitaker, *Common Threads: Pueblo and Navajo Textiles in the Southwest Museum* (Los Angeles: Southwest Museum, 1998).
52. Reichard, *Navajo Religion*, 468.
53. Walters, "The Navajo Concept of Art," 29.
54. D. Y. Begay, "Shi' Sha' Hane (My Story)," in *Woven by the Grandmothers*, ed. Bonar, 27.
55. Ann Lane Hedlund, " 'More a Survival than an Art,' " in *Woven by the Grandmothers*, ed. Bonar, 48; Moore, "Elle Meets the President," 25.
56. Wesley Thomas, "Shił Yóół T'ooł: Personification of Navajo Weaving," in *Woven by the Grandmothers*, ed. Bonar, 33.
57. Laurie D. Webster, "Woven by the Grandmothers," *American Anthropologist* 100, no. 4 (December 1998): 1000.
58. The originals are maintained in the National Archives in Washington, D.C. The exhibition signage indicated that the Navajo copy, which went to Chief Manuelito, signer for the Navajo people in 1868, is lost, so the tribe does not have its own copy of either document.
59. Francis Paul Prucha, *American Indian Treaties: The History of a Political Anomaly* (Berkeley: University of California Press, 1994), 26, 31.
60. Ibid., 3.
61. *Johnson and Graham's Leasee v. William McIntosh*, 21 U.S. (8 Wheaton) (1823), in Francis Paul Prucha, ed., *Documents of United States Indian Policy*, 2nd ed. (Lincoln: University of Nebraska Press, 1990), 35–37. See Robert A. Williams Jr., *The American Indian in Western Legal Thought: The Discourses of Conquest*

(New York: Oxford, 1990), particularly chapter 7, "The Colonists' War for America"; Mary Lawlor, "Indigenous Internationalism: Human Rights and the UN," *Comparative American Studies* 1, no. 3 (fall 2003): 2–4. Also see the concluding chapter of this book for a discussion of Marshall's rulings and the writers he looked to in drafting them, including Francisco de Vitoria and Thomas Aquinas.

62. Prucha, *Documents of United States Indian Policy*, 35–37.
63. Ibid., 58–60. *Cherokee Nation v. Georgia*, 30 U.S. (5 Peters), in Prucha, *Documents of United States Indian Policy*, 58–60. As I note in the chapter 5, Marshall's term reflected a division in the Court over the Cherokee status. The chief justice's own view was that the tribes were dependent on the United States, politically, economically, and, in fact, geographically, while several dissenting justices wanted to recognize them as distinct nations.
64. Iverson, *Diné*, 39.
65. The citation is from *United States v. Wheeler*, March 22, 1978 (435 U.S. 323–324), in which the Supreme Court looked back to the 1849 and 1868 Navajo Treaties to rule on the question of whether a Navajo man could be tried in federal court after a Navajo court had already convicted him of a lesser offence in relation to the same incident. The Court ruled against double jeopardy, since, according to the treaties, the tribal court was separate and autonomous from the federal court. See Prucha's summary in *American Indian Treaties*, 399.
66. "Treaty with the Navajo, 1849," in *Indian Affairs: Laws and Treaties*, vol. 2, ed. Charles J. Kappler (Washington, D.C.: U.S. Government Printing Office, 1904), 583–585.
67. Prucha, *American Indian Treaties*, 257. On the intercourse acts, see chapter 4 in this book; and Prucha, *Documents of United States Indian Policy*, 17–21.
68. Peter Iverson notes that "the Navajos, not surprisingly, did not accord [the 1849] agreement any of the respect they later felt for the treaty of 1868. They understood it [as] . . . an arrangement negotiated in haste and signed under duress" (*Diné*, 41).
69. Kappler, *Indian Affairs*, 1016.
70. References to the Long Walk are evident everywhere in public discourse and iconography on the reservation. For a useful collection of published renditions of the experience, see Johnson, ed., *Navajo Stories of the Long Walk Period*.
71. David Eng, "Melancholia in the Late Twentieth Century," *Signs: Journal of Women in Culture and Society* 25, no. 4 (2000): 1276.
72. Simon Ortiz, "Towards a National Indian Literature: Cultural Authenticity in Nationalism," *MELUS* 8, no. 2 (summer 1981): 9; Eng, "Melancholia in the Late Twentieth Century," 1276.
73. Ortiz, "Towards a National Indian Literature," 9.
74. Peter Iverson writes that among its other effects, the collective experience of adversity that came with the Long Walk and with subsequent forms of colonial oppression prompted more mutual identification among Navajo people than had existed in the past (*Diné*, 205). What had been, in David Brugge's words, "semi-sedentary bands and local family groups" reshaped itself through the process of resisting colonial domination into "the largest tribe living on the largest reservation in the United States" (Brugge quoted in Iverson, *Diné*, 205). Iverson argues that even now the Diné tend to function as "a series of autonomous groups with highly localized leadership patterns" (*Diné*, 25).

Nevertheless, the treaty exhibit celebrates an achieved rather than a "traditional" national status, an achievement that mitigates against the blurring of cultural distinctiveness threatening from every direction, in 1868 as now.

75. Eng and Kazanjian, "Introduction: Mourning Remains," in *Loss*, ed. Eng and Kazanjian, 5–7.

76. "Indigenization" in the sense I use it here is taken from Arjun Appadurai's *Modernity at Large*, 32 and 90. For a discussion of the open-endedness of history in the melancholic imagination, see Eng and Kazanjian, "Introduction: Mourning Remains," 5.

77. Author notes, February 28, 2003, 3.

78. James Clifford, "Four Northwest Coast Museums," in *Exhibiting Cultures: The Poetics and Politics of Museum Display*, ed. Ivan Karp and Stephen D. Levine (Washington, D.C.: Smithsonian Institution Press, 1991), 215.

79. See Shiprock Chapter Web site, http://shiprock.nndes.org; and Iverson, *Diné*, 12–16. Through linguistic evidence, anthropologists and archaeologists have identified this place as the arctic region of western Canadian. Western historiography has commonly dated Diné arrival in the Southwest in the late fifteenth and early sixteenth centuries. Diné creation stories, as the opening pages of this chapter indicate, describe the tribe's origins in lower worlds, out of which they gradually emerge. The process is commonly understood as autochthony, or the development in place from earlier forms; but Peter Iverson suggests that it might be construed as a journey as well, or a series of journeys, a theory that does not necessarily conflict with those proposed by Western scholars. Whether the northern cite referred to in the story of Tse Bi'it A'i flying the Diné people to the present location should be understood as a place of origin is another matter. Iverson refers to a story in which a group of Diné journey south to north to find relatives from whom they are separated, either in a massive fire or by some other means (*Diné*, 13). The debate, of course, has implications that exceed academic needs to distinguish antiquity from early modernity in schemes of Diné history. Attitudes on the issue can have substantial bearing on federal rulings over tribal issues, on donations from the private sector for tribal projects, and on public sentiment in general toward Navajo tribal sovereignty. Iverson writes, "We have every right to be skeptical about orthodox archaeological accounts in which Navajos arrive essentially intact as a linguistic community, but curiously empty-handed otherwise. In these renditions, the Diné too often lurch onto the Southwestern stage as nomadic vagabonds . . . [and] other communities must teach them how to survive. Such scenarios doom the Navajos to second-class citizenship, demote them to newcomers in a new land, and relegate them to the category of upstarts whose eventual ambition becomes arrogance" (*Diné*, 14).

80. See http:/shiprock.nndes.org.

81. See http://ewebs.realtimesites.net/ds-Contemporary/cont-j-6/ImagesCust/429376117-09-27-2004-15-36-14k.pdf.

82. Seth Mydans, "Gangs Reach a New Frontier: Reservations," *New York Times*, March 18, 1995, 1; "On Indian Reservations in the West, Violent Crime Soars," *New York Times*, August 16, 1998, 28; Naftali Bendavid, "Violent Crime Rising on Indian Reservations, *New London Day*, May 3, 1998, A3; Eric Henderson, Stephen J. Kunitz, and Herrold E. Levy, "The Origins of Navajo Youth Gangs," *American Indian Culture and Research Journal* 23, no. 3 (1999): 243–264.

83. Larry DiGiovanni, "Navajos' Oldest Fair Talks 'Regime Change,'" *Gallup Independent*, May 29, 2003.
84. Shelton is remembered as a tyrannical figure who was not adverse to taking violent action in asserting his control in the Shiprock region and beyond. For a description of Shelton, his work, and his reputation on the Navajo reservation, see Iverson, *Diné*, 110–112 and 126.
85. Iverson, *Diné*, 108–136.
86. See, for example, David E. Wilkins, "Governance within the Navajo Nation: Have Democratic Traditions Taken Hold?" *Wicazo Sa Review* 17, no. 1 (spring 2002): 91–129.
87. Ranajit Guha, *Dominance without Hegemony: History and Power in Colonial India* (Cambridge, Mass.: Harvard University Press, 1997), xii.
88. Washington Matthews, *The Night Chant: A Navajo Ceremony* (Salt Lake City: University of Utah Press, 1995; reprint of New York: Knickerbocker Press, 1902), 159.
89. As Overstreet notes, "scholarly documentation of the Nightway remains surprisingly sparse" ("The Navajo Nightway and the Western Gaze," 61). See Overstreet ("The Navajo Nightway and the Western Gaze," 71) for a summary of the detailed accounts provided by Matthews, *The Night Chant*, 159–197 and 197–212.
90. James Faris, *The Nightway: A History and a History of Documentation of a Navajo Ceremonial* (Albuquerque: University of New Mexico Press, 1990), 235, 71.
91. Faris, *The Nightway*, 79.
92. Overstreet, "The Navajo Nightway and the Western Gaze," 59.
93. Reichard, *Navajo Religion*, 476–477; Matthews, *The Night Chant*, 9.
94. Reichard, *Navajo Religion*, 76; Matthews, *The Night Chant*, 9.
95. Overstreet, "The Navajo Nightway and the Western Gaze," 59.
96. See http://ewebs.realtimesites.net/ds-Contemporary/cont-s-8/ImageCust/158552677-02-07-2002-14-15-15r.doc.
97. Overstreet, "The Navajo Nightway and the Western Gaze," 60, 61; Faris, *The Nightway*, 3.
98. Faris, *The Nightway*, 120.
99. Faris, *The Nightway*, 26; Overstreet, "The Navajo Nightway and the Western Gaze," 72.
100. Overstreet, "The Navajo Nightway and the Western Gaze," 71.

CHAPTER 3   WIND RIVER LESSONS

1. The Western Shoshones are related to the Eastern Shoshones and share linguistic, religious, and other cultural inheritances, but they have a different history and occupy reservations west of the Rocky Mountains, in Nevada, Idaho, and parts of Utah. The Southern Arapahoes, like their Northern relatives, occupied territories in the lower Great Basin and eastern Plains until they were assigned a reservation in Oklahoma in the 1860s by the U.S. government. Loretta Fowler, *Arapahoe Politics, 1851–1978: Symbols in Crises of Authority* (Lincoln: University of Nebraska Press, 1982), 44, 229.
2. The Northern Arapahoes were removed to Wind River from their homelands in the southern plains region in what had been described to them as a temporary move before being granted their own reservation, a promise that was never fulfilled. Henry E. Stamm, *People of the Wind River: 1825–1900* (Norman:

University of Oklahoma Press, 1999), 129–130; Janet Flynn, *Tribal Government: Wind River Reservation* (Lander, Wyo.: Mortimore Publishing, 1998), 36; Elinor Markley and Beatrice Crofts, *Walk Softly, This Is God's Country: Sixty-Six Years on the Wind River Indian Reservation* (Lander, Wyo.: Mortimer Publishing, 1997), 12.

3. Flynn, *Tribal Government*, 34; Winnie Bausch et al., eds., *Riverton: The Early Years, 1906–1953* (Riverton, Wyo.: Riverton Historical Research Committee, 1981), 7–12.

4. Flynn, *Tribal Government*, 34; Bausch et al., *Riverton*, 10–11; Stamm, *People of the Wind River*, 243.

5. John Wilson, letter to Thomas Ewing, Secretary of the Interior, August 22, 1849, in Dale Morgan, ed., "Washakie and the Shoshoni: A Selection of Documents and Records of the Utah Superintendency of Indian Affairs (Part I, 1849–1852)," *Annals of Wyoming* 25 (July 1953): 149.

6. Stamm, *People of the Wind River*, ix.

7. For the story of the Church of the Creator's efforts to establish its headquarters in Riverton and the community's adamant reaction against the idea, see a series of articles in the two town newspapers: the *Ranger* from December 9, 2002, through January 21, 2003, and *Wind River News* from December 12, 2003, through January 23, 2003.

8. Stamm, *People of the Wind River*, ix.

9. The Northern Arapahos have their iconic figures of negotiation and peace too. Black Coal, like others of his tribe and like many Shoshones, spent time working as a scout for the U.S. military in the late nineteenth century and helped in particular with capture of Native Americans in the northern plains who were trying to escape General Crook's efforts to put them on reservations. As Janet Flynn has written, "Black Coal is remembered for his role in helping to bring [Euro-American] education to the reservation. His donations of land and other assistance helped found St. Stephen's Catholic Mission, the largest of the three . . . established at Wind River." His gravestone, an obelisk in the tribal cemetery, is inscribed, "Erected by the Northern Arapahoes, In honor of a Brave and Honest Man" (Flynn, *Tribal Government*, 17). Sharp Nose, another nineteenth-century leader, had also been a scout before becoming an important chief on the reservation. He assisted the U.S. Army in Nebraska by providing key intelligence on Cheyenne villages that the U.S. Cavalry sought to subdue. He taught an army lieutenant the basics of Plains Indian sign language, which for a time was the standard text for the U.S. military in the region (Markley and Crofts, *Walk Softly, This Is God's Country*, 92–93).

10. Several different spellings of her name are used, even among contemporary writers. "Sacajawea" is generally considered the Shoshone spelling and translates as "Boat Launcher." "Bird Woman" is the English equivalent of the Hidatsa "Sacagawea." "Sakakawea" is a variant spelling of the Hidatsa name and is common in North Dakota, particularly in the area of the Mandan, Hidatsa, and Arikara Reservation at Fort Berthold. Lewis and Clark multiply these spellings many times over, each of them using at least five or six variations of the name in their journal entries. See Harold P. Howard, *Sacagawea* (Norman: University of Oklahoma Press, 1971), 16 n1; Russell Reid, *Sakakawea: The Bird Woman* (Bismarck: State Historical Society of North Dakota, 1986), 10–11.

11. Howard writes in his book that at this point in her life, she "was now one of Charbonneau's chattels." Howard's account of this exchange is that "he had probably acquired her in a gambling game or by barter" (*Sacagawea*, 17). Howard's is considered by several contemporary academic historians to be one of the more respected narratives of Sacajawea's life and role in the Lewis and Clark expedition. While his book presents the evidence for both sides of the debate described below concerning the date of Sacajawea's death, he subscribes to the conclusion of most Euro -American historians, namely, that she died in 1812, shortly after the expedition ended.

12. See James P. Ronda, *Lewis and Clark among the Indians* (Lincoln: University of Nebraska Press, 1995), 258; Gary Moulton, ed., *The Journals of Lewis and Clark*, vol. 3 (Lincoln: University of Nebraska Press, 1988), 171n; Elliot Coues, ed., *History of the Expedition under the Command of Lewis and Clark*, vol. 1 (New York: Dover Publications, 1950), 190n; Clark Wissler, *Indians of the United States* (Garden City, N.Y.: Anchor Books, 1966); T. A. Larson, "Where Is Sacajawea Buried?" in Sacajawea Collection, Shoshone Tribal Cultural Center, Fort Washakie, Wyoming; Blanche Schroer, "Sacajawea: The Legend and the Truth," *Wyoming* (winter 1978): 20–28, 37–43; and Howard, *Sacajawea*, 191. The other argument claims that Sacajawea died in 1884 at Wind River, after living there for many years.

13. Grace Hebard's *Sacagawea: Guide of the Lewis and Clark Expedition* (Los Angles: Arthur H. Clark Co., 1932) was to a great extent based on interviews with Shoshone people living at Wind River who told Hebard that they had known Sacagawea, also known by them as Porivo and Wadze-Wipe, or Lost Woman, during her later years. Hebard's argument has not been given much credit by other historians, who claim that she ignored the evidence of contemporary witnesses Henry Brackenridge, John Luttig, and John Bradbury that Sacagawea died much earlier. Hebard has also been criticized for wrongly assuming that Sacagawea was mistaken for one of Charbonneau's other wives by Brackenridge, Bradbury, and Luttig. See Howard, *Sacajawea*, 157–158. For a summary of Hebard's oral sources, see Howard, *Sacajawea*, 178–184.

14. The year 1945 is the date given for Roberts's death, which occurred while he was still working at Wind River, in *Wind River: The People and Place*, published by the North American Indian Heritage Center, St. Stephens, Wyoming, in 1989. Harold Howard writes in his book, *Sacajawea*, that Roberts remained at the reservation for forty-nine years after his arrival in 1883, which would mean that his time there concluded in 1932 rather than 1945. No sources for these dates are given in either text.

15. Roberts narrates his experience in "The Death of Sacajawea," *Indians at Work: A News Sheet for Indians and the Indian Service* 2, no. 16 (April 1, 1935). A blown-up print of his article is on display at the Shoshone Tribal Cultural Center.

16. Eva Emery Dye, *The Conquest: The True Story of Lewis and Clark* (Chicago: A. C. McClurg, 1902).

17. Markley and Crofts, *Walk Softly, This Is God's Country*, 133.

18. On La Malinche's reputation, see, for example, Tzvetan Todorov, *The Conquest of America* (New York: Harper and Row, 1987), 100–102; and Octavio Paz, *The Labyrinth of Solitude* (New York: Grove Weidenfeld, 1985), 65–88. Daniel Richter offers an illuminating discussion of the myths and more plausible events of Pocahontas's life with the English in *Facing East from Indian Country:*

A Native History of Early America (Cambridge, Mass.: Harvard University Press, 2001), 69–78. Other useful discussions of Pocahontas's reputation appear in Mary Dearborn, *Pocahontas's Daughters: Gender and Ethnicity in American Culture* (New York: Oxford University Press, 1986); Asebrit Sundquist, *Pocahontas & Co.: The Fictional American Indian Woman in the Nineteenth Century* (Atlantic Highlands, N.J.: Humanities Press, 1987). Frances Karttunen's *Between Worlds: Interpreters, Guides, and Survivors* (New Brunswick, N.J.: Rutgers University Press, 1994) provides fascinating, detailed accounts of the complex relationships conducted between Natives and Europeans by a series of guides and interpreters, including Sacagawea, Charbonneau, Malinche, and Cortes.

19. Six statues have been erected to Sacajawea in different parts of the United States since 1904. In addition, four mountain peaks, two lakes, a state park, a spring, at least five historical markers, an airplane, and a Girl Scout Camp have all been named after her. She has also been the subject of three musical compositions, several paintings, a museum, the design of a silver service, and much other memorabilia. All of these memorials have been sponsored or produced by European Americans. For a list, see Howard, *Sacajawea*, appendix A.

20. See Paula Gunn Allen, *The Sacred Hoop: Recovering the Feminine in American Indian Traditions* (Boston: Beacon Press, 1986), 27.

21. Concerning Sacajawea's place in the expedition, William Clark wrote in his journal for the expedition that "her presence reconsiles all the Indians as to our friendly intensions, a woman with a party of men is a token of piece [*sic*]." See Gary Moulton, ed., *The Journals of the Lewis and Clark Expedition*, vol. 2 (Lincoln: University of Nebraska Press, 1986), 266. Later, as they entered the Columbia River, Clark noted that the Umatilla people were apparently pacified at the sight of Sacajawea: "as soon as they saw the Squar wife of the interperters they pointed to her and informed [the others who had not seen her.] [T]hey imediately all came out and appeared to assume new life, the sight of This Indian woman, wife to one of our interprs. confirmed those people of our friendly intentions, as no woman ever accompanies a war party of Indians in this quarter [*sic*]." See Gary Moulton, ed., *The Journals of the Lewis and Clark Expedition*, vol. 5 (Lincoln: University of Nebraska Press, 1988), 306.

22. Howard, *Sacajawea*, 185.

23. From this point on, she figures as a much more self-directed character. Taking her daughter and adopted son with her, she travels to Montana and lives with a group of Comanches, marrying a man named Jerk Meat, who is kind and generous to her. Sometime after his death, she briefly joins the Fremont expedition of 1843 and finally settles during her last years at Wind River. This account thus constructs Sacajawea as one who is in a position to make some choices and who, in doing so, separates herself from the man who determined an entire phase of her life. In this narrative, the Fremont expedition figures as simply a temporary vehicle for passage to Wind River rather than another opportunity for contributing to official U.S. exploration of the West. Hebard, *Sacagawea*; Mae Cody, "Sacajawea," in Sacajawea Collection, Shoshone Tribal Cultural Center; Charles Eastman letters in Hebard Collection, University of Wyoming Library, Laramie, Wyoming; and Howard, *Sacajawea*, 175–182.

24. See William Bevis, "Homing In," in *Recovering the Word: Essays on Native American Literature*, ed. Arnold Krupat and Brian Swann (Berkeley: University of California Press, 1987), 580–620.

25. Washakie quoted in Flynn, *Tribal Government*, 15. Markley quotes Washakie as saying the following, although they do not provide a source, date, or occasion for the statement: "One thing I tell them and tell them, the Whites are your true friends. Be true to them. One thing more I want to see and my heart will be at peace. I want to see the church and the school built for my people by the 'white robes.' To you, John Roberts [Episcopal missionary at Wind River in the late nineteenth century; husband and father of the authors, respectively], I give the land" (*Walk Softly, This Is God's Country*, 122).

26. Dale L. Morgan, ed., "Washakie and the Shoshoni: A Selection of Documents from the Records of the Utah Superintendency of Indian Affairs (Part X–1867–1869)," *Annals of Wyoming* 30 (April 1958): 83.

27. Stamm, *People of the Wind River*, 25; Markley and Crofts, *Walk Softly, This Is God's Country*, 117.

28. Markley and Crofts, *Walk Softly, This Is God's Country*, 119, Stamm, *People of the Wind River*, 26.

29. Don D. Fowler, ed., "Notes on the Early Life of Chief Washakie, Taken Down by Captain Ray," *Annals of Wyoming* 36 (April 1964): 34–42; Stamm, *People of the Wind River*, 26–27. Stamm adds that Washakie's times with Bridger "provided the requisite experiences in hunting, while participation in raiding parties . . . proved [the] warrior abilities" necessary for the Shoshone youth to prepare himself for marriage. The ties between the two men are evidenced as well by the fact that Mary Washakie, the chief's daughter, became Bridger's third wife.

30. Stamm, *People of the Wind River*, xii. According to a contemporary, Washakie occupied this central role without speaking or understanding the English language. P. L. Williams, "Personal Recollections of Wash-A-Kie, Chief of the Shoshones," *Utah Historical Quarterly* 1, no. 4 (October 1928): 103.

31. F. H. Head, letter to N. G. Taylor, Commissioner of Indian Affairs, July 30, 1867, in Morgan, ed., "Washakie and the Shoshones (Part X)," 60. The particular problem at issue, which Head describes in his letter to the commissioner of Indian Affairs, is that the government had built a road through the territory claimed by the four tribes along the Powder River route to Montana and had explained to them that the road was necessary as the only means for whites to access the Montana gold mines. The Indians easily discovered that this was untrue, since the road was barely used by anyone but soldiers. The soldiers used up local game, gave the Native people whiskey, "seduced from them numbers of their squaws, and otherwise maltreated them." As a result, the tribes took up arms against the military in preference to dying by starvation and maltreatment. Head expressed agreement with Washakie's opinion on the origins of the renewed hostilities and added that the bloodshed had been worth nothing because the road was not used by any emigrants or miners, given that the Missouri River had been found navigable shortly after the road construction began and that the road itself was longer and more difficult to travel than others that pre-existed it. He wrote, "What is known as the Powder River road is one of the most complete and expensive humbugs of the day" (61).

32. Williams, "Personal Recollections of Wash-A-Kie," 101.

33. Stamm, *People of the Wind River*, 51.

34. Morgan, ed., "Washakie and the Shoshoni (Part X)," 85–86; Stamm, *People of the Wind River*, 54–55.

35. Stamm, *People of the Wind River*, 82.

36. Frantz Fanon, *The Wretched of the Earth* (New York: Grove Press, 1963), 149–150.

37. Stamm, *People of the Wind River*, 104.

38. Ibid., 249.

39. L. Fowler, *Arapahoe Politics, 1851–1978*, 48–51.

40. P. L. Williams points out that the Treaty of 1868 provided for the potential assignment of other tribes to the Wind River Reservation, "if acceptable to the Indians" ("Personal Recollections of Wash-A-Kie," 102). Article II of the treaty text, after describing the boundaries of the reservation, states that this territory "is set apart for the absolute and undisturbed use and occupation of the Shoshonee Indians herein named and for such other friendly tribes or individual Indians as from time to time they may be willing with the consent of the United States to admit amongst them." Quoted in Morgan, ed., "Washakie and the Shoshonie (Part X)," 68. Washakie, speaking for the Shoshone people, was not "willing" to have the Arapahoes share the reservation, but agreed to the arrangement under pressure from the government.

41. L. Fowler, *Arapahoe Politics, 1851–1978*, 64–65, 67, 91. Relative to other individuals, Washakie nevertheless continued to be an important figure at Wind River. Dale Morgan notes that Washakie's "ascendancy, . . . except for a brief period during the Civil War, [was] maintained to the end of his life." Morgan, ed., "Washakie and the Shoshoni (Part I)," 143.

42. Stamm, *People of the Wind River*, 226.

43. L. Fowler, *Arapahoe Politics, 1851–1978*, 80.

44. Stamm, *People of the Wind River*, 94.

45. David Eng and David Kazanjian, "Introduction: Mourning Remains," in *Loss: The Politics of Mourning*, ed. Eng and Kazanjian (Berkeley: University of California Press, 2002), 5.

46. Stamm, *People of the Wind River*, 50. On the formation and membership of the Peace Commission, see Robert M. Utley, *The Indian Frontier of the American West, 1846–1890* (Albuquerque: University of New Mexico Press, 1984), 108–109.

47. Utley, *The Indian Frontier of the American West*, 1.

48. Robert DesJarlait, "The Contest Powwow versus the Traditional Powwow and the Role of the Native American Community," *Wiscazo Sa Review* 12, no. 1 (spring 1997): 116.

49. Clyde Ellis, " 'We Don't Want Your Rations, We Want This Dance': The Changing Use of Song and Dance on the Southern Plains," *Western Historical Quarterly* 30 (summer 1999): 134.

50. DesJarlait, "The Contest Powwow versus the Traditional Powwow," 117.

51. Kathleen Bragdon, *Native People of Southern New England* (Norman: University of Oklahoma Press, 1996), 200–203; Jill Lepore, *The Name of War: King Philip's War and the Origins of American Identity* (New York: Vintage, 1998), 7, 97.

52. Ellis, " 'We Don't Want Your Rations,' " 136–137; DesJarlait, "The Contest Powwow versus the Traditional Powwow," 118–119.

53. James Axtell, *The Invasion Within: The Contest of Cultures in Colonial North America* (New York: Oxford University Press, 1985), 107, 142, 246; Francis Jennings, *The Invasion of America: Indians, Colonialism, and the Cant of Conquest* (New York: Norton, 1975), 248.

54. Ellis, "'We Don't Want Your Rations,'" 137–141; Francis Paul Prucha, ed., *Documents of United States Indian Policy* (Lincoln: University of Nebraska Press, 1990), 160, 186; Clyde Holler, *Black Elk's Religion: The Sun Dance and Lakota Catholicism* (Syracuse: Syracuse University Press, 1995), 134; James Collins, *Understanding Tolowa Histories: Western Hegemonies and Native American Responses* (New York: Routledge, 1998), 62, 111, 183; Peter J. Powell, *Sweet Medicine: The Continuing Role of the Sacred Arrows, the Sun Dance, and the Sacred Buffalo Hat in Northern Cheyenne History*, vol. 1 (Norman: University of Oklahoma Press, 1979), 340–345; David Whitehorse, *Pow-wow: The Contemporary Pan-Indian Celebration* (San Diego: San Diego State University Publications in American Indian Studies, No. 5, 1989), 5; Benjamin Kracht, "Kiowa Pow-wows: Continuity in Ritual Practice," *American Indian Quarterly* 18, no. 3 (summer 1994): 322, 324, 327.

55. Ellis, "'We Don't Want Your Rations,'" 138–140; Kracht, "Kiowa Powwows," 322, 323.

56. Markley and Crofts, *Walk Softly, This Is God's Country*, 57; Flynn, *Tribal Government*, 48.

57. Whitehorse, *Pow-wow*, 13.

58. Whitehorse, *Pow-wow*, 8–12; William Powers, *War Dance: Plains Indian Musical Performance* (Tucson: University of Arizona Press, 1990), 50–60; Barre Toelken, "Ethnic Selection and Intensification in the Native American Powwow," in *Creative Ethnicities: Symbols and Strategies of Contemporary Ethnic Life*, ed. Stephen Stern and John Allan Crala (Logan: University of Utah Press, 1991), 137–156; Rachel Buff, *Immigration and the Political Economy of Home: West Indian Brooklyn and American Indian Minneapolis, 1945–1992* (Berkeley: University of California Press, 2001), 25–26, 34, 36; Patricia Barker Lerch and Susan Bullers, "Powwows as Identity Markers: Traditional or Pan-Indian?" *Human Organization* 55, no. 4 (1996): 390–391; DesJarlait, "The Contest Powwow versus the Traditional Powwow," 118–119; Ann Axtmann, "Performative Power in Native America: Powwow Dancing," *Dance Research Journal* 33, no. 1 (summer 2001): 10–12; Ellis, "'We Don't Want Your Rations,'" 134–138.

59. The latter idea is commonly attributed to James H. Howard, whose 1955 essay, "The Pan-Indian Culture of Oklahoma," published in *Scientific Monthly* 18, no. 5 (1955): 215–220, is often considered the source of a trend in anthropological writing that perpetuated the general idea that the sharing of tribal dance, music, and performance styles was a progressive movement that had a momentum to it which would eventually result in the erasure of tribal cultural particularity, at least in terms of identity formation, and lead ultimately to assimilation. William Powers is perhaps the most well known of those anthropologists to reject this argument, although he credits his position to earlier writers, particularly Joan Ablon, Nancy Lurie, Robert K. Thomas, and Carol Rachlin. See Powers, *War Dance*, chapter 7, "Pan-Indianism Reconsidered"; Ablon, "Relocated American Indians in the San Francisco Bay Area: Social Interaction and Indian Identity," *Human Organization* 24 (1964): 296–304; Lurie, "An American Indian Renaissance?" *Midcontinent American Studies Journal* 6, no. 2 (1965): 25–50; Thomas, "Pan-Indianism," *Midcontinent American Studies Journal* 6, no. 2 (1965): 75–83; and Rachlin, "Tight Shoe Night," *Midcontinent American Studies Journal* 6, no. 2 (1965): 84–100.

60. Ellis, "'We Don't Want Your Rations,'" 134; DesJarlait, "The Contest Powwow versus the Traditional Powwow," 120–124. The relatively few scholars of

powwow generally agree on the point that one of the central effects of pow-wows across North America is the representation of tribal identity, for the benefit of tribal members themselves as well as to enhance recognition by non-Indians. Because of the prevalence since the 1950s of inter-tribal pow-wows and the common practice at individual tribal powwows of welcoming Natives from other tribes to participate, James Howard argued some time ago that powwows evidence how specific tribal identities have been disintegrating over the course of the last several decades into a general and diffuse, "pan-tribal" Indianism. See Howard, "The Pan-Indian Culture of Oklahoma." As Karl Eschbach and Kalman Applbaum aptly describe Howard's argument in "Who Goes to Powwows? Evidence from the Survey of American Indians and Alaska Natives" (*American Indian Culture and Research Journal* 24, no. 2 [2000]: 68), it suggests that powwows "emerged as a way station on the road to as-similation" and that since then this point of view has been seriously chal-lenged by many scholars, including William Powers, Anita Herle, Nancy Lurie, James Hirabayashi, William Willard, and Luis Kemnitzer.

61. Ellis, "'We Don't Want Your Rations,'" 142; Buff, *Immigration and the Political Economy of Home*, 36, 152; Powers, *War Dance*, 161; Whitehorse, *Pow-wow*, 12; Kracht, "Kiowa Powwows," 322, 335.
62. Daniel Gelo, "Powwow Patter: Indian Emcee Discourse on Power and Iden-tity," *Journal of American Folklore* 112, no. 443 (winter 1999): 43.
63. Ibid., 42.
64. Victoria Sanchez, "Intertribal Dance and Cross Cultural Communication: Traditional Powwows in Ohio," *Communications Studies* 52, no. 1 (spring 2001): 51–52; Gloria Young, "Dance as Communication," *Akwe:kon Journal* 11, no. 3–4: 9, 15.
65. Eschbach and Applbaum, "Who Goes to Powwows?" 68. Eschbach and Appl-baum reference Philip Deloria's *Playing Indian* (New Haven, Yale University Press, 1998) to make this point.
66. Sanchez, "Intertribal Dance and Cross Cultural Communication," 52.
67. Ibid., 53, 60.
68. The powwow was preceded by a three-day Shoshone Reunion hosted by the tribe, which drew over three hundred members of Shoshone-speaking tribes and bands throughout the West. *Wind River News*, June 26, 2003, 1.
69. Ellis, "'We Don't Want Your Rations,'" 148.
70. Buff, *Immigration and the Political Economy of Home*, 169.
71. Ibid., 149–159, 166–167.
72. Ibid., 151.
73. Whitehorse, *Pow-wow*, 1.
74. Author notes on conversation with Ernie Over, June 26, 2003.
75. I take the term "playing Indian" from Philip Deloria's *Playing Indian*. Al-though he does not address rendezvous, DeLoria's study of Anglo imitations of stereotyped Native dress, speech, and behavior in the United States offers very useful analyses of such appropriations in a number of other contexts, in-cluding powwows.
76. "During the height of the [rendezvous] system, from 1825 to 1840," Henry Stamm writes, "Trappers, Nez Perces, Flatheads, Crows, Bannocks, Utes, and Shoshones met once or twice every summer at designated sites in the Green River, Bear River, Snake River, or Wind River drainages." Thus the ren-dezvous "became an important part of the yearly travels of many Shoshone bands." Stamm, *People of the Wind River*, 15, 19–21.

77. Axtmann, "Performative Power in Native America," 8.
78. Michel De Certeau, *Heterologies: Discourse on the Other* (Minneapolis: University of Minnesota Press, 1986), 227.
79. Eng and Kazanjian, "Introduction: Mourning Remains," 5.

CHAPTER 4   KEEPING HISTORY AT ACOMA PUEBLO

1. After this chapter was written, the Acoma Pueblo Museum burned to the ground. It has very recently been rebuilt and is scheduled to reopen in September of 2005. A vigorous and costly effort is under way to buy back and transport to the new museum ancient Acoma materials currently out of tribal hands and held across the United States and elsewhere. When this collection is completed, the museum's holdings will therefore be significantly greater than they were in the old museum I describe here.

2. *Southwest Indian Country Traveler,* a local journal of the tourist trade, notes that among the many tourism sites in the "vast region west of Albuquerque . . . [t]he most popular attraction is the Pueblo of Acoma's historic Sky City" (early spring 2003: 6).

3. In 1979, when Peter Matthiessen tried to visit Acoma, it was still not open to tourism, and, with his Mohawk traveling companion Craig Carpenter, he was effectively shunned from the mesa. They were pleased with this experience, and in spite of the denied access, Matthiessen did gather a very distinct impression of the Acoma Pueblo and its peoples' attitudes toward strangers. In *Indian Country* (New York: Viking Penguin, 1984) he recorded this peculiar tourist experience in the following way: "Although it could trade on what must be the most striking location of all the pueblo villages of the Southwest, Acoma has so far resisted the temptation of both electricity and running water, and its people are silent and reserved. Resistance to the intrusion of our truck was so manifest in the dead silence of the stone dwellings in the rock that we turned around and left immediately, on a shared impulse, feeling exhilarated rather than rejected, as if we had glimpsed a rare vanishing creature without scaring it away" (301). The anecdote demonstrates the historical inclination of Acoma Pueblo to distance itself from the larger society of the United States and to not show itself to foreign audiences. Although the mesa is now open to tourism, the experience, as my argument attempts to show, does not allow visitors to see much more than Matthiessen saw.

4. The Native American Church developed in the early twentieth century and combines elements of Sun dance religion, peyotism, and Christianity. It is still practiced by many people at the present time, but legal issues concerning preservation of and access to sacred places as well as the consumption of peyote have in many instances complicated the performance of rituals. See Vine Deloria Jr., "Trouble in High Places," in *The State of Native America: Genocide, Colonization, and Resistance,* ed. M. Annette Jaimes (Boston: South End Press, 1992); James S. Slotkin, *The Peyote Religion* (Glencoe, Ill.: Free Press, 1956); David F. Aberle, *The Peyote Religion among the Navaho* (Chicago: Aldine, 1966).

5. The contrasts between these monuments have been analyzed in, for example, Marita Sturken, "The Wall, the Screen, and the Image: The Vietnam Veterans Memorial," *Representations* 35 (summer 1991): 118–142; and Grant Scott, "Meditations in Black: The Vietnam Veterans Memorial," *Journal of American Culture* 13, no. 3 (fall 1990): 37–40.

6. See, for example, Vine Deloria, *God Is Red: A Native View of Religion* (Golden, Colo.: Fulcrum Publishing, 1994), 154–155; Peggy Beck, Anna Lee Walters, and Nia Francisco, *The Sacred: Ways of Knowledge, Sources of Life* (Tsaile, Ariz.: Navajo Community College Press, 1995), 27–28; and Ramon Gutiérrez, *When Jesus Came, the Corn Mothers Went Away: Marriage, Sexuality, and Power in New Mexico, 1500–1846* (Stanford University Press, 1991), see particularly Gutiérrez's chapter "The Pueblo Indian World in the Sixteenth Century," 3–36.

7. See, for example, Leslie Marmon Silko, "Language and Literature from a Pueblo Indian Perspective," in *Nothing but the Truth: An Anthology of Native American Literature*, ed. John L. Purdy and James Ruppert (Upper Saddle River, N.J.: Prentice Hall, 2001), 160–161; Deloria, *God Is Red*, 99–100; and Maria Josefina Saldaña-Portillo, *The Revolutionary Imagination in the Americas and the Age of Development* (Durham, N.C.: Duke University Press, 2003), 236. Paula Gunn Allen, in her introduction to *Spider Woman's Granddaughters: Traditional Tales and Contemporary Writing by Native American Women* (New York: Fawcett Columbine, 1989) notes that it is nevertheless possible to make "mistakes" in the storytelling process (1). Also see Andrew Wiget, "Telling the Tale: A Performance Analysis of a Hopi Coyote Story," in *Recovering the Word: Essays on Native American Literature*, ed. Brian Swann and Arnold Krupat (Berkeley: University of California Press, 1987), 311; and Arnold Krupate, "Post-structuralism and Oral Literature," in *Recovering the Word*, ed. Swann and Krupat, 118–119.

8. Simon Ortiz, "Towards a National Indian Literature: Cultural Authenticity in Nationalism," *MELUS* 8, no. 2 (summer 1981): 9.

9. Ibid.

10. Ibid.

11. Another version of this story turns up in Willa Cather's novel of the region, *Death Comes for the Archbishop* (New York: Random House, 1990). In Cather's version, he is thrown from the cliff for murdering a child because he has made a mistake in serving a meal.

12. Acoma Business Enterprises, "Sky City: Acoma at the crossroads of nature, heritage and the spirit of fun" and "Acoma Sky City: Old and New," www.skycitycasino.com.

13. Accounts created by the government for the sale and lease of individually owned Indian lands held in trust as a result of the Dawes Act are called "Individual Indian Money" accounts, and they have been managed from the beginning by the Bureau of Indian Affairs. Because of generations of mismanagement, they are at the center of an ongoing, much publicized class-action suit against the Department of the Interior initiated by Elouise Cobell, a member of the Blackfeet Tribe, in 1996 on behalf of five hundred thousand Native Americans. The current status of the case is still unclear, since the data of the accounts needed for the courts to determine the extent of mismanagement has not been presented by the bureau or the secretary of the Interior. For further information, see www.indiantrust.com.

14. See above, note 1.

15. Igor Broes, "Acoma Business Enterprises Awarded Roadrunner Recognition from Quality New Mexico," *Southwest Indian Country Traveler* 10, no. 1 (2003): 6.

16. Ibid.

17. Michel de Certeau, *The Practice of Everyday Life*, trans. Steven Randall (Berkley: University of California Press, 1984), xiii.

18. Ranajit Guha, *Dominance without Hegemony: History and Power in Colonial India* (Cambridge, Mass: Harvard University Press, 199), 7.
19. Taiaiake Alfred, "Sovereignty," in *A Companion to American Indian History*, ed. Philip J. Deloria and Neal Salisbury (London: Blackwell, 2002, 460–474), 460–461.
20. David E. Wilkins, *American Indian Sovereignty and the U.S. Supreme Court: The Masking of Justice* (Austin: University of Texas Press, 1997), 23–24, 74–75; Felix Cohen, *Handbook of Federal Indian Law* (Washington: U.S. Government Printing Office, 1945), x.
21. Francis Paul Prucha, *Documents of United States Indian Policy* (Lincoln: University of Nebraska Press, 1990), 17–21.
22. The complexity and confusion of federal Indian law has been noted by many legal scholars. See, for example, Cohen, *Handbook of Federal Indian Law*, viii; Wilkins, *American Indian Sovereignty*, 1; Stephen L. Pevar, *The Rights of Indians and Tribes* (Carbondale: Southern Illinois University Press, 1992), ix.
23. *Johnson and Graham's Lessee v. William McIntosh*, 21 U.S. (8 Wheaton) (1823), in Prucha, *Documents of United States Indian Policy*, 35–37; Robert A. Williams, *The American Indian in Western Legal Thought: The Discourses of Conquest* (New York: Oxford University Press, 1990), 289, 308.
24. Lindsay G. Robertson's *Conquest by Law: How the Discovery of America Dispossessed Indigenous Peoples of Their Lands* (New York: Oxford University Press, 2005) provides the most complete history of the case to date and is an indispensable work for an understanding of its complexities and of the political as well as legal manipulations it involved, not the least of which resulted in the legal precedent that has served to justify the taking of Native American lands to the present time. His discussion of the partnership between McIntosh and the plaintiffs appears in chapter 3, "Before the Court," 51–53. Eric Kades also provides new evidence on the bad faith involved in *Johnson* in "The Dark Side of Efficiency: *Johnson v. M'Intosh* and the Expropriation of American Indian Lands," *University of Pennsylvania Law Review* 148, no. 4 (April 2000): 1065–1190. Kades describes the faking of the dispute between parties in *Johnson* on page 1092.
25. Prucha, *Documents of United States Indian Policy*, 36.
26. Lindsay G. Robertson writes in "*Johnson v. M'Intosh* Reargument: Brief for the Appellants," *Kansas Journal of Law & Public Policy* (summer 2000) [9 Kan. J.L. & Pub. Pol'y 852], 858–872:

> In the United States, since 1859, Johnson has been cited in reported opinions in approximately thirty-two federal district court, forty-six federal circuit court, and thirty-eight federal Supreme Court cases, one third of the last decided since 1973. In virtually all of these, the Court defers to the Johnson Court's description and interpretation of British colonial policy vis a vis the legal consequences of discovery. Tee-Hit-Ton Indians v. United States is the most notorious. In Tee-Hit-Ton, the Supreme Court of the United States denied a Fifth Amendment takings claim brought to protest the United States' removal of timber from "aboriginal" Indian land in Alaska on the ground that the "aboriginal Indian interest in land" is "mere possession. . . . After conquest they were permitted to occupy portions of territory over which they had previously exercised "sovereignty," as we use that term. This is not a property right but amounts to a right

of occupancy which the sovereign grants and protects against intrusion by third parties but which right of occupancy may be terminated and such lands fully disposed of by the sovereign itself without any enforceable obligation to compensate the Indians. This position of the Indian has long been rationalized by the legal theory that discovery and conquest gave the conquerors sovereignty over and ownership of the lands thus obtained. The great case of Johnson v. McIntosh . . . denied the power of an Indian tribe to pass their right of occupancy to another. It confirmed the practice of two hundred years of American history "that discovery gave an exclusive right to extinguish the Indian title of occupancy, either by purchase or by conquest." *Tee-Hit-Ton Indians v. United States,* 348 U.S. 272, 279–80 (1955) (870–871).

27. *Cherokee Nation v. Georgia,* 30 U.S. (5 Peters) (1831); Marshall quoted in Prucha, *Documents of United States Indian Policy,* 58–60.

28. *Worcester v. Georgia,* 31 U.S. (6 Peters) (1832), in Prucha, *Documents of United States Indian Policy,* 60–62. *Worcester* is echoed in the Court decision in the case of *United States v. Kagama* of 1886: "Because of the local ill feeling, the people of the states where they are found are often their deadliest enemies. From their very weakness and helplessness, so largely due to the course of dealing of the federal government with them, and the treaties in which it has been promised, there arises the duty of protection, and with it the power. This has always been recognized by the executive and by congress, and by this court, whenever the question has arisen," *United States v. Kagama,* 118 U.S. 384 (1886), cited in Andrea M. Seielstad, "The Recognition and Evolution of Tribal Sovereign Immunity under Federal Law: Legal, Historical, and Normative Reflections on a Fundamental Aspect of American Indian Sovereignty," *Tulsa Law Review* 36, no. 3 (spring 2002): 685.

29. *United States v. Wheeler,* 435 U.S. at 323, quoted in N. Bruce Duthu, "Incorporative Discourse in Federal Indian Law: Negotiating Tribal Sovereignty through the Lens of Native American Literature," *Harvard Human Rights Journal* 13 (2000): 150.

30. Duthu, "Incorporative Discourse in Federal Indian Law," 150.

31. Ibid., 151.

32. Peter d'Errico, "Native Americans in America: A Theoretical and Historical Overview," in *American Nations: Encounters in Indian Country, 1850 to the Present,* ed. Frederick Hoxie, Peter Mancall, and James Merrell (New York: Routledge, 2001), 483.

33. *McClanahan v. Arizona Tax Commission,* 411 U.S. 164, 93 S.Ct. 1257, 36 L.Ed.2d 129 (1973), 172. The full text, where these phrases appear in Marshall's decision, reads: "The trend has been away from the idea of inherent Indian sovereignty as a bar to state jurisdiction and toward reliance on federal pre-emption." [Marshall's footnote here reads: "The source of federal authority over Indian matters has been the subject of some confusion, but it is now generally recognized that the power derives from federal responsibility for regulating commerce with Indian tribes and for treaty making." See U.S. Constitution, Art. I, §8, cl. 3 and Art. II, §2, cl. 2. See also *Williams v. Lee,* 358 U.S. 217, 219, 79 S.Ct. 269, 270, 3 L.Ed.2d 251 n. 4 (1959); *Perrin v. United States,* 232 U.S. 478, 482, 34 S.Ct. 387, 389, 58 L.Ed. 691 (1914); Federal Indian Law 3.] See *Mescalero Apache Tribe v. Jones,* 411 U.S. 145, 93 S.Ct. 1267, 36 L.Ed.2d 114. The modern cases thus tend to avoid reliance on platonic notions

of Indian sovereignty and to look instead to the applicable treaties and statutes which define the limits of state power. Compare, e.g., *United States v. Kagama*, 118 U.S. 375, 6 S.Ct. 1109, 30 L.Ed. 228 (1886), with *Kennerly v. District Court*, 400 U.S. 423, 90 S.Ct. 480, 27 L.Ed.2d 507 (1971). The Indian sovereignty doctrine is relevant, then, not because it provides a definitive resolution of the issues in this suit, but because it provides a backdrop against which the applicable treaties and federal statutes must be read. It must always be remembered that the various Indian tribes were once independent and sovereign nations, and that their claim to sovereignty long predates that of our own government. Indians today are American citizens. See U.S. Constitution, §1401(a)(2). They have the right to vote and to use state courts, and they receive some state services. But it is nonetheless still true, as it was in the last century, that "the relation of the Indian tribes living within the borders of the United States . . . [is] an anomalous one and of a complex character. . . . They were, and always have been, regarded as having a semi-independent position when they preserved their tribal relations; not as States, not as nations, not as possessed of the full attributes of sovereignty, but as a separate people, with the power of regulating their internal and social relations, and thus far not brought under the laws of the Union or of the State within whose limits they resided." *United States v. Kagama*, 118 U.S., at 381–382, 6 S.Ct., at 1112.

34. Robert Allen Warrior, *Tribal Secrets: Recovering American Indian Intellectual Traditions* (Minneapolis: University of Minnesota Press, 1995), xxi.
35. Alfred, "Sovereignty," 465.
36. Ibid., 471.
37. D'Errico, "Native Americans in America," 496–497.
38. Ibid., 497.
39. The Passasamoquoddy, Penobscots, and Maleet of Maine and later the Mashantucket Pequots documented their histories in their homelands sufficiently to gain federal recognition, after which point they used the eighteenth-century federal legislation to reclaim lands taken from them by Massachusetts (later Maine) and Connecticut, respectively, in violation of the constitutionally mandated federal authority over Indian commerce.

CHAPTER 5   INDIGENOUS INTERNATIONALISM

1. Thomas Jefferson, *Notes on the State of Virginia* (Chapel Hill: University of North Carolina Press, 1955), 96; Daniel Webster, in *Johnson and Graham's Lessee v. William McIntosh*, 21 U.S. (8 Wheat.) 543 (1823), quoted in Lindsay G. Robertson, *Conquest by Law: How the Discovery of America Dispossess Indigenous Peoples of Their Lands* (New York, Oxford University Press, 2005), 69–70.
2. For a comprehensive and illuminating discussion of Marshall's motivations and political considerations in deciding *Johnson v. McIntosh, Cherokee Nation v. George, and Worcester v. George,* see Robertson, *Conquest by Law,* chapters 4 and 5.
3. In addressing the first meeting of the Permanent Forum on Indigenous Issues on the closing day, Kofi Annan quoted the president of the Economic and Social Council, Ivan Simonovic, whose opening remarks to the forum included a welcoming to the "United Nations family." Kofi Annan, " 'You Have a Home at the United Nations' Says Secretary-General, as Indigenous Forum Concludes First Session," United Nations Press Release SG/SM/8249 HR/4603, May 24, 2002, 1.

4. In "The Rights of Peoples (in Particular Indigenous Peoples)," in James Crawford, ed., *The Rights of Peoples* (Oxford: Clarendon Press, 1988), 17–126, Richard Falk writes, "One of the earliest tensions in classical international law is between the territorial sovereignty of governments and the status of individuals and groups as beneficiaries of human rights"; he adds that the rise of human rights law in the period since World War II "has challenged [the] deference to governmental supremacy" that had developed since the middle of the nineteenth century (17).

5. Robert A. Williams Jr., *The American Indian in Western Legal Thought: The Discourses of Conquest* (New York: Oxford University Press, 1990), 96. My discussion of this history, and of Vitoria in particular, relies heavily on the excellent scholarship of Williams, whose writings are crucial for an understanding of the prehistory of contemporary international law concerning indigenous peoples.

6. Robert A. Williams Jr., "The Medieval and Renaissance Origins of the Status of the American Indian in Western Legal Thought," *Southern California Law Review* 47, no. 1 (November 1983): 64.

7. Ibid., 94.

8. Ibid., 51.

9. Alexander, pontiff from 1492 to 1503, issued Intercaetera divina in 1493, which, revised by the Treaty of Tordesillas in 1949, gave Spain the rights to any lands it discovered to the west of a north-south boundary line running 360 leagues west of the Cape Verde Islands. See Williams, *The American Indian in Western Legal Thought*, 44, 80.

10. Williams, *The American Indian in Western Legal Thought*, 44.

11. Ibid., 44–47.

12. For interpretations of Vitoria's work that understand it as sympathetic to indigenous peoples, see, for example, Glenn Morris, "International Law and Politics: Toward a Right to Self-Determination for Indigenous Peoples," in *The State of Native America: Genocide, Colonization, and Resistance*, ed. M. Annette Jaimes (Boston: South End Press, 1992), 60–61; Felix Cohen, *Handbook of Federal Indian Law* (Washington, D.C.: U.S. Government Printing Office, 1945), 46–47; Vine Deloria Jr., *Behind the Trail of Broken Treaties: An Indian Declaration of Independence* (Austin: University of Texas Press, 1991), 89–90, 129; and James Brown Scott, quoted in Williams, "The Medieval and Renaissance Origins of the Status of the American Indian," 69.

13. Cohen, *Handbook of Federal Indian Law*, 47.

14. Williams, "The Medieval and Renaissance Origins of the Status of the American Indian," 70.

15. Ibid., 83.

16. Ibid., 95.

17. Francis Paul Prucha, *Documents of United States Indian Policy* (Lincoln: University of Nebraska Press, 1990), 36.

18. Webster quoted in Williams, *The American Indian in Western Legal Thought*, 310; also see Robertson, *Conquest by Law*, 70.

19. Robertson, *Conquest by Law*, 101.

20. Russell Barsh, "Indigenous North America and Contemporary International Law," *Oregon Law Review* 62 (1983), 112.

21. Marshall quoted in Prucha, *Documents of United States Indian Policy*, 36.

22. Marshall quoted in Cohen, *Handbook of Federal Indian Law*, 292.

23. Williams, *The American Indian in Western Legal Thought*, 231.
24. Deloria, "Trouble in High Places: Erosion of American Indian Rights to Religious Freedom in the United States," in *The State of Native America*, ed. Jaimes, 272–273; Robertson, *Conquest by Law*, 117–141.
25. Marshall quoted in Prucha, *Documents of United States Indian Policy*, 58.
26. Ibid., 59.
27. Ibid.
28. Deloria, *Behind the Trail of Broken Treaties*, 115. Deloria gives some of the text of Justice Thompson's dissenting opinion: "The terms state and nation are used in the law of nations, as well as in common parlance, as importing the same thing; and imply a body of men, united together, to procure their mutual safety and advantage by means of their union. Such a society has its affairs and interest to manage; it deliberates, and takes resolutions in common, and thus becomes a moral person, having an understanding and a will peculiar to itself. . . . [A] weak state, that, in order to provide for its safety, places itself under the protection of a more powerful one, without stripping itself of the right of government and sovereignty does not cease on this account to be placed among the sovereigns who acknowledge no other power" (116).
29. For a comprehensive, stimulating discussion of the dominant theories of conquest of non-normative peoples during the crusades and, particularly, the highly influential theories of Pope Innocent IV, see Williams, *The American Indian in Western Legal Thought*, 1, 44–50.
30. Deloria, *Behind the Trail of Broken Treaties*, 115.
31. James Anaya, *Indigenous Peoples in International Law* (New York: Oxford University Press, 1996), 16.
32. Ibid., 183.
33. Falk, "The Rights of Peoples (in Particular Indigenous Peoples)," 17.
34. See United Nations Commission on Human Rights, Leaflet 8, 3.
35. Elsa Stamatopoulou, "Indigenous Peoples and the United Nations: Human Rights as a Developing Dynamic," *Human Rights Quarterly* 16, no. 1 (1994), 60.
36. Ibid., 60–61.
37. Stamatopoulou, interview with author, February 3, 2002; Robert T. Coulter, "Recollections of the Early Years of Indian Involvement in the International Community, 1974–1983," published as "Les Indiens sur la scène internationale: Les premiers contact avec l'Organisation des Nations unies 1974–1983," in *Destins croisés: cinq siècles de rencontres avec les Amérindiens*, by Coulter (Paris: Albin Michel/UNESCO Publications, 1992), 333–348.
38. For a very interesting personal narrative of the beginnings of indigenous nongovernmental organizations' relations with the United Nations, see Coulter, "Recollections of the Early Years of Indian Involvement," 5.
39. Coulter, "Recollections of the Early Years of Indian Involvement," 6.
40. Anaya, *Indigenous Peoples in International Law*, 46.
41. Coulter, "Recollections of the Early Years of Indian Involvement," 10, 12.
42. Ibid., 16.
43. Stamatopoulou, "Indigenous Peoples and the United Nations," 68.
44. United Nations Commission on Human Rights Web site, GIP leaflet 5, 1.
45. Ibid., leaflet 5, 2.
46. Wilton Littlechild describes the precise mandate of the Permanent Forum in "Draft Report of the Permanent Forum on Indigenous Issues" (unpublished draft report for the United Nations Economic and Social Council,

E/CN.19/2002/CRP.1): "It is to a) Provide expert advice and recommendations on indigenous issues to the [Economic and Social] Council, as well as to programmes, funds, and agencies of the United Nations through the Council; b) Raise awareness and promote the integrations and co-ordination of activities relating to indigenous issues within the United Nations system; c) Prepare and disseminate information on indigenous issues" (2).

47. United Nations Commission Human Rights, *Guide for Indigenous Peoples* (Geneva: Office of the High Commissioner for Human Rights, 2001), leaflet 6, 2.

48. Ibid., leaflet 5, 3.

49. Russell Barsh, "Indigenous Peoples and the UN Commission on Human Rights: A Case of the Immovable Object and the Irresistible Force," *Human Rights Quarterly* 18, no. 4 (1996), 782–813, esp. 785. The Commission on Human Rights' *Guide for Indigenous Peoples*, leaflet 5, 3, stipulates that "more than 100 organizations representing indigenous peoples [have by 2002] received approval to participate in the drafting process." For other references to the complexity of bureaucratic processes in the Working Group of the Commission on the Draft Declaration at its beginnings, see Roderic Pitty, "Indigenous Peoples, Self-Determination, and International Law," *International Journal of Human Rights* 5, no. 4 (2001): 45; and Stephen Quesenberry, "Recent United Nations Initiatives Concerning the Rights of Indigenous Peoples," *American Indian Culture and Research Journal* 21, no. 3 (1997): 237–238.

50. Barsh, "Indigenous Peoples and the UN Commission on Human Rights," 782.

51. Falk, "The Rights of Peoples (in Particular Indigenous Peoples)," 19.

52. Barsh, "Indigenous Peoples and the UN Commission on Human Rights," 800.

53. Ibid., 788.

54. Ibid., 790; Stamatopoulou, "Indigenous Peoples and the United Nations, 72.

55. In a general sense, the entire history of colonization of indigenous peoples on the part of European nations has tended to deny the very existence of indigenousness through assimilationist and more violent policies of extermination. Particular contemporary cases, however, have brought the question to the foreground in international forums and have yet to be resolved. Elsa Stamatopoulou writes in "Indigenous Peoples and the United Nations" that "China, India, Bangladesh and originally the Soviet Union . . . [have denied] that they had any indigenous peoples on their territory" (72).

56. Pitty, "Indigenous Peoples, Self-Determination, and International Law," 61, summarizes several indigenous statements that make this point.

57. See the Commission on Human Rights' *Guide for Indigenous Peoples*, leaflet 5, 1.

58. Barsh, "Indigenous North America and Contemporary International Law," 124.

59. The relations between individual and collective rights have been the subject of much dispute and analysis in recent years. For some particularly interesting discussions see Falk, "The Rights of Peoples (in Particular Indigenous Peoples)"; Cindy Holder and Jeff Corntassel, "Indigenous Peoples and Multicultural Citizenship: Bridging Collective and Individual Rights," *Human Rights Quarterly* 24, no. 1 (2002): 126–151; Will Kymlicka, *Multicultural Citizenship: A Liberal Theory of Minority Rights* (Oxford: Clarendon Press, 1995); and Dalee

Sambo Dorough's comments in Andrea Muehlebach, " 'Making Place' at the United Nations: Indigenous Cultural Politics at the U.N. Working Group on Indigenous Populations," *Cultural Anthropology* 16, no. 3 (2001): 415–448.

60. Ashis Nandy, "Shamans, Savages, and the Wilderness: On the Audibility of Dissent and the Future of Civilizations," *Alternatives* 14, no. 3 (1989): 275.

61. Ibid.

62. Ibid., 263, 265.

63. Ibid., 270.

64. Ibid., 265.

65. Ibid.

66. Ibid., 263.

67. See the introduction to this book.

68. Nandy, "Shamans, Savages, and the Wilderness," 265.

69. As Maria Josefina Saldaña-Portillo tells us in relation to the Zapatistas—"a discretely new form of Indian specificity"—that this group of different indigenous origins, in seeking to represent its history in the global political sphere, translates it "into a recognizable idiom for the conquerors," but this translation does not by any means prompt a shift in subjectivity such that the speakers and those they represent begin to become what Nandy calls priests. Saldaña-Portillo, *The Revolutionary Imagination in the Americas and the Age of Development* (Durham, N.C.: Duke University Press, 2003), 236–237.

70. Chris Tennant, "Indigenous Peoples, International Institutions, and the International Legal Literature from 1945–1993," *Human Rights Quarterly* 16, no. 1 (1994): 3.

71. Ibid., 16–17.

72. Ibid., 17.

73. Tennant bases his periodization on the 1971 commissioning of José R. Martinez Cobo's "Study on the Problem of Discrimination against Indigenous Populations" by the Sub-Commission on Prevention of Discrimination and Protection of Minorities; his study outlined many of the problems for indigenous peoples in their dealings with state governments and sought to begin a process of honoring indigenous interests more substantially. UN Doc. E/CN.4/Sub.2/1986/7 and Add. 1–4. The study was launched in 1972 and was completed in 1986, "thus making it the most voluminous study of its kind, based on 37 monographs," according to "The Concept of Indigenous Peoples" (PFII/2004/WS.1/3), a 2004 background paper compiled by the secretariat of the Permanent Forum for the Workshop on Data Collection and Dissagregation for Indigenous Peoples, which was held in January of that year. This background paper describes Martinez Cobo's working definition of indigenous peoples, which was adopted by the Permanent Forum:

> After long consideration of the issues involved, the Special Rapporteur who prepared the above-mentioned study offered a working definition of "indigenous communities, peoples and nations." In doing so he expressed a number of basic ideas to provide the intellectual framework for this effort, which included the right of indigenous peoples themselves to define what and who is indigenous. The working definition reads as follows:
> "Indigenous communities, peoples and nations are those which, having a historical continuity with pre-invasion and pre-colonial societies that developed on their territories, consider themselves distinct

from other sectors of the societies now prevailing on those territories, or parts of them. They form at present non-dominant sectors of society and are determined to preserve, develop and transmit to future generations their ancestral territories, and their ethnic identity, as the basis of their continued existence as peoples, in accordance with their own cultural patterns, social institutions and legal system.

"This historical continuity may consist of the continuation, for an extended period reaching into the present of one or more of the following factors:

a) Occupation of ancestral lands, or at least of part of them;

b) Common ancestry with the original occupants of these lands;

c) Culture in general, or in specific manifestations (such as religion, living under a tribal system, membership of an indigenous community, dress, means of livelihood, lifestyle, etc.);

d) Language (whether used as the only language, as mother-tongue, as the habitual means of communication at home or in the family, or as the main, preferred, habitual, general or normal language);

e) Residence on certain parts of the country, or in certain regions of the world;

f) Other relevant factors.

"On an individual basis, an indigenous person is one who belongs to these indigenous populations through self-identification as indigenous (group consciousness) and is recognized and accepted by these populations as one of its members (acceptance by the group).

"This preserves for these communities the sovereign right and power to decide who belongs to them, without external interference."

Tennant characterizes Martinez Cobo's language regarding indigenous peoples as "noble primitivization," echoing the fraught concept of "noble savagism" and all its historical-cultural baggage.

74. Gayatry Spivak, "Can the Subaltern Speak?" in *Marxism and the Interpretation of Culture*, ed. Cathy Nelson and Lawrence Grossberg (Urbana: University of Illinois Press, 1988), 271–316.

75. Tennant, "Indigenous Peoples, International Institutions," 38.

76. Ibid., 33.

77. Ibid., 37; Nandy, "Shamans, Savages, and the Wilderness," 263.

78. Tennant, "Indigenous Peoples, International Institutions," 7.

79. See www.ohchr.org/english/issues/indigenous/guide.htm.

80. Muehlebach, " 'Making Place' at the United Nations," 1.

81. Ibid., 2.

82. Ibid.

83. Annan, " 'You Have a Home at the United Nations,' " 2.

84. *Indian Country Today*, June 5, 2005.

Index

About the Author

Mary Lawlor is associate professor of English and director of American studies at Muhlenberg College in Allentown, Pennsylvania.